To Sin Against Hope

To Sin Against Hope

Life and Politics on the Borderland

BY

ALFREDO GUTIERREZ

VERSO

London • New York

To Rose's daughter Marisol and to my sons,
Samuel, Luis, Ben and David that they may
understand the journey that brought us here.

First published by Verso 2013
© Alfredo Gutierrez 2013

1 3 5 7 9 10 8 6 4 2

Verso
UK: 6 Meard Street, London W1F 0EG
US: 20 Jay Street, Suite 1010, Brooklyn, NY 11201
www.versobooks.com

Verso is the imprint of New Left Books

ISBN-13: 978-1-84467-992-8

British Library Cataloguing in Publication Data
A catalogue record for this book is available from the British Library

Library of Congress Cataloging-in-Publication Data
Gutierrez, Alfredo, 1945–
To sin against hope : life and politics on the borderland / by Alfredo Gutierrez.
   pages cm
Includes bibliographical references.
ISBN 978-1-84467-992-8 (alkaline paper)
1. Gutierrez, Alfredo, 1945- 2. Political activists—Arizona—Biography. 3.
Mexican Americans—Arizona—Biography. 4. Mexican Americans—Civil
rights—Arizona. 5. Civil rights movements—Arizona. 6. Immigrants—
Civil rights—Arizona. 7. Legislators—Arizona—Biography. 8. Arizona.
Legislature. Senate—Biography. 9. Arizona—Politics and government—1951-
10. Mexican-American Border Region—Politics and government. I. Title.
   F815.3.G88A3 2013
   328.73'092—dc23
   [B]
   2013007252

Typeset in Sabon by Hewer Text UK Ltd, Edinburgh
Printed in the US by Maple Vail

Contents

CHAPTER I

To Sin Against Hope

I was born in Miami, Arizona, on Depot Hill, which rises dramatically from the rail's edge next to the passenger depot. Miami was also the town where my father was born—and from where he was deported. One day in 1932, he boarded a train into exile in Mexico, and it was a dozen years before he returned.

The Miami, Arizona, where I grew up in the 1950s was booming. Three major mines were operating twenty-four hours a day, with hundreds of workers lined up at the gates for every shift. At the end of every shift they stormed out, covered with grime and dust, and headed into a town full of bars, churches and thriving family-owned stores that met every conceivable need. There were whorehouses: three big ones in the 1950s. The biggest of all had a gambling hall full of poker tables, the town's longest bar, and on weekends a barroom full of drunken cowboys and miners. I was a shoeshine boy, and I soon learned that whorehouses, especially the Pioneer, were the best places to wait for someone to claim a jackpot or stroll down the stairs, smile and all, having just visited the ladies. These guys were ready for a shine and ready to tip.

My other job was delivering the newspaper each morning. My route was the one with canyons, winding dirt trails, concrete staircases built by miners at the turn of the century that went a thousand steps up sheer hillsides, and Mexican families grateful that the old man was working underground so they could afford the paper. Every morning I visited houses that sat precariously on lots carved into the canyons, and every weekend I knocked on each door to collect. It was on those Saturday mornings that I came to understand what it really cost to work those mines. There were families smiling, stomachs full and ready to head out to the company store . . . but perhaps two houses down the canyon your friend would whisper that it might be best if you came back later. Kids would gather at the bottom of the hill to recount the events, of fathers staggering home at daybreak, mothers in tears, a young guy threatening to kill his father if the old man hit her again.

And you knew when the work was running thin, or when it was time to pay for the daughter's wedding or the kids' new shoes or the new room—families were always growing in mining towns. You knew because when times were tough, who needed an anti-union, right-wing newspaper that barely noticed the world of the miners?

My father's deportation story was not particularly unusual in Arizona's mining towns at that time. It was just part of the landscape, one of the sacrifices Mexicans risked in order to work in the mines, join the union, get steady pay and a company doctor, raise the kids, maybe send them to college and get them out from underground. My father was deported in 1932. It was at the height of anti-immigrant hysteria that had been growing for two decades. Madison Grant's highly influential book, *The Passing of the Great Race*, had been published in 1916. Grant described the United States as the highest accomplishment of the Nordic race of northern and western Europe, a place where Democracy flourished because it had been founded by this Nordic white race. The greatest danger America faced was the immigration of non-Nordic people. They would pollute the purity of America and debase the values, morals, and intelligence of the American people. Mexicans fit Grant's definition of a "population of race bastards" as an example of a people whose inferior Indian blood would dominate whatever good white blood there may have been in a mestizo.[1] The mestizo, in his view, was a moral cripple incapable of democratic government.

Grant was perhaps the best known and most often cited scientific racist of the era, a leader of the eugenics movement in America. A powerful voice advocating for the passage of the restrictive anti-immigration Quota Law of 1924, he argued successfully in a majority of the states for coercive sterilization laws and worked with Marcus Garvey to facilitate the return of former slaves to Africa. Grant's public persona was not defined by simple racism. He was a friend of Teddy Roosevelt, is often credited as a founder of the American conservation movement, helped create Denali and Glacier National Parks, and counted among his friends President William Taft, John D. Rockefeller, and Andrew Carnegie. Even Adolf Hitler recognized his genius, calling *The Passing of the Great Race* "my bible."[2]

But Grant's was not the only voice calling for extreme measures against dark-skinned immigrants. C. M. Goethe, later the august founder of Sacramento State College, estimated that "the average American Family had three children while the Mexican family had nine or ten offspring. At this rate the former couple had 27 great-grandchildren while the latter had 729. Within a few generations Mexicans would control the United States through sheer weight of numbers." The danger of being inundated by Mexican bad blood was imminent and profoundly alarming. Roy Garis, an expert in eugenics and a professor of economics at Vanderbilt University, wrote of Mexicans:

Their minds run to nothing higher than animal functions—eat, sleep, and sexual debauchery. In every huddle of Mexican shacks one meets the same idleness, hordes of hungry dogs, and filthy children with faces plastered with flies, disease, lice, human filth, stench, promiscuous fornication, bastardy . . . These people sleep by day and prowl by night like coyotes, stealing anything they can get their hands on, no matter how useless to them it may be . . . Yet there are Americans clamoring for more of this human swine to be brought over from Mexico.[3]

The Chinese Exclusion Act of 1882 and later legislation had closed the door to Asians, and the Literacy Act of 1917 had been passed to try to exclude illiterate peasants, but waves of Jews, Poles, Italians, Irish, and Greeks continued landing on America's shores. In 1921 and again in 1924 Congress passed Quota Laws that established a maximum number of immigrants by national origin. The quotas were based upon the demographic makeup of the United States in 1890—prior to the great waves from southern Europe. The intent was obvious: America had been founded as a white Nordic country, and Congress intended to keep it that way.

As it happens, Western Hemisphere immigration was excluded from the quotas established in 1921 and 1924. Between 1921 and 1930 there were numerous attempts to impose quotas on Mexican immigration. Representative John Box of Texas, a Methodist minister and a founder of Southern Methodist University, argued on the floor of the House in 1928 that "every reason which calls for the exclusion of the most wretched, ignorant, dirty, diseased and degraded people of Europe or Asia demands that the illiterate, unclean, peonized masses moving this way from Mexico be stopped at the border." But in this and other instances, the quotas were blocked in the Senate by Southerners and Westerners who were protecting the agricultural lobby and its flow of cheap labor. Immigration policy in the 1920s officially welcomed only the Nordic race, but the Mexican "back door" was left open.

Then came the Depression. The repatriation campaigns of the Great Depression were initiated by the Hoover Administration as an attempt to do something, no matter how ineffective, in response to the growing wave of unemployment sweeping the country. Like Obama's deportations in his first term, they began in response to accusations of inaction against hordes of criminal Mexicans crossing the border and stealing jobs. In both cases, it was perhaps the president's choice of chief enforcer of immigration laws that signaled the willingness to use the blunt force of government. William Doak was appointed Secretary of Labor by Hoover in 1930. Doak was a leading figure in the Brotherhood of Railroad Trainmen union and a prominent figure in the campaign against immigrants. (Janet Napolitano, appointed Secretary of Homeland Security by Obama in 2009, had deployed the National Guard on the Mexican border as governor of Arizona from 2003 to 2009. She had signed into law the most severe employer sanctions bill in the nation and had approved measures making migrants smuggled in as much felons as traffickers.)

Shortly after taking office, Doak centered his attention on deporting aliens who were or had been in the workforce. In his annual departmental report of 1931, he wrote that the purpose of the Department of Labor, which then enforced immigration laws, was

> to foster, promote, and develop the welfare of wage earners of the United States . . . it is a mere corollary of this duty and purpose to spare no reasonable effort to remove the menace of unfair competition which actually exists in the vast number of aliens who have in one way or another, principally by surreptitious entries, violated our immigration laws . . . the force and effect of these provisions would be largely defeated if they were not accompanied by

5

provisions for the deportation of those found in the country as having entered in violation of these restrictions.

In 1930 the Border Patrol numbered 781 agents. President Hoover offered Doak unqualified support for his campaign, and pledged an additional "245 more agents to assist in the deportation of 500,000 foreigners."[3] Even 1,000 agents were insufficient for the magnitude of the task. Doak, undeterred, launched initiatives to expand the reach of the Border Patrol, measures that would continue to be refined by successive administrations, including Obama's.

The belief that deteriorating employment was a consequence of immigration reached hysterical levels. Congressman Martin Dies of Texas introduced a thick raft of bills aimed at making the life of immigrants miserable. Dies' racist and anti-Semitic views were well known. He proposed forcibly deporting all of the 6 million aliens he claimed resided in the United States. There were raids, roundups, and mass deportations in almost every state in the Union. Local committees, mayors, sheriffs, and governors escalated the rhetoric of hate. In Los Angeles, the chairman of a local committee, Charles Visel, proposed a campaign of extensive newspaper publicity, threatening detention and deportation to "scare-head" Mexicans to self-deport without the necessity of formal proceedings.[4] The city saw nationally publicized raids in which streets were closed off, cars stopped and searched, and those who looked "Mexican" apprehended. Colorado's governor, Edwin C. Johnson, threatened "to call the National Guard to round up foreigners and expel them from the state." Latinos lived with the ever-present fear of detention and deportation. To seek help from a welfare office or a county hospital was to run great risks.

The description of raids conducted by local law enforcement fully authorized by high officials reads disturbingly

like the front-page stories of today, as with the raids of
Maricopa County Sheriff Joe Arpaio (the bombastic Arizona
poster boy of the nativist movement). If anything, there was
a bit more frankness and clarity in the rhetoric of the 1930s.
There was no pretense that the expulsions were aimed solely
at "illegals," leaving little doubt that the corrupting influence of Mexican morals, values, and inferior culture
threatened America's very existence. Even Arpaio tiptoes
more delicately through the racial and ethnic maze than did
his more honest predecessors. While governor of Arizona,
President Obama's Homeland Security secretary was careful
enough to call on the National Guard only to keep the
foreigners out, and not to round them up.

Miami on the eve of the Depression was a thriving boomtown
of 12,500 in a state that was barely being born. The 1930
Census recorded a population of 48,000 for Arizona's capital
city, Phoenix. Tucson was the second largest city in the state,
with 32,000. Miami had been founded near the claims of
major mining companies in 1909 as the real-estate play of an
eastern speculator. His name was Cleve Van Dyke, and by
1929 he had made a fortune on his private town. But when the
Depression came, all of the mines in the Globe-Miami Basin
of Gila County closed. Then as now, there was someone to
blame. Miami's newspaper, the *Arizona Silver Belt*, reviled the
Mexican community of Miami, often in front-page editorials.
In April of 1930, the *Silver Belt* told its readers:

> The experience of the country is that almost any form of
> European immigration is preferable to that from Mexico. It
> has been found that Mexicans are less assimilable and show
> a greater tendency to tear down American living and wage
> standards than any class of Europeans. Go to any commu-
> nity, such as the Globe-Miami district, where there are large

European elements among the population as well as Mexicans, and ask any native citizen or business man which of these alien residents is least desirable . . . and the answer almost invariable [sic] will be "the Mexicans." . . . Thousands of white miners in Globe-Miami district, not to mention other copper-producing sections of the state, have been displaced by these Mexicans.[5]

And raising the specter of Mexican political domination of Arizona, the *Silver Belt* appears to have pioneered the arguments against Mexican babies and Mexican birth rates that cause panic and dread in the hearts of nativists today:

It won't be long until more babies of Mexican parentage will be born in Arizona each year than the white race. The state board of vital statistics for the year 1929 show there were 9,521 babies born in Arizona. Of that number 4,754 were white. Babies of Mexican parentage numbered 3,706, or 40% of the total. . . . During the last few years the percentage in favor of the Mexicans has steadily increased . . . How long will the Caucasian strain in Arizona retain political control after the majority of the citizenship is of Mexican blood? The answer is, not for long.[6]

Soon enough, the white establishment, responding to Doak's call for local participation, began forming a mechanism to repatriate the Mexicans. In Miami it took the form of the Gila County Welfare Association. As the name implies, the association coordinated welfare efforts for unemployed miners, but its duties quickly evolved to include coordinating the dragnets that led to repatriations and deportations. The term "voluntary departure" is the Orwellian phrase adopted by the Obama Administration for using local police to apprehend undocumented persons under any pretext, jail them in massive private prisons for extended periods while they await judicial proceedings, and then offer to release them immediately if they agree to a "voluntary departure" from the country. The phrase was invented in the 1930s to support the fiction that only criminal aliens were being forcibly removed. All other Mexicans were allegedly leaving in response to the Depression, and not as a consequence of a national public policy to scapegoat them and whip up local vigilante hysteria to round them up and force them out.

My maternal grandmother, Antonia, was born in Metcalf, Arizona, on the thirteenth of June, 1895. Metcalf was a mining camp founded in the late 1800s and abandoned in 1936. It now lies buried under the ore waste from the larger Morenci mine. We can trace the family on her mother's side to 1878, when the family lore says that her grandmother Isabel Luna and her two grown sons, Jose Maria and Estanislao, rode into Clifton, Arizona, on an oxcart from Chihuahua. We know the name of my father's grandfather, Fidel Samudio, but little else. How the family name came to be Gutierrez remains a mystery. Antonia and my grandfather Samuel Gutierrez were married in Miami in 1914. My father was born a year after the marriage of Antonia and Samuel.

Antonia remarried a few years later and had three more children with her second husband. This man, Fortunato Vega, was living proof of how wild and wide-open the boom years had been in Miami. Fortunato was a professional gambler. Apparently a pretty good one—he supported a wife and five children playing cards in local saloons. Unfortunately, however, he had never bothered to become a citizen. He soon became the target of the Gila County Welfare Association, and the family was subjected to immense pressure from the Welfare Association to voluntarily deport. In the midst of the depression, gambling had come to an end. Food donations and the occasional day job depended on the Association, and there were to be none for an illegal family. It was only a matter of time before the family was forced from Miami.

And so it was that in March of 1932, my father, then seventeen years old, and the rest of the family—except for Fortunato, all citizens of the United States—boarded a train in the Miami town depot and began their journey to Fortunato's rural ranchería at El Fuerte, in the Mexican state of Sinaloa. The *Arizona Silver Belt* celebrated the deportations:

> Mexicans were scurrying for seats in the passenger coaches Saturday afternoon, happy and excited in the thought that they were returning to their native Mexico. Hundreds of friends were at the siding to bid them farewell. All Aboard! There was a final exchange of salutations. Harried handclasps were made through the window. The train began to move. "Vamos! Adios! Adios!"[7]

Even forty years later my father's eyes would well up with tears as he recalled that day. He carried that memory of betrayal throughout his life.

In less than two years Fortunato would be dead. My grandmother Antonia decided that immediately after his burial they would return to Miami. But my father stayed in Mexico another eight years. He and his brother José, neither of them the children of Fortunato, had been unwelcome mouths to feed in the Vega ranchería, and José had quickly made his way back to Arizona. My father also left El Fuerte, but he stayed in Sinaloa. He got a job in Culiacan, Sinaloa's capital, as a clerk for the Mexican government, became involved with local politicians, worked the railroad, and along the way met a woman he fell in love with.

This woman would endanger his relationships with his family for years. He and his mother were never close again.

The problem was that Julia, my mother, was an older, "experienced" woman, divorced with two children, and, perhaps most hurtful to a devoutly Catholic family, a Protestant—and as if that weren't enough, she was greeted when they returned to Miami with suspicious murmurings that she was secretly a Jew. The rabidly anti-Catholic policies of the Calles Administration in Mexico had resulted in the bloody rebellion known as the Cristero War (1926–29). There were rumors among devout Catholics of secret cabals of conversos and the complicity of cristianos, as Evangelical Christians are called, in the Calles Administration. The term "conversos" denoted Jews who were forced to publicly convert to Catholicism by the Holy Inquisition in fourteenth-century Spain but continued to practice their religion in secret. Historians believe that a large percentage of Spanish conversos escaped to the New World and continued their secret practices. My father's maternal grandfather, José Carbajal—an important union organizer in the Morenci-Clifton mining area—was himself suspected by Antonia to have been a converso. My grandmother described how he would gather with other men on Friday evening and sing a kind of prayer in an unknown language, and light candles.

And in 1944, when he finally decided to come back to Miami, my father revived all those rumors by bringing, well, a harlot, a Protestant, and possibly a Jewess home from exile.

CHAPTER 2

Return from Exile

I was born in 1945 in a wooden house that sat at the very edge of a hill half ripped apart to make room for the railroad line that carried the copper to market and had only a decade earlier carried the Mexicans into exile. World War II created a shortage of both copper and the laborers who excavate it. Recruiters began roaming northern Mexico seeking men to work the mines, especially among those who had been deported. These were experienced at piercing deep into the earth, needed no training, and, equally importantly, most of them spoke English.

Each time I meet with students of Mexican extraction, I implore them to go home and ask their parents about the crossing. The stories of our parents' and grandparents' sacrifice should never be forgotten. Unfortunately, I was never able to persuade my father to talk much about it. He was, I think, ashamed to have come back to the town that had feted his exile only a few years before. But when he made the decision to return he was older, and responsible for four children: two were my mother's from her earlier marriage, and two more were born in Los Mochis, Mexico. The wages at Ferrocarriles de México, the nationalized Mexican railroad where he was a freight agent in their Culiacán, Sinaloa depot, could never compare to what the Miami Copper Company promised him. My mother begged him to go back. The future for the children in Mexico was bleak at best. So he accepted the offer. They went by train to the border and took a bus from Nogales to Miami. They entered the country illegally. The two youngest children were citizens by virtue of their father's status . . . but he had been expelled without regard to his citizenship.

All he told me was that he just didn't trust the government any longer, so they walked across, following a well-beaten path that skirted the port of entry and the requirement for papers. They were shown the way by a fellow miner who had taken the path many times. His name was Alfredo Horcasitas. That's how I came to be named Alfredo. My mother, probably at my father's request, would also talk little about the trip. In answer to my inquiries she would only say, "*Sí, sí, era muy duro pero era un sacrificio que tuvimos que hacer.*" Yes, it was very hard, but it was a sacrifice we had to make. And when I questioned further, "Why?" her answer was always the same: "*Por tí, tontito.*" For you, little dummy.

My mother and father have passed away. My two sisters have as well; my brother who was born in Los Mochis was only two when he crossed and has few memories of the trip. My oldest brother is very ill, and frankly, he too resists discussing the experience. I will never know, and I will never share with my children those sacrifices in the rich detail they deserve, explaining exactly what it cost so that they might enjoy lives of middle-class comfort, extraordinary educations, and a future.

My birth certificate says that I was born in the company hospital. Family lore says I was born in that house on top of Depot Hill with the help of a *partera*, a midwife. The Union had yet to wrest health care from the company in 1945, so the likelihood is that I was taken to the hospital afterwards for the birth certificate. Health care was a decade away, but the Union had already accomplished significant victories. The International Union of Mine, Mill and Smelter Workers was sometimes called the Mexican Union, because unlike other unions it actively recruited Mexicans and fought vigorously against the practice of paying Mexican workers less for a day's work than white workers would earn. It did not matter to the company if a person was just off the boat from Italy, Serbia, Hungary, or Finland: they still got paid $1.15 more per shift than a Mexican. And it did not matter to the company if the Mexican worker was recently arrived from Mexico or a citizen for generations. White was white and Mexican was Mexican. The practice was ordered halted by the federal government in 1944 in response to a grievance filed by the Union, along with the threats of slowdowns and strikes. War and the Mine Mill, as the Union was known, convinced the National Non-Ferrous Metals Commission to find "a consistent pattern of discriminatory rates" at Miami Copper Company and Inspiration Consolidated Copper Company, also in Miami. The Commission ordered equal pay for equal work.[1] The company's entrenched racism was not so easily extinguished, however. They equalized the workforce during the war, but shortly afterwards furtively returned to their old habits. As late as 1963 the Union was in federal court alleging wage discrimination. The federal district judge entered a decision in September of 1973 ordering back pay. In November 1978, Inspiration Consolidated Copper Company finally sent a memo to all Mexican-American and Indian employees, notifying them that they were eligible for back pay.

The Mine Mill was the successor to the Western Mining Federation that initiated the strikes in the Clifton-Morenci mining district of Arizona in 1915, and also the strike in Bisbee. It was the Bisbee strike that led to the infamous deportations of at least 1,200 miners, mostly Mexicans. The striking miners were forced at gunpoint into cattle cars owned by the mining company's private railroad, transported to the desert near Columbus, New Mexico, and abandoned there. As word of the mass kidnapping spread throughout the country a national scandal ensued. President Wilson sent the Army to build a shelter and to feed and care for the men and ultimately to assure their safe return to Bisbee. The Mine Mill was born in controversy, embraced Mexican workers, and from the beginning was depicted by the mining companies and by the rival "white" unions as radical, leftist, and communist. The Mine Mill was indeed the most militant union, and it was also the leading advocate for the rights of local Mexican families, continually subject to discrimination and segregation.

The entry into the town from the big city of Phoenix some seventy miles away was through west Live Oak Street. West Live Oak had been populated by Mexicans and the few "colored" families in town since its founding by Cleve Van Dyke. Van Dyke died as the war ended. His son-in-law Watson Fitz assumed control of the Miami Townsite Company, and Fitz, unlike Van Dyke, wanted money fast. With the war over, the town anticipated that the sinewy, dangerous mountain road that connected Phoenix to Miami would finally be improved and visitors would soon be arriving. When they did arrive, they would unfortunately have to pass through a gauntlet of Mexican and colored families that lived along west Live Oak before arriving at the bustle of bars, gambling salons, whorehouses, and businesses that lined downtown Miami. Thus Mexicans, colored folk, and the fast money they were in the way of became the motivations for Miami's major urban renewal and racial cleansing project. Fitz announced the commercial and residential development in 1947, promising "large restricted home sites": the fact that Mexican and colored families were renting those home sites and had been doing so for years made little difference. They would have to move.

The campaign against the Mexican and colored families moved quickly. A prominent Mexican American, A. J. Flores, was recruited to lead the charge and "get rid of the shacks." As a kid I never heard anyone say a kind word about A. J. Flores. He was considered a pariah, a quisling, a sell-out, and worse. I was surprised to discover, when I read a transcript of a conversation with him recorded in 2001, fifty years after the demolition of those homes, that A. J. was still trying to defend himself:

> The Mexicans had no aspirations. They liked living in shacks or else they would have done something about it. They didn't want anything better. They didn't care enough to take care of their own homes. If the Town did nothing, Mexicans and Negroes would continue to live that way. It was time to bring in someone to take care of that area. The Town had to raise the quality of life there and they had to control the town's growth to make it livable.[2]

I hope A. J. was paid a lot of money. He was held in contempt by the miners and constantly ridiculed behind his back. That should be expensive. In the late 1990s, after years of economic decline, on the verge of becoming a ghost town and with few folks remaining who remembered the relocations, Miami elected a very bitter A. J. as town mayor. Most folks in Miami had forgotten why the cloud of suspicion hovers about A. J., but obviously he never will.

The Union mounted a major effort to stop the relocation, but it had no influence with the town fathers, and they were unable to curb Watson Fitz's lust for quick money. After the relocation, the Union committed itself to gaining control of city hall. It would take them over a decade to do it. There was one, not so small, secondary consequence of the relocation for us: we moved from Depot Hill into a "shack" in Davis Canyon, one of those colored and Mexican canyons that families from west Live Oak were forced into. Many of the black families left altogether after the wave of hate that spread through the town. The small two-room house was nestled against a hillside abutting a natural cave. The cave, once plastered and ventilated, became the third room of the house. I lived in that house until I left for the Army years later.

The highway entering Miami from Phoenix, even before it reached the renewal project of west Live Oak, would edge next to a dry wash for perhaps a half-mile. If you were to peer down into the wash you would see a teeming camp of shacks, beat-up trailers, tents, outhouses, campfires, and half-clothed kids running amuck. That was Mackey's Camp. The "okies" of the camp were all white. There were perhaps a hundred or more transient families in the camp, kept there—the Union men said—so that the company would have a ready supply of strike-breakers should the Mine Mill decide to call a Bolshevik strike. Some of the "okie" families moved into the Mexican canyons when the west Live Oak renewal project made homes available. Most just drifted away to destinations unknown. Watson Fitz and the town fathers apparently never thought to forcibly remove the white squatters, and A. J. never publicly demanded that the town get rid of their shacks.

When I was just a kid I remember the great joy when my older brothers would take me to the YMCA swimming pool on Saturday. It was only years later that I realized my father refused to join my mother's Christian activities because the Christians who ran the Y would only let the Mexicans swim for a few hours on Saturday night. That was the night they drained the pool. He refused to join his mother at Catholic mass as well. The mass was in Latin in those days, so language was no excuse to segregate, but segregate they did. The Mexicans sat on the left side and the whites on the right. The practice apparently began in the 1920s when Thomas O'Brien, superintendent of Inspiration Mine and president of the Valley National Bank, complained that the Mexicans were dirty, stank, and were stealing women's purses. He threatened the priest with withholding his offering unless something was done. Segregation under God and separate lines for communion, whites on the right and Mexicans on the left, was the result.[3]

The school system was integrated after my second year at Bullion Plaza Elementary, the Mexican school. The summer before the integrated school year was to begin there was much debate at the union hall and at El Divino Salvador, the Spanish-language Presbyterian Church, about the plan. My mother was vehemently opposed to her children going to school with *"gringos patas saladas."* The phrase translates literally as salty-legged gringos. It meant that gringos were unwashed, filthy, and full of fleas. They were also, according to the church ladies, rude, uncivilized, lazy, and not bright enough to get out of a dry creek when it rained. The Union had demanded that schools be integrated, and a court in Phoenix had finally ordered it, but my mother wanted that judge to come and see how the gringos who lived in filth at Mackey's Camp allowed their children to dress and act. The judge never came, integration proceeded without incident, fleas never infested her children, and Mackey's Camp soon disappeared.

The noted demographer and historian David Hayes-Bautista graphs the dramatic changes in the population of Latinos between 1930 and 1940. In California there were nearly 200,000 Latino immigrants in 1930 and only 168,848 US-born Latinos, according to the Census. By 1940, immigrant Latinos had dropped significantly to slightly over 100,000, but the number of children born in the US had zoomed upwards to 262,100.[4] The decade of deportations had indeed taken its toll, and one measure was the absolute drop in number of immigrants who remained in the country. But those who did were fruitful and multiplied. The California experience can be generalized to the less populated Arizona of the 1930s and '40s. The immigrants who stayed lived in fear of deportation, and those that returned lived with the constant dread of being rediscovered. And in a place like

Miami they were culturally isolated as well. The only newspaper in Spanish was a Phoenix-based weekly paper, and the English dailies cared little about the Mexicans. There was no Spanish-language television, just a weekly hour-long radio program on KIKO hosted by an American-born Mexican who played records donated or lent to the station. There was the "Mexican" movie theater, the Lyric, that changed movies every week and sometimes showed news trailers as well. Folks brought with them a memory of Mexico that would remain fixed for a very long time. On occasion one of the immigrant families would make a trip to Mexico. The family would be inundated with requests for food and goods that were unattainable in Miami—and always for newspapers, books, and records. When we returned from a trip to Culiacán we were greeted by half the town flocking to hear gossip and news, and some people even got a handwritten note from a friend or relative *del otro lado*, from the other side. North of the border, mangos were magic, papayas unheard of, *dulce de membrillo*, *cajeta*, *machaca de burro* (dried donkey meat has very little fat or gristle and makes the best *machaca*, my father would assure us), and *pitayas,* or cactus fruit, all had to be smuggled in. But that was easily done, and of course it made them all the more exotic and valuable.

Cultural isolation also meant that the prejudices and fears that may have driven someone to this country could persist unchallenged. Mexico's violent Cristero Rebellion that raged between 1926 and 1929 was the prism through which many Mexicans who fled during the late 1920s would see each other. They arrived with stories of abuse and atrocities committed by and against devout Catholics. The Catholics believed that the vicious atheism and anti-Catholicism of the Calles era was manipulated by the Jews and the Protestants; these were still among us, and had to be watched. The Protestants, on the other hand, thought the Cristeros were murderous fanatics hiding among the seemingly civilized Catholic congregation, and *they* had to be watched. And as far as I could tell there were no clandestine Jewish conversos at all, except in the imagination of my grandmother and her devout, aging friends.

El Divino Salvador, the Spanish-language Presbyterian church, was dedicated in 1921. Our Lady of the Blessed Sacrament was built in 1917. By the time I was a kid the Mexican Protestants had multiplied and built Methodist, Baptist, and Pentecostal churches. Every month or so, traveling tents full of preachers and healers would make their way up the hill. The Protestants were the minority, and though they seemed not to have a secret handshake they did put on a knowing look when they encountered each other, and they often met in each other's homes to spread the Gospel along with rumors about Catholics. My mother was a *costurera*, a seamstress who sewed the dresses for *quinceañeras* and weddings, especially for the Protestant girls. The Christian ladies would gather in our tiny house, drink coffee, and talk darkly about the guns in the basement of the Catholic church. They all had Catholic friends, but they were sure that hidden amongst them were the ringleaders of the next rebellion. But who were they? That was the subject of much speculation. Theological issues were also passionately debated. The eternal fate of Jerry Lopez was the theological subject for months.

Jerry and Noni Lopez and their beautiful children were faithful members of the Presbyterian Church. Noni was a wonderful piano player, conversant with all the Spanish hymns, who would often be asked to play in the Methodist and Baptist churches as well. She was loved and admired. Jerry drove the beer truck that replenished the supply after payday's drunken debauchery had left every bar and whorehouse short. Though Jerry did not drink himself, wasn't he doing the devil's work by driving that truck? One Saturday morning as he was making his usual deliveries he was slammed into by a mining

ore truck and killed. Was he struck down by divine intervention, or was he a good Christian man who tithed each week
and worshipped with his family? Would the Lord forgive him?
Had he, at least a moment before death, asked for forgiveness?
Did he need to be forgiven? Was he eternally damned, or did
he sit on God's right hand? In their Christian zeal, Protestants
had thrown Purgatory overboard, so there was no easy answer
for the ladies.

Noni had the good sense to pack up the kids and move to
Phoenix.

By 1954 most Hispanics in the United States were citizens
by virtue of birth. Again, using Hayes-Bautista's study of
California Hispanics as a guide, in 1950 there were 189,800
immigrant Latinos in California and an astounding 819,000
US-born Hispanics. The trend would continue for at least
another decade; by 1960 the number of immigrant Hispanics
was 282,400, but the number of children born in the US was
nearly 1,750,000. The term "Hispanic" had not yet come into
use. The term most whites used for Latinos was simply "Mexicans." The Mexicans, on the other hand, invented hyphens
and phrases to describe themselves. "Mexican-American" and
"Americans of Mexican descent" were the favorite two. The
pressure to "be white," as assimilation or Americanization
were commonly called, was relentless. Perhaps that is why the
announcement in 1954 of Operation Wetback and the extension of the Bracero Program so electrified the immigrant
community and caused such soul-searching, turmoil, and ultimately deep divisions.

The dual, conflicting programs came at a time when the
proportion of foreign-born and thus "illegal" immigration
was at a low point, while the goal of Americanization seemed
achievable to national organizations such as the League of
United Latin American Citizens and the GI Forum. It was
another betrayal. To the generation of immigrants it meant

they were coming back—the soldiers, the border patrol, the vigilantes, all riding on the wave of hate that was sure to follow the announcements. The Americanizers, the national Latino organizations, supported Operation Wetback and massive deportations, but they bitterly opposed the Bracero Program. They understood that the continuation of the Bracero Program meant that Mexican culture, from language and music to food, would be replenished by the hundreds of thousands of contract laborers who would stay in the country and the thousands more to be invited each year. George I. Sánchez is often referred to as the dean of Mexican-American scholars and a respected intellectual who reached national prominence with the publication of his history of Mexican Americans, *Forgotten People*, in 1940. Sánchez, an active member and former director of the League of United Latin American Citizens, captured the fears of the Americanizers in this anguished quote in the *New York Times*:

> No careful distinctions are made between illegal aliens and local citizens of Mexican descent. They are lumped together as "Mexicans" and the characteristics that are observed among the wetbacks are by extension assigned to the local people. . . . From a cultural standpoint, the influx of a million or more wetbacks a year transforms the Spanish-speaking people of the Southwest from an ethnic group which might be assimilated with reasonable facility into what I call a culturally indigestible peninsula of Mexico. The "wet" migration . . . has set the whole assimilation process back at least twenty years.[5]

To be fair, most prominent Latino labor leaders opposed the Bracero Program as well. Examples are Ernesto Galarza, a leader in the National Farmworkers Union, an author and a respected social scientist, and Maclovio Barraza, a leading organizer with the Mine Mill; but their opposition was specific to the issue of wages and abuse. The Americanizers, on the other hand, saw a threat to their coveted but elusive welcoming into the white world.

The Bracero Program formally began with an agreement between Mexico and the United States signed on July 23, 1942. The agreement was highly controversial in Mexico. An earlier contract-labor program entered into during World War I had gone badly. When the Great War broke out, growers claimed that the conflict had removed thousands of their workers, and they successfully pressed the US government into adopting a guest-worker program. Assurances that the workers would be given decent accommodation and other guarantees were widely ignored. There were also (apparently unfounded) reports that the contract workers were being pressed into military service against their will. The World War I program was terminated by the Mexican government less than two years after it was launched.[6]

The Arizona Cotton Growers Association became the cause of the worst scandal in the program's short history. The Cotton Growers hired a recruiting firm, Nogales Labor Association, to induce workers to come to the Salt River Valley with promises of good wages, steady work, and money to return to Mexico when the war ended. The Growers routinely violated their contractual obligations. They also recruited more workers than were needed for the harvest, forcing wages downward. Some even set up company stores and forced workers to purchase from them. When the war ended and recession ensued, the growers claimed poverty and simply abandoned the workers. Ten thousand Mexican workers were left penniless and near starvation surrounding Phoenix, a city whose official population in 1920 was only 29,053. Under pressure from the Mexican and American governments, the Growers reached a new accord promising to pay the workers their overdue wages and train fares to Mexico. The Growers then refused to comply with the contract. They were, after all, only Mexicans. The Mexican government was forced to launch a welfare program for the workers and pay their train fares.[7]

The Bracero Program began with another act of gall and shameless greed by Arizona growers. In July of 1941, the Farm Bureau Federation of Arizona made a formal request of the United States Employment Service to import 18,000 Mexican contract workers. Though the request was denied, it initiated a discussion within the Farm Security Administration on the shortage of harvest labor. As a consequence of Arizona's petition, a formal request was made to the Mexican government by the Roosevelt Administration for a major guest-worker program to meet wartime shortages. Mexico's initial resistance was overcome by appropriate assurances. The opposition of organized labor in the US was ignored, and the bloody flag of war was waved to ensure approval in both countries. The wartime emergency program would outlast World War II and the Korean War and be on hand to greet the Vietnam War.[8] Though it was the circumstance of war that supplied growers with the Mexican contract labor they desired, these employers had their own reasoning for wanting Mexicans in the field. Americans, they claimed, lacked the Mexicans' skill, stamina, dependability, and natural proclivity for stoop labor. Mexicans were built by the Lord to be perfect beasts of burden, their stature was close to the ground and they could remain stooped for hours without ill effect. They were accustomed to the hot, arid climate of Arizona and California, they were honest, and they were cheap. By the way, according to the farm industry, Americans are still fat-fingered, incompetent weaklings, too clumsy to pick fruit, and Mexicans are still hardworking, stooped, honest, and cheap.

The response by Mexican workers eager to apply aston-
ished the Mexican government. Initially it opened a single
recruitment center in Mexico City. It became a Mecca for
thousands upon thousands of workers seeking work in the
United States. Mexico City estimated that its population
increased by 50,000 because of the center. Lacking the abi9lity
to feed clothe or house the human wave that confronted it the
government quickly changed course and opened centers
throughout the country and far from the seat of government.[9]

Allegations that the international agreement was being
violated came quickly. One stipulation was that braceros be
paid the prevailing wage. But flooding a farming area with
desperate contract laborers willing to work at poverty wages
and in inhumane conditions was bound to push the prevailing
wage down, so that the guarantee insisted upon by the Mexican government proved useless. The record of abuse of
braceros was dismal by the mid-1950s. Yet the only aggressive
response on the part of the Mexican government was to cancel
all agreements to place contract workers in the state of Texas
immediately after World War II. Stories of inhumane treatment and blatant racism became a fixture in the Mexican
press. One newspaper, *Mañana*, referred to Texans as "Nazis,"
who if they weren't "political partners of the Führer of
Germany were nevertheless slaves to the same prejudices."[10]
By 1954 there was an unmistakable bracero presence in
almost every barrio in the southwest. Anyone recently arrived
from Mexico, with or without papers, was suspected of being
a bracero or a wetback, and often the terms were interchange-
able. By the time I was nine and ten years old the discussion of
what to do about braceros was the principal conversation in
church socials, the union hall, and my mother's sewing, gossip,
and coffee sessions. The pressure to "Americanize" was strong
and constant, and unquestionably the presence of recently
arrived Mexicans reinforced the racism that permeated the

white world. On the other hand, the examples of wanton abuse of Mexican workers outraged the union men.

Congressional hearings to reconsider the Bracero Program began as early as 1951, but it was clear from the beginning that the Truman Administration and the Congress were simply doing the bidding of the growers.[10] The negotiations between Mexico and the United States came to an impasse in the fall of 1953 over Mexico's insistence that the extension include upward wage adjustments. On January 15, 1954, the United States unilaterally broke the impasse by simply announcing that "illegal entrants" into the US would be provided with emergency agricultural guest-worker status. Emergency status rules required that undocumented workers in the US touch Mexican soil before their adjustment could be complete. At San Ysidro and San Diego, approximately 3,200 men stormed across the border to Mexico and were immediately granted emergency status by the Border Patrol. At Calexico there were wild scenes of Mexican workers being held by one arm by Mexican police and pulled by the other into the United States by the Border Patrol. In the days that followed, growers delivered thousands of undocumented workers to Calexico to be "dried out," or given special status, and 14,000 braceros whose permits had expired were given extended status. On January 28, Mexico relented and the Bracero Program survived.[11] The United States government would remain the chief recruiter and defender of worker abuse for the agricultural industry for the next thirteen years. Historian Juan Ramón García quotes a grower as saying: "We used to buy our slaves, now we rent them from the Government."[12]

What did happen in Congress was the successful blending of anti-communist hysteria and national immigration policy. The Internal Security Act of 1950 authorized the prosecution of anyone affiliated with a socialist or communist organization or deemed subversive in any way. The Act would be used to destroy progressive unions like the Mine Mill that championed human rights in the southwest, and to label the few outspoken Latino leaders that rejected Americanization as communists. The McCarran-Walter Act of 1952 (passed over President Harry Truman's veto) was an omnibus immigration bill that authorized the denaturalization of immigrants and decreed that any "unnaturalized" alien who had entered the US since 1924 could be summarily deported regardless of family, employment, character, or contribution to the country.

Apparently to counter criticism that the US government was complicit in the mongrelization of America, President Dwight Eisenhower's administration declared war against the same "wetbacks" they were actively recruiting. Eisenhower chose a former general, Joseph Swing, to lead the task of removing millions of those "wetbacks." General Swing had been the president's roommate at West Point, had accompanied General Pershing in the failed "punitive expedition" against Pancho Villa, was a former commander of the 101st Airborne, and had performed distinguished service in the Pacific. Most importantly, he remained a close friend and confidant of the president. General Swing designed a secret military plan code-named "Operation Cloudburst," calling for 4,000 soldiers to be deployed from Yuma, Arizona. The State Department and the ambassador to Mexico were adamantly opposed to the military solution. Swing himself would later testify that a military solution was "perfectly horrible."[13] Upon retirement from the Army in 1954, Swing was appointed Commissioner of Immigration and quickly named two retired generals as his assistants. "Operation Wetback" would be as close to a military response to the "illegal invasion" as politics and good diplomatic manners permitted.

Operation Wetback was planned with the knowledge and approval of the Mexican government. The State Department worked closely with the Mexicans to make sure that there were adequate facilities for the detention and transportation of the deportees deep into Mexico. There was little coverage by the Mexican press of the mass roundups. I assume that the Mexican government, still fully capable of controlling the press, made sure that the citizenry was not outraged by the coverage.

General Swing, on the other hand, adopted the public relations technique used so effectively in the repatriations of the 1930s, "scare-heading." The most important scholar of the program, Juan Ramón García, writes,

> The carefully planned media blitz accomplished its purposes. First of all, by sensationalizing the activities and deployment of the Border Patrol it created the impression that a veritable army was being assembled. In order to maintain that impression, "maximum security prevailed throughout the operation . . . Information concerning exact officer strength and the organization of the units was kept strictly within the ranks of the officers assigned to the operation. Cleverly worded press releases plus an ostentatious display of men created an impression of greater strength than actually existed." The press was misled into overestimating the size of the actual force. Even those papers hostile to the drive inadvertently helped contribute to the illusion by constantly using such superlatives as "hordes" and "battalions" when writing about small groups of officers.[14]

And according to General Swing, scare-heading worked. The Border Patrol Management Report claimed that in Texas, 63,000 "illegal aliens" returned to Mexico voluntarily, and in California the number was so great that "it was impossible to count them."[15] And that was before the operation officially began.

On June 9, 1954, Attorney General Herbert Brownell

announced that the first deployment of Operation Wetback would launch on June 17 in California and Arizona. The day after the announcement, the Border Patrol set up roadblocks in the two states and began stopping trains and demanding papers of anyone who looked Mexican. That same day, June 10, the governors of both states received letters requesting the cooperation of local law enforcement agencies to assist in the "mass roundups."[16] The locals responded enthusiastically. Get the wets was the order of the day.

In my little town the news spread quickly, and quiet, organized panic reigned among the undocumented and those who remembered earlier deportations. The men gathered in our front yard under a chinaberry tree, sitting on chairs, boxes, and on the ground. The house was too small, it was obvious they didn't want the kids to overhear, and my mother would have taken a frying pan to the first one who lit a cigarette indoors. The gathered kids knew it was important by their whispering and dour, sometimes angry faces. I remember that this climate of secrecy and fear lasted weeks.

At that first meeting under the chinaberry tree, the group included the few men who had been deported, plus a handful of others who were undocumented or whose wives were undocumented. The deported believed that they had been betrayed in the 1930s by their own compatriots—fingered by Mexicans who wanted their jobs or their house or were repaying insults perceived or real. They could never forget that the Gila County Welfare Board hired Mexicans to bring the news that they had been identified as illegal and warn that the family had best accept "voluntary departure" or else suffer the consequences. It was important, especially to the undocumented, that their status remained a secret lest it all begin again; but they needed help. They turned to the Mine Mill. In 1950 the Congress of Industrial Organizations, better known as the CIO, had expelled the Mine Mill in the heat of postwar anti-communist hysteria. The national leadership of the Mine Mill had been declared communists under the authority of the Internal Security Act, and even some presidents of union locals and regional organizers were subpoenaed and forced to appear before the House Un-American Activities Committee. When Mine Mill's leadership and rank and file refused to cooperate, it became clear that the Union's days were numbered. Roberto Barcon, the president of Local 589 in Miami, and Maclovio Barraza, the regional organizer for the copper strip that spanned southeastern Arizona and western New Mexico, had both been hauled before congressional committees and declared communists. Perhaps that made them pariahs to some, but to my father and to the undocumented that made them trustworthy. A chapter of the League of Latin American Citizens, LULAC, had been active in Miami since 1941, and many of its members and founders were also members of the Mine Mill, but it was LULAC that enthusiastically supported Operation Wetback. The delicate discussion with Barcon and Barraza was how to get the Union's help without triggering LULAC's hysterical self-loathing. The answer lay in the Asociación Nacional México-Americana. ANMA was a national organization chartered in a founding convention in Phoenix in 1949 to defend the rights and culture of Mexican working men and women. Its membership was drawn from the progressive unions under attack as leftist and communist, including the Longshoremen, the Furniture Workers Union, the Cannery Workers, the Electrical Workers Union, and of course the Mine Mill. Throughout its short history, ANMA would champion the rights of braceros (though adamantly opposing the Bracero Program) and the rights of the undocumented. Two of the organizers who had attended that founding convention in Phoenix were Barcon and Barraza.

The Union and ANMA set up a network of observers from

their locals in Phoenix, Tucson Superior, and Hayden. There were only two roads up the hill. If the Border Patrol or the military were on their way, calls would come directly to the Union office, and the men and their families would have time to disappear into the hills. During this entire period my mother and father imposed strict rules on us: school, church, and home. My friend Fred Barcon, son of Roberto, lived at the very bottom of Davis Canyon where it met Miami's main thoroughfare, Sullivan Street. He remembers soldiers and patrols on the streets of Miami. My father recalled that there were only a few times they hid the undocumented. Everyone with "*papeles*," papers, or temporary residence was required to present themselves at the county courthouse for review. ANMA members and the Union representatives, often one and the same, were vigilant so that no one was unjustly deported.

No one recalls a single deportation or scare-headed departure from Miami during Operation Wetback.

Operation Wetback soon came to an ignoble end. The Border Patrol commissioned Mexican and US ships to transport Texas deportees from Port Isabel, Texas, to Veracruz, Mexico. In September of 1956, during a shipment of human cargo to Veracruz, a riot protesting conditions on board broke out, a mutiny followed, and in the course of events seven men drowned. Not even Mexico's institutionalized dictatorship could restrain the press. The incident became a major embarrassment to the ruling PRI party, and the international accord was promptly suspended by the Mexican government.

Operation Wetback, the very phrase, still has a certain allure for nativists. The anti-immigrant movement cherishes nostalgically the image of generals in jeeps ordering millions of Mexicans at gunpoint into trucks, buses, rail cars, and naval vessels and pushed deep into Mexico from where they would never return. Evidence of abuse is dismissed with the sophomoric notion that if they hadn't entered the country illegally they wouldn't have been abused.

The reality of course was that Operation Wetback was the public relations ploy that kept the country distracted while the Bracero Program was being extended and enlarged. According to Ramos, General Swing's troops knew "they lacked the manpower to conduct such a widespread operation. What they planned to do was to deluge the southwestern region with advance publicity about the upcoming campaign against 'illegals.' . . . it was hoped that the threat of mass deportation and their increasingly unwelcomed status as 'invaders' would serve to pressure many of them into leaving the country voluntarily."[17] The general, confronting what he called the "wetback invasion,"[18] swaggered across the southwest, commanding a PR machine that provided a constant onslaught of movie theater newsreels and photos showing thousands of Mexicans lined up listlessly while armed, clean-shaven, light-skinned, uniformed Americans directed them out of the country. The general himself claimed that Operation Wetback had resulted in the departure of 1,300,000 illegal aliens, but some estimates reckon figures of up to 3 million.[19]

The Bracero Program collapsed from the cumulative weight of abuse on both sides of the border. The Mexican recruiting stations were replete with corruption. The poorest of Mexico's poor were forced to pay bribes for the privilege of being half-starved in Mexican recruiting centers, paraded naked for perverse "medical examinations," sprayed with DDT, herded like animals into rail cars, and transported to border towns where the nightmare continued . . . and that was only on the Mexican side. Ill treatment by farmers and complicit rural sheriffs was the daily bread of braceros. These problems were covered widely, both in the Mexican and US press. Churches and labor unions maintained campaigns of constant criticism, calling for the halt of the program, but no one in officialdom seemingly cared either in Mexico City or Washington.

Organized labor's attempts at organizing braceros or forcing them from the country failed, though occasionally violent confrontations between braceros and union men flared in the fields.[20] CBS News' now classic television special "Harvest of Shame," presented by Edward R. Murrow, was broadcast the weekend after Thanksgiving in 1960. It showed how the feast everyone had just enjoyed came to be on their table. It shocked the nation. The publication of Ernesto Galarza's *Strangers in Our Fields* caused an uproar in 1956. Then the DiGiorgio Corporation, the giant farming business that was the focus of Galarza's contempt, had the rashness to sue Galarza, and the controversy expanded. After twenty-two years, the mounting evidence of abuse could no longer be denied.

Four million, three hundred ninety-five thousand, six hundred twenty-two: that is the undisputed number of braceros that were contracted. Though they represented every region of Mexico, they came inordinately from the central and southern states. Northern Mexicans had been crossing the border since the Mexican-American War: they knew the paths of the "migra," the rhythms of the agricultural migratory stream, the ways of the urban Mexican Americans, they had developed the skills to survive and in many cases remain permanently in the United States. Braceros from the southern and central states, on the other hand, had little experience *en el otro lado*. They would be given a subsidized crash course by the American government, complete with prejudice, discrimination, and abuse. There is simply no data on how many braceros stayed, married, had children; how many sent for their families, invited friends, adopted this country as their own, and joined their northern *paisanos* in the thriving communities they had built throughout America. Of one thing we can be sure, there were millions of them, and their children were millions more and now add their grandchildren—and they were all invited in by the United States of America.

And throughout this time the pressure on children to "be white" was extreme. Being white would prevent you from being seen as a Mexican. Having the right accent, which meant no accent, dressing snazzy, being clean-cut, never but *never* speaking Spanish within earshot of white people, always saying loudly you were an American, but, if confronted about your surname or your skin color, conceding you were Mexican-American or better yet an American of Mexican descent . . . Those were the constant instructions on how to pass for white. In segregated Bullion Plaza Elementary, the Mexican school, the teachers would tape your mouth shut if you spoke Spanish. Your name was "Americanized": Alfredo became Alfred, Guillermo became William, Federico was Fred, all names ending with an "o" were just shortened, so Ernesto became Ernest. Pánfilo was screwed, they changed his to Perry. Girls were not exempt, María was Mary and Rosa became Rose. Yahaira was a challenge. Her white name became Joann.

Accents were a real problem. Second- and third-generation kids came from households that spoke Spanish at home, so even they would pronounce English with an accent. Television, the great teacher of English and leveler of accents, was only barely becoming affordable to most mining families in the 1950s; movies were affordable perhaps once a week, and kids were in school for only a few hours a day. Thus accents, which we did not know we had, were reinforced constantly. It was the persistence of accents that led to some of the most ridiculous exercises in whiteness. One ludicrous idea was teaching kids to speak in "round sounds." To this day I don't know if this was a local invention or whether some lame-brained linguist actually developed this method. Open your mouth slightly, then form an "O" with your lips extended outward, then speak while keeping your mouth in that O shape. Try it. It will indeed reduce your accent, but it will also make you sound like a fastidious and pretentious fool. In elementary school it could make you the object of derision and get you a good whuppin' from the other Mexican kids as an added benefit.

Enforcing accentless English were kids policing other kids. To mispronounce a word, wash for watch, eschool for school for example, would lead to guffaws and mockery. "*¡Qué feo lo mascas!*" "You chewed that up ugly" was a favorite phrase. Kids recently arrived or kids who came from homes where only Spanish was spoken were ridiculed to the point that they were afraid to speak.

Going to the Mexican movies at the Lyric would signal to the whole town you were a Mexican, and not really a Mexican American or an American of Mexican descent. Just a Mexican, and it was becoming increasingly clear to the kids that being Mexican was not a good thing. The Lyric closed, because the Mexican families who had enjoyed the movies every week had transmogrified into Mexican Americans or better yet Americans of Mexican descent, and in their new identities wouldn't be caught dead in a Mexican theater. Taking bean burros or *tacos de papa* for lunch at school was an open admission that you were a Mexican, as was humming or singing any ranchera or corrido. "Cielito Lindo" was acceptable to the white teachers, and at least once a year they trotted a bunch of Mexican kids to the auditorium to sing it for them. I still hate "Cielito Lindo," and don't call me Alfred. My mother spoke little English, and my father worked long shifts and was always volunteering for overtime. I would accompany my mother to pay the bills and do the shopping as the translator and cultural guide. It could get a bit embarrassing when inquiring about feminine products and underclothes.

It fell to me because my sister, god bless her, was embarrassed by our mother's Spanish. There was little doubt my mother was a Mexican.

Girls loved Max Factor. Especially the bleaching cream. It would whiten them up. In the late 1950s Rose Escobedo was the first Mexican-American cheerleader at Miami High School. Years later she told me that at the time she attributed her breakthrough to Max Factor. She used it all week before the tryouts. If girls were lighter-skinned, putting henna in their hair could give it a reddish tone and make them look, well, Italian maybe.

I was a problematic student in high school. My older brother was a record-breaking track star, a varsity football player, and a pretty good student. My sister was every teacher's pet. Given my behavior, I was ordered to the principal's office routinely, and given a "good talking-to" before being expelled for a day or so. Principal Nick Ragus, whose preferred method of counseling students was the loud, intimidating rant, would remind me each time: "You know why you're not like your brother and sister? You don't have red hair! You don't have freckles! You look like a Mexican! You better straighten out!" My mother suggested henna.

Mexican restaurants started serving Spanish food, especially if they wanted to attract white clientele and the folks who aspired to be white. Amazingly, Spanish food, it turned out, was exactly the same as the tacos and enchiladas they served the week before. La Casita in Globe, famous for its menudo, red chile, enchiladas con huevos, and, of course, always serving its homemade tortillas with a generous slathering of butter, declared its cuisine Spanish-American. The food is just as wonderful today, and the neon sign on the window has long ago been boxed and taken away, consigned to the trash heap like a bad memory. In Miami, the town's most popular restaurant, El Rey, where I followed both of my brothers scrubbing floors and washing dishes, proclaimed with its own sign that what it called a "regular burro," red chili and beef with refried beans and longhorn cheese mixed together in a heavenly concoction, was really Spanish-American. And down in Phoenix, the El Rey on South Central was the final defiant restaurant in Arizona refusing to serve blacks. It became the site of continuous protests by the NAACP until the tiny, family-owned storefront relented at last. It never regained its popularity with the white downtown crowd, but it survived in business for years afterward serving pretty good Mexican food, especially its chile colorado with frijoles de la olla. A big hand-lettered sign painted onto the south-side wall of the homely white building reading "Mexican Dishes" survived until El Rey closed in the early seventies, but the neon sign that announced Spanish-American food on the window under a big colorful poster of a sombrero came down soon after its ignorant last stand against integration. Up the street from the infamous El Rey was the Spanish Kitchen. The chief cook was Sra. Duran, whose daughters Rosie and Esther would become icons of the Latino civil rights movement in Arizona. The menu at the Spanish Kitchen was tacos dorados, chile verde, menudo, gorditas, and many other northern Mexican delicacies. There wasn't a paella or even a Spaniard in the kitchen. Discomfort with calling someone or even something Mexican lingered for many years. As late as 1970 the city of Scottsdale held a downtown fair featuring "Spanish food." The menu as listed in the advertising section of the *Arizona Republic* was tacos, tostadas, burritos, and enchiladas with rice and beans.

In February of 1988, Arizona's Secretary of State Rose Mofford assumed the governorship upon the impeachment of Evan Mecham (who had a habit of calling African Americans "pickaninnies"[21]). I became part of a hastily assembled team who would lead her transition. Governor Mofford was a native of Globe, six miles from Miami, born in 1922 and clearly a woman of her generation. From time to time, facing a controversial issue that could have an impact on her future electoral plans, she would turn to me and ask, "What do the Spanish think of this, Alfredo?" The appropriate response would have been "How the hell should I know?" but instead I would gently ask in response, "You mean the Mexicans, don't you?" and she would grumble her agreement.

Nationally, LULAC and the GI Forum preached patriotism and whiteness and embraced Operation Wetback. They were at the forefront of the campaign to Americanize us. LULAC was then, and is still today, the oldest and largest Latino civil rights organization in the country. LULAC's record of struggle is impressive. The GI Forum was formed after World War II in response to blatant discrimination against Latino veterans. In fairness to both organizations, their obsession with whiteness was only to help young people survive and succeed in an exceedingly hostile climate. The concern for "being white," however, dates back to the Treaty of Guadalupe Hidalgo. The treaty that ended the Mexican and American War guaranteed that Mexicans who lived in the territories that would become the United States would do so "with the enjoyment of all the rights of citizens."[22] The assumption of the Mexican negotiators was that those residing in their former territories would simply become US citizens. They were snookered. US citizenship at the time was primarily limited to white persons, and Mexicans, as anyone can plainly see, are a marvelous mess of African, Indian, Spanish, and whatever else happened to land on that shore. They were closer to uniformly mestizo. An international treaty notwithstanding, prior to the adoption of the fourteenth amendment of the Constitution, each individual state determined the citizenship status of Mexicans. Mexicans deemed mestizo or Indian in appearance were categorized as Indians, and in most states were denied citizenship, property rights, the right to testify in court or ever to become a naturalized citizen. Those declared black were subject to applicable laws during a period when slavery was still legal in most states.[23] For the next century, Latinos would be challenging state laws in court and pleading with the US Census to be categorized as white. LULAC, formed in 1929, waged a heroic battle to establish and maintain that Mexican Americans in the US have the full rights of citizens, regardless of their mestizohood, and that meant "being white."

The goal of being white may have had roots in the struggle for civil rights, but by the 1950s it had become an obsession to be accepted as American albeit of Mexican descent, and to be distinguished—as George Sánchez reminded us—from "illegal aliens" and wetbacks. The historian David Gutiérrez quotes as follows a LULAC delegate to their 1946 convention:

> The American citizen of Mexican ancestry is weak because he is a minority citizen. Discrimination will pursue him until he blends with the majority group of this country enough to lose his present identity. This is a discouragingly slow process . . . [but] if we fail to do it we shall continue to be discriminated against, insulted and abused; and complaining of injustice in the name of democracy will not help us. We shall simply be begging for things that must be paid for.[24]

Being white was not about assimilation and acculturation. That was taking place, and would have taken place even without the punitive campaign by LULAC and the GI Forum. No, from the point of view of these organizations, "being white" meant losing our identity. Melting away. The blatant discrimination and prejudice of the time did not discourage them. The *pachucos* were perhaps the most extreme manifestation of resistance to the enforced dogma. Pachucos were a Mexican youth subculture that burst upon the scene in Los Angeles. Though few in number, their impact was powerful. They dressed in a distinctive, flamboyant fashion, especially the men: exaggerated "zoot suits" with a coat reaching almost to the knee and baggy pleated pants that rode high above the waist, spectacularly colorful satin shirts with ties to match and, topping it off, a jauntily slanted wide-brimmed hat, with a feather that curved beautifully over it. They spoke in a special patois they called caló, primarily Spanglish with a decidedly urban black influence. The patois included the term "chicano" when referring to themselves. In 1942 twenty-two pachucos were charged with murder in a case, the Sleepy Lagoon trial, that became a national scandal. In 1943, confrontations between US marines and sailors and pachucos in Los Angeles sparked a week of riots in L.A. and other cities in the country. Soldiers and sailors were ordered to stand down only after Mexico had lodged a formal diplomatic complaint, and President Roosevelt intervened.[25] The Los Angeles Police Department released "A Report on the Mexicans" in 1943 that described Mexicans as naturally given to violence, with "biological urges to kill, or at least let blood." That tendency arose from the "Asiatic nomads" from which we were descended and from the "Indian blood" running through us. The Mexican's "utter disregard for the value of life" was, the report asserted, "well known to everyone."[26] Once the asiatic connection was established and the violent stereotype reaffirmed, it was inevitable that the pachucos would be identified as part of an elaborate communist plot. The citizens' committee formed to defend the accused in the Sleepy Lagoon case included prominent Mexican-American Angelenos like Josefina Fierro de Bright, and major celebrities Rita Hayworth and Anthony Quinn; it was promptly declared a "Communist front organization" by the Los Angeles police chief, C. B. Horrall.[27] All of this attention served to spread the fashion and the patois to every barrio in America and, in the eyes of many young Latinos, to transform pachucos into outlaw heroes.

Pachuco influence was still strongly felt in the 1950s. Dressing like a pachuco in that decade meant wearing high-riding khaki pants, thick-soled work shoes with steel-tipped heels, white T-shirts, and a little *tandita* on top. A tandita was a cockily placed, fancy fedora. The style and the slang had the pleasant effect of driving Americanizers insane, but frankly, the pachuco threat had dissipated by the 1950s and was by then but an irritating side show. The Americanizers were single-mindedly dedicated to extinguishing the Mexican identity in America, and they seemed poised to succeed.

I finished high school in 1963 and, like my two older brothers before me, promptly enlisted in the Army. By the time I came back, the Americanizers were on the run, and the rumble of change and the talk of revolution were everywhere.

CHAPTER 3

War and Chicanos

At seventeen I thought it natural to hitchhike the six miles to Globe, Arizona, walk into the recruiter's storefront, and enlist in the military. There were no thoughtful conversations at the kitchen table with my mother and father asking me to carefully think it through, nor was anyone in my family dismayed. It was, I guess in retrospect, what was expected of me. My father had been exiled for most of World War II; his brother José enlisted almost immediately upon his return from Mexico; the oldest of my two brothers, Gilberto, enlisted when he turned seventeen, became a Ranger, and took part in both combat paratrooper jumps in the Korean conflict; my brother Arnoldo enlisted when he graduated from high school and spent the next twenty years on active military duty—so I guess that ride to Globe was destined. There was perhaps one more reason that my enlistment would elicit so little discussion in the family. By 1963 there was only one whorehouse left in the town, the Keystone, but business was so bad or the moral opprobrium so great that it was only open on Friday and Saturday nights. The rest of the week it just sat there at the bottom of Davis Canyon, empty, intriguing, and inviting. The stories of the painted ladies, their exotic toys, and the luxuries that surrounded them was the stuff that drove adolescents into a frenzy. One night the temptation overcame us ruffians. We broke in through a bathroom window, three of us, spent an hour or so upending the place and were disappointed by a drab cheap hotel with rooms the size of cells, steel frame beds and mattresses that stank of urine and disinfectant. There was a box of whiskey, gin, and rum in the kitchen. We stole it and lugged it up the canyon to Cabezón's house. The police came to my house and picked me up the following morning. It turns out that Cabezón had been unhappy with our paltry loot, and after the Bear and I left, he decided to go back to the Keystone, this time with a diablito, a hand truck, and his little brother. They somehow loaded up the oversize refrigerator on the hand truck and proceeded to push it down an alley and up the canyon. Cabezón was a short little fellow with an inordinately large head, hence the nickname. He must have been quite a sight pushing a refrigerator twice his height up the road. It was not long before the police took them away, and it was apparently not long after that before Cabezón gave me and the Bear up. Cabezón got probation. The Bear and I went before the superior court judge in Globe, and, given our past colorful history with Judge McGhee, he gave us an ultimatum: either the military or six months at the notorious juvenile detention center known as Fort Grant. For me it was a godsend. I intended to sign up for the Marines as soon as I was out of high school. The Bear adamantly rejected the deal, Man you're gonna be gone a long time, they could shoot you or cut your legs off and stick you in a wheelchair, ¿estás loco o qué? Me, I'm gonna be back in six months and I'm gonna kill pinche Cabezón." Thus began the Bear's long life of crime and incarceration. Fortunately he never got around to killing Cabezón.

The family has plenty of heroes, but my time in the Army was free of courageous charges, spectacular parachute jumps, extraordinary sacrifice, or even a glimpse of combat. When I got to Globe, the Marine recruiter was at lunch, so I ended up in the Army Infantry. A childhood of hunting rabbits and wild javelina pigs made shooting a big, round, slow-moving target at a hundred yards a cinch, so they declared me a sharpshooter. I was apparently smart enough to easily pass their battery of tests, so they made me a Mental Hygienist. Mental Hygiene was the Army's euphemistic way of describing a small independent unit whose responsibility was to remove primarily combat command officers from the front who had, in the eyes of their superiors, gone stark raving mad and were threatening the wellbeing of the troops. I guess I wasn't that smart because it took me some time and some straight talk to understand what a unit like that needed with a sharpshooter. Thankfully, I never shot a lunatic officer, though I did meet a number of candidates.

And upon the end of my term I respectfully declined reenlistment. The war gave me a heightened understanding that the work of killing and death was not my work. In time I would conclude it should be nobody's work.

War and the role of Latinos in America's wars was to become one of the major themes of the Chicano Movement. Vietnam would divide America. It would rip through the Latino community as well, but there it would also call into question what was increasingly seen as the embarrassing pandering of the Americanizers and its deadly consequences.

Wherever Latino veterans gather there will inevitably be a conversation about our proud presence in every conflict since the Revolutionary War. David Hayes-Bautista's *El Cinco de Mayo: An American Tradition* details the Californios who proudly volunteered and valiantly fought with the Union Army.[1] Abraham Lincoln and Benito Juárez were the two most admired figures to the Californio community. Latinos volunteered proudly for World War II and the Korean War from every city and town in the southwest. After I was discharged, it was easy to find the "Mexican" VFW or American Legion post in almost every community, large or small, that I would find myself in. The battlefront may have been integrated, but the veteran organizations, their rituals, and the drinking that went along with them never were. Vietnam was different, and so were the Chicano veterans. Rather than be the occasion for proud nostalgic storytelling, and, in many cases, liquored-up fantastical tales of heroism and suffering (my post had an informal rule that after ten p.m. or five beers, drunken exaggerations were forgiven), Vietnam provoked heated debate. I believe a large percentage of Chicano Vietnam vets soon withdrew from the posts, because any expression of doubt about the war's justice would provoke outbursts from older vets. Questioning whether Latinos were being killed at an inordinately high rate could ignite angry charges of cowardice and questionable patriotism. It had been the unchallenged dogma of that generation that Latinos volunteered for war, volunteered for the most dangerous units, and fought hard. If you were killed in combat, so be it. That was the price of courage.

And the price was high. In October of 1969 the Congressional Record published a study, *Mexican-American Casualties in Vietnam*, by Ralph Guzman. The analysis found that:

Mexican-American military personnel have a higher death rate in Vietnam than all other servicemen. Analysis of casualty reports for two periods of time: one between January 1961 and February 1967 and the other between December 1967 and March 1969 reveals that a disproportionate number of young men with distinctive Spanish names do not return from the Southeast Asia theater of war. Investigation also reveals that a substantial number of them are involved in high-risk branches of the service . . . It is significant that the percentages of Spanish surnamed casualties for each period remains nearly constant at 19.0 percent.[2]

According to the 1960 US Census, only 11.8 percent of the total southwestern population had distinctive Spanish surnames. Guzman speculates that over-representation in death may be due to the fact that few Mexican Americans were in college, and thus they were unable to receive deferments available to others, or it may be due to factors "that motivate Mexican Americans to join the Armed Forces, [of which] some may be rooted in the inherited culture of these people." He goes on to say that "still others wish to prove their Americanism. Organizations like the American GI Forum, composed of ex-GIs of Mexican-American identity, have long proclaimed the sizable military contributions of the Mexican-American soldier. According to the American GI Forum and other Mexican-American groups, members of this minority have an impressive record of heroism in time of war. There is a concomitant number of casualties attending this Mexican American patriotic investment."[3]

Among Chicano activists, the study would be quoted as if it were Biblical verse in a gathering of evangelical zealots. "One in five" of those killed in Vietnam were Chicanos, was the rallying cry of the Chicano Moratorium against the war. "One in five" was the proud assertion offered at American Legion Post 41, and presumably at every other Mexican post and at every meeting of LULAC and the GI Forum, to prove that we were indeed courageous, patriotic Americans willing to sacrifice our young in defense of this country. Defending, even praising the disproportionate killing of Mexican-American soldiers was probably an untenable position to take from the beginning. Ultimately, the Vietnam experience and the activism of the Chicano Movement would end the rhetoric of being white and of delivering oneself to Americanism at the expense of one's Latino identity. It would also besmirch the argument that you demonstrated your patriotism by sending your children to war, knowing there existed a statistically higher chance that they would be killed.

A passionate redefinition of being Mexican-American, and a wave of radical activism that seemed like a necessary rite of passage, took hold in college campuses across the southwest in the mid-1960s. The Chicano Movement, as the decentralized, often angry, amorphous movement came to be known, was the product of a long, slow boil. The kids were pissed, and they were primarily pissed at the established Mexican-American leadership.

The principal organizations that constituted the Mexican-American leadership in the post–World War II era were LULAC and the GI Forum. The activists of the Chicano Movement were raised in a social and political environment that those two organizations helped create. The Chicano generation was the beneficiary of their accomplishments and the inheritor of their legacy, such as it was. LULAC was founded in 1929 in the very heart of discrimination, Corpus Christi, Texas. Membership was limited to American citizens. It has a remarkable record of accomplishment. LULAC was organizing boycotts and sit-ins in the 1930s to integrate lunch counters and public accommodations; it was responsible for the first major legal challenge against segregated "Mexican" schools, Salvatierra v. Del Rio Independent School District in 1931; in 1945 it successfully challenged the segregated schools of Orange County, California; it filed fifteen challenges in Texas that finally ended school segregation there; and in 1946 it filed Mendez v. Westminster, which ended 100 years of segregated schools in California. It was the Mendez case that would serve as the key precedent to the Brown v. Board of Education case that ended legal segregation in the rest of the country. LULAC marched, protested, filed lawsuits, and advocated for the rights of Latinos throughout its history. So how does such a defender of human rights become a major tormentor of the undocumented and the chief proselytizer of being white in America?

The Mexican-American obsession with being white probably begins with the bungled negotiation that produced the Treaty of Guadalupe Hidalgo. The Mexicans in the conquered territories were guaranteed the enjoyment of all rights of citizens. The problem of course was that in the United States only white persons could enjoy all of the rights of citizens. The first major test of the whiteness of Mexicans occurred in California twenty years after it became part of the United States. The citizenship of a wealthy Californio and one of the state's major land barons, Pablo de la Guerra, was challenged in 1870 when he was called to sit on a jury. De la Guerra, whose family arrived in Santa Barbara before the British colonies declared their independence, had served in California's first Constitutional Convention. Stripped of his citizenship, he became ineligible to own land, vote, hold office, or even sue his accusers. De la Guerra was clearly not white, and possibly even "three-fourths Indian."[4] He was said to be the victim of "caste creep," wherein Indians and mulattos tarnish the purity of white blood.[5] Fortunately, de la Guerra had the resources to hire attorneys and fight back. Ultimately, the court decided that he was "white enough" and restored his citizenship, but it also set a dangerous precedent: the court appropriated for itself the right to determine racial composition and exclude from citizenship any Mexican who was not "white enough."[6]

In 1897 a federal district court in San Antonio took an entirely different tack. Ricardo Rodriguez, who was applying for citizenship, was carefully targeted by nativists who were seeking to create a legal precedent stating that all non-white Mexicans were ineligible. Rodriguez was a "copper-colored or red-skinned man with dark eyes, straight black hair and high cheekbones." He would also testify that he was neither of the "original Aztec race nor the Spanish race," but was a "pure-blooded Mexican." Rodriguez was not trifling with the question of race, and neither was the judge. Judge T. S. Maxey found that Rodriguez had a right to citizenship based on the Treaty of Guadalupe Hidalgo and subsequent international agreements. Period. Judge Maxey did not consider the question of Rodriguez's red skin, the placement of his cheek-bones, or his racial composition as relevant.[7]

Unfortunately, the Rodriguez case did not settle the matter. The state constitution of California adopted in 1849 gave the right of citizenship only to white Mexicans. Mestizos, Indians, and blacks were excluded.[8] The 1836 Constitution of the Republic of Texas gave citizenship to Mexicans who were not Indian or black, and the territorial constitution of Arizona limited citizenship to white males and white Mexican males.[9] Courts and state commissions and laws would continue to try to exclude anyone who was discernibly mestizo. The delicate legal status of Mexican Americans augured toward protecting one's legal whiteness. In 1930 the United States Congress considered a bill imposing quotas on Mexican migration. For the first time in history, Mexican Americans appeared in Congress to testify, mostly in support of the legislation. The testimony in part was that LULAC, then barely a year old, was dedicated to developing "within the members of our race the best and purest and most perfect type of true and loyal citizen of the United States of America." [10]

That same year, as the anti-immigrant campaign was nearing its peak, the US Census announced that it was reclassifying "Mexicans" from the white category to a new "Mexican" category. The census would now enumerate race as: a. White, b. Negro, c. Mexican. Predictably, LULAC mounted a concerted effort to overturn that decision. In 1936 the city of El Paso announced that Mexicans would henceforth be categorized as colored. LULAC organized a successful campaign to reverse El Paso's decision and, prompted by that victory, filed a court challenge to the US Census classification of Mexicans as, well, Mexicans.[11]

LULAC took up the objective of being white as a civil rights strategy. Being anything other than white placed the whole community in a legally precarious position. Unfortunately, in time being white became a single-minded strategy for destroying Mexican identity. Since its foundation, the "LULAC Code" had urged: "Be proud of your origin . . . respect your glorious past and help defend the rights of your people . . . learn how to master with purity the most essential languages—English and Spanish." But historian David Gutiérrez tells us that in the early 1950s those provisions were stricken from the code. In fact, in LULAC's "Aims and Purposes" published in 1954, all references to the Spanish language completely disappeared, replaced by a pledge to "foster the acquisition and facile use of the official language of our country that we may thereby equip ourselves and our families for the fullest enjoyment of our rights and privileges and the efficient discharge of our duties to this, our country."[12]

At its ugliest, during the 1950s, LULAC's obsession with being white was the handmaiden to the practices of humiliating children who spoke Spanish, of punishing anyone appearing too Mexican, and of supporting blatant discrimination against the recently arrived because they replenished the *mexicanidad* of the community. In time LULAC's obsession appeared to the students of the Chicano Movement as self-loathing. Eventually, however, the abuses of the Bracero Program, the blatant racism in the execution of Operation Wetback, the troubling casualty rates in Vietnam, and finally the confrontation with the Chicano Movement caused LULAC to reconsider their fifty-year longing to be just like the Anglos . . . maybe even to *be* them.

In the 1950s, the American GI Forum was in the news even more than LULAC. I suspect that just about every Mexican American heard the story of Private Felix Longoria. He was killed by a sniper in the Philippines, his body was returned to his family in his hometown of Three Rivers, Texas, and the local Funeral Home owner refused to bury him, because "the whites won't like it," he reportedly told Longoria's widow.[13]

The American GI Forum, founded only months earlier, immediately launched a protest and also formally asked Senator Lyndon Johnson to intervene. In the midst of the controversy, Mrs. Longoria and her children were refused lunch at the local diner, because they were Mexican. The case of Private Longoria became a national scandal, and the president of the GI Forum, Dr. Hector P. García—a charismatic, brilliant, articulate voice on behalf of Mexican-American veterans—quickly became the most recognizable Mexican-American civil rights leader of the decade. As a result of the Forum's efforts, Pvt. Longoria became the first Mexican-American soldier buried at Arlington National Cemetery.

García articulated the plight of the Mexican American unlike anyone before him. He commanded media attention like no Mexican-American civil rights leader ever had. Forum members paraded at every opportunity and surrounded Dr. (former Major) García each time he spoke. In the 1950s the guys had yet to grow a paunch, they still wore their uniforms handsomely and executed parade orders crisply. García and the Forum loved the press, and the press loved them back. Unfortunately, García and the Forum suffered from the same schizophrenia as their counterparts at LULAC. García railed against the "wetback tide" and lobbied against illegal immigration. In 1954, the Forum published a propaganda booklet still ballyhooed by nativists: "What Price Wetbacks?" "Illegal immigration represents the fundamental problem facing the Spanish-speaking population of the southwest," it read. It argued that poverty, sickness, and low educational achievement was a consequence of those Mexicans crossing without papers, but then went further than the other Mexican organizations. The Forum offered policy solutions that read as though they were manufactured in Bush or Obama's Department of Homeland Security fifty years later: "enforceable penalties for harboring or aiding an alien . . . confiscation of vehicles used to transport aliens and . . . enforceable penalties for the employment of illegal aliens."[14] The Forum was composed of veterans of America's wars; all were required to be citizens, and reeked of patriotism. This made them particularly credible when, in the midst of the Cold War and the Red Scare, they raised without a scintilla of evidence the specter of communist infiltration among their reasons to oppose the "wetback tide."[15] Until now, wetbacks had been merely filthy, disease-ridden, ignorant, and lazy—but after the Forum's attack they were potentially a terrorist threat as well.

So imagine you are a kid in the 1950s, and what seems an unstoppable onslaught of messages from every front is telling you that you have to be like them, not like you, and even your own family is telling you that for your own good you have to be Alfred, not Alfredo, and that Alfred should be careful where he speaks Spanish and to whom and never ever even hint that his family had been deported and to proclaim loudly albeit untruthfully that everyone in the family including the dog was made in America. Even a kid wonders why the leaders of the Mexican-American community mostly attack Mexicans, even though they are careful to point out they only attack the wetback kind. In the 1940s and '50s the border was not yet a war zone. Folks went back and forth with relative ease, the neighbors may have arrived without papers and stayed, heck, half the town may have arrived without papers. As a little kid I used to ask my father what a wetback was, and he would explain that the origin of the word referred to crossing the Rio Grande with no papers, but now it meant all Mexicans without papers. Mexicans without papers were wetbacks. I think that made sense when I was five or six. By the time I was twelve or so I began to wonder whether this Dr. García guy had his head screwed on right. And perhaps only years afterwards did I grasp that these so-called leaders of the Mexican-American community had, for doubtless the most selfless of reasons, adopted the rhetoric of the nativists in order to achieve ends opposed by the nativists. They were cowed, I thought, by the seeming power and popularity of hate, so they hoped to sound just like the racists in order to demonstrate that they and presumably the cleaned-up, round-sounding English-speaking Americans of Mexican descent whom they claimed to speak for weren't really like those dirty Mexicans the racists hated. The logic was as convoluted as my attempt to explain it. The tactic was foolish, and ultimately discredited. Unfortunately, in the century to come, mainstream Washington-based Latino and immigrant rights groups would adopt the shameful tactic and suffer the same fate.

In the tough mining town of Miami, the anti-immigrant hysteria played out with a difference. In much of the southwest, perhaps the only voices Latinos heard speaking out on their behalf were those of the compromised, often servile LULAC and GI Forum. In Miami and in a few other places across the country there were alternative voices. Their message, because it was diametrically opposed to the prevailing dirge, was all the more startling. And to young Mexican Americans, uncomfortable with the constant pressure to conform, it would have sounded all the more intriguing and exciting. In Miami, it was the Union.

By 1950 the Miami Copper Company had opened a new open pit mine in the Sleeping Beauty mountain ridge, about twenty miles from the town. The company had reached a sweetheart deal with United Steelworkers to be the lead union and for the first time to accept Mexican members, my father among them. The company was responding to intense pressure to break the Mine Mill union, because of its "subservience to the Communist Party." *Time* magazine, in the 1950s perhaps the most powerful single publication, described how the Mine Mill was tossed out of the CIO:

The C.I.O. was cleaning out one more Red-infested corner of its labor empire. This time the man in the corner was 39-year-old Maurice Travis, boss of the militant Mine, Mill and Smelter Workers . . . "Only the Communist assumption that what is good for the Soviet Union is good for American labor could justify Mine-Mill's position. Only constant subservience to the Communist Party can explain it." Mine-Mill, said Potofsky [the CIO official who presented the indictment against the Mine Mill], was dominated and its policies set by a four-member steering committee, which took its orders from . . . the hierarchy of the Communist Party. The Reds ran the union newspaper, its organizing staff and its leadership . . . Travis denied the charges, declared that the hearing was a "kangaroo court." But C.I.O. President Philip Murray gave him short shrift. He threw Mine-Mill out of the C.I.O.[16]

Red-infested or not, the Mine Mill remained for another fifteen years the voice of the Mexican community in the mining strip of Arizona and eastern New Mexico. The leadership of Local 586 in Miami, Roberto Barcon, Kikes Pastor (father of future Congressman Ed Pastor), Elias Lazarin, and the regional organizer Maclovio Barraza, were treated with deference in the town. Barcon and Barraza were both named communists by a Congressional committee, which led to the often-whispered wisdom, "If Barcon and Barraza are communists, then communists must be some pretty good people." The Union responded to every act of discrimination in the town. In time the schools were integrated, the Y's Christian pool became open to Mexicans every day of the week, and the Irish priest deigned to give Mexicans communion from the same silver service as he did the white folk. The Union maintained its fierce opposition to the dual pay system in any form and challenged the Company on discriminatory promotion practices. The skilled crafts—electricians, carpenters, welders—always a bastion of white workers as long any old-timer could remember, opened to its first Mexican members. Arnold Rojas, a lifelong Union member, became the first Latino electrician at Inspiration Consolidated Copper Company, and my father the first at Miami Copper Company's Sleeping Beauty Mine.

Mine Mill was instrumental in forming a progressive Mexican-American national organization that would unabashedly fight for the rights of Mexican workers and families, be they documented, undocumented, or braceros. The Asociación Nacional México-Americana (ANMA) formed in response to angry Union members who were beaten and abused by the sheriff of Grants, in New Mexico. A legal defense was mounted on their behalf, a successful political campaign to defeat the sheriff was organized. In the aftermath the Union came to the realization that a national organization to aggressively defend the rights of Mexican-American working people was needed.[17] The initial membership was drawn from the members of Mine Mill and from the progressive unions that had also been forced out of the CIO by anti-communist hysteria. ANMA grew quickly. Within four years there were local branches in almost every Western community in which progressive labor had a presence: Los Angeles, San Francisco, El Paso, Phoenix, Denver, Tucson, Albuquerque, and of course every mining community in the southwest. One of ANMA's significant organizers was a very young former president of the Longshoremen's local in San Francisco, the future founder of the Mexican American Political Association and soon to become one of the most important political and community leaders of the Latino community: Bert Corona.

ANMA aggressively fought discrimination on every front and—unlike LULAC, the Forum, and even the predecessor to Cesar Chavez's United Farm Workers, the National Agriculture

Workers Union—organized braceros to fight the wanton abuse to which they were often subjected.[18]

Mine Mill and ANMA were both important players in the making of perhaps the most significant and realistic film of Mexican life in mining towns, depicting for the first time the powerful role of women in Mexican life: *Salt of the Earth*. On the morning of October 15, 1950, the miners at the underground Empire Zinc mine in Hanover, New Mexico, mounted a picket line at the gates. Mine Mill had demanded an end to the dual wage system, wherein Mexican workers were paid less than their white counterparts for doing the same job, and for their wages to be raised to the industry standard. The company refused. The strike began when the workers surfaced from below. The strike was not unlike any other in the parched hills of the mining strip that ran from northern Mexico, through Arizona, and into western New Mexico. Strikes were a tough drama that dominated the region while they lasted, but the mining towns' isolation meant that they rarely received much notice in the major cities. What transformed the Empire Zinc strike was the company's decision that it would reopen with non-union labor. In preparation for what they perceived as their ultimate defeat of Mine Mill, the Company asked for an injunction against further picketing by the Union. On June 12, 1951, a federal judge dutifully granted it.[19]

The Union's meeting that evening was contentious and angry. It was doubtful that future action would be possible. Defeat seemed imminent. But the gloom lifted when the wife of one of the workers pointed out that the injunction was against striking miners. The wives were not miners, "so they could picket and the Sheriff would have no authority to stop them." Macho Mexican men first scoffed at the notion, but when they realized the women were serious, mockery gave way to stunned disbelief, followed by vociferous objections. The meeting lasted for hours. "We had a hard time convincing the men but we finally did, by a vote," Braulia Velázquez, an outspoken wife, would comment later. An unusual provision in the Mine Mill's bylaws made the difference. Local 890's auxiliary members, the miner's wives, were allowed a vote, and they voted overwhelmingly to take over the picket line. The women were at the company's gates at sunrise. They would stay there until the end of the strike. [20]

The sheriff and the company representatives stared at the women in the picket line, uncertain how to respond. A few days later they regained their composure, wrangled an arrest order from the local county attorney and sent the sheriff's deputies to arrest the picketers, who were all women, many with children. The deputies threw gas grenades into the crowd of women, then charged at them. There was bitter resistance; according to the deputies, "we keep arresting them but they keep moving in . . ." Fifty-three women were ultimately arrested and jailed, where they proceeded "to raise hell the entire day. The deputies jailed the children as well as the women and the conditions were intolerable. According to the Sheriff they made the 'worst mess.' He released all 53 along with their children that evening. The following morning they were at the picket line as a national scandal erupted."[21]

Rosie the Riveter did what she was told on behalf of the United States of America, always depicted as a smiling, red-cheeked, young white woman beloved by everyone. Esperanza the Picketer was brown, spoke English with an accent, did not do what the authorities asked, was angry, demanded equality, and acted on behalf of a union that had been declared communist by the red-baiters in Congress. Women like her were not conforming to the preachings of the Americanizers.

ANMA launched a national campaign in support of the strike. By 1951 ANMA had locals throughout the southwest. ANMA adopted Mine Mill's method of organizing families, as Bert Corona, the northern California lead organizer, explained: "In Oakland for example we had about one hundred and fifty families. In San José, about four hundred families joined ANMA . . . we built quite a chapter in San Francisco organizing between three hundred and four hundred families. ANMA supported equal pay for equal work for Mexicans, and it supported equal rights for men and women." He recalls, "Several ANMA chapters had strong women leaders. In San José, for example, Dora Sanchez . . . was the heart and soul of ANMA. The INS tried to deport her husband . . . In San Francisco key women leaders were Aurora Santana de Dawson, Elvira Romo, and Abigail Alvarez." ANMA was fiercely proud of its Mexican heritage, it was uncompromising in its support for liberation movements throughout Latin America, and it displayed an internationalist, pan-Latin perspective (the Guatemalan consul in northern California attended meetings to describe how the US government was trying to overthrow the democratically elected administration of President Jacobo Arbenz). It participated in demonstrations supporting the Cuban Liberation movement headed by a then obscure guerrilla leader named Fidel Castro, it opposed nuclear armament and supported the peace movement. ANMA's reach was impressive, and its support for the strike meant that this industrial action would soon be a cause célèbre in Latino communities across the southwest.[22]

The strike also caught the attention of Hollywood. Three filmmakers, all blacklisted in Hollywood for their leftist views and activities, worked with Union organizers and the members of Local 890 to present a true picture of the confrontation at Empire Zinc. It was a radical departure from Hollywood filmmaking. Only a handful of trained professional actors were in the film, including the Mexican film actress Rosaura Revueltas and a blacklisted actor, Will Geer. Almost every other role was played by town folks, mostly members of Local 890. The scriptwriter himself insisted on sharing the story with the strikers, seeking their approval at every stage. ANMA and Mine Mill became as committed as the filmmakers to seeing the project through to completion. Alleged Commie filmmakers in cahoots with a Commie-led union would not go unnoticed for long. An influential, nationally syndicated columnist, Victor Riesel, wrote a blistering column in February 1953, nearly a year before the film's release. The column offered a taste of what was to come. Riesel claimed that the "pro-Soviet" Mine Mill was paying for the film, implied that the filming near Los Alamos might involve atomic spying, and finally that the film would feature "abuse of the foreign-born in the US" and depict "Americans as ogres who exploit peoples who are not all-Caucasian."[23] The film was unrelentingly and viciously attacked by the right, while conservative theater artists' unions refused to authorize projectionists to show the film. Theater owners backed off from commitments to show the film, blaming it on the theater artists' unions. One year after its release the movie had been shown in exactly thirteen theaters.[24]

Salt of the Earth may have been a financial disaster, but it has an extraordinarily powerful moral force. The story of the women who seized control of the strike at the moment it teetered on the brink of doom is compelling. In 1954 it was revolutionary. I saw the movie when I was eleven or so in the Union hall. I was stunned. Up there on the screen were real Mexicans, in a story that I understood and believed. The kitchen was a real Mexican miner's kitchen, that was no Hollywood kitchen, and the town was no movie set, heck, those were the houses in the Canyons that I knew. I could not believe what I was seeing. Esperanza was beautiful, courageous, heroic, and real. The "Latin" women I had seen in American movies had fruit baskets on their head, fiery tempers, big hips swaying to a marimba band, and never got their man. The men were violent criminals, snarling, "Badges, we don't need no steenking badges," or shuffling behind the white hero, "*Sí señor, sí señor*, I cleen up after you." But these men looked like real miners, and they were depicted with dignity. I think that even at eleven I understood that this was a subversive movie, although I probably did not understand the explosiveness of showing women as a powerful force equal to any man. What I did understand was that these people on the screen were not cowering or apologizing for who they were. They were proud folks, miners, demanding to be treated with dignity and respect. They were us. And not one of them spoke in round sounds.

In the years to come I met and worked with many of the young folks who played significant roles in the Chicano Movement. Again and again, *Salt of the Earth* would weave into the conversation, and the phenomenon of seeing it for the first time would always be described as a revelatory experience, an empowering one. In the 1960s *Salt of the Earth* became a cult favorite of the Chicano Movement, rarely shown in union halls by then but popular in student unions.

In retrospect it seems miraculous that ANMA could have existed at all in the red-baiting 1950s . . . but it did not exist for very long. The government that grew to love LULAC and invited Dr. García to the White House would not allow an alternative this radical to thrive. As early as 1954 some ANMA chapters closed. Bert Corona explained that "as a result of McCarthyism and the Cold War atmosphere of the 1950s it became even more difficult for progressive unions to help support ANMA." Significant ANMA figures were declared communists. In those days, being declared a communist was similar to being named an "Islamic terrorist" after 9/11. Others, like Corona himself, were harassed, and "ANMA eventually declined because the FBI intimidated its members and destroyed the organization," Corona lamented. The last ANMA chapter closed in 1957.[25]

California was always different and better. I think that the whole Chicano generation came up thinking that. Texas was just as grubby and racist as Arizona, but our hope and our future lay in California. The Sleepy Lagoon scandal would have unquestionably met with condemnation by the Mexican-American leadership had it happened in Arizona or Texas, but in California it led to an indignant community accusing the police of brutality and the county attorney of an abuse of power. The citizens' committee did not flinch; it carried forward until it overturned the Sleepy Lagoon boys' conviction on appeal.[26] Wow! And for years afterwards the guys were in love with Rita Hayworth.

The Community Services Organization, best known by its initials CSO, was also uniquely Californian. In 1947 the progressive Ed Roybal, unrelentingly critical of McCarthyism and a veteran of World War II, ran for the Los Angeles City Council. No Latino had served on the Council since 1888. Roybal lost, but his supporters—buoyed by the camaraderie and the experience—formed the CSO. Its initial objectives were to pay the campaign's debts and register voters for the next encounter. The next encounter came in 1949, when Roybal trounced his opponent by a vote of 20,472 to 11,956. Shocking then, perhaps more so today, 82 percent of eligible voters went to the polls.[27] CSO delivered. Soon after its formation CSO attracted the attention of Saul Alinsky and the Industrial Areas Foundation. The IAF had money and organizational expertise, and the CSO had an ambitious agenda. CSO focused on voter registration and citizenship classes, and it embraced every resident of the barrio. Unlike with LULAC and the GI Forum, there were no citizenship requirements; citizens, residents, and the undocumented were all welcome. The IAF funding made it possible for the CSO to hire and train organizers to carry out its work. Herman Gallegos became the national president of CSO, and among the organizers he chose were two talented young people: Dolores Huerta and Cesar Chavez.

The Mexican-American Political Association was launched in 1959 in Fresno, California. There are a lot of folks who believe that that was it. The moment. The moment that Mexican Americans had had it with the Americanizers and were ready to push back. The lesson of ANMA's demise was all too clear. If you step out too far, the FBI and the government will destroy you. Prior to ANMA no one even risked putting Mexican-American in their name. Perhaps by 1959 the Red Scare was subsiding, perhaps the organizers knew the risks and just didn't care. The organizers of MAPA, prominent among them Bert Corona, Herman Gallegos, and Ed Roybal, tried first to set up a national organization. Meetings throughout the southwest led to an impasse because of something Bert Corona recalled as foolish. Except for the Californians everyone else demanded that "Mexican" not be part of the organization's name. They proposed Latin American, Spanish-Speaking, Hispanic . . . anything but Mexican.[28] Corona may have thought it foolish at the time, but the name was the metaphorical line in the sand that ended the era of the Americanizers. Over the course of the next few years MAPA was on fire, responding to police brutality and miscarriages of justice, organizing workers, demanding an end to discrimination from city councils throughout the state, launching citizenship drives, registering voters, and, of course, supporting candidates seeking elected office. Bert Corona recalled: "The 1960s saw the greatest increase in Mexican Americans running for office in California." MAPA was the most significant Latino political organization for the next decade in California.

There may not be a precise moment from which to date the Chicano Movement, but I believe that MAPA and the whirlwind of activism it created opened the door for young Chicanos, most of them second and third generation, all brought up in the oppressive 1950s, to express themselves . . . and boy, did we. My introduction to the movement came in a bar in Seoul or Saigon, probably in 1965, where Latino soldiers would hang out and the talk about back home would dominate every conversation. It was there that I first heard about a guy named Cesar Chavez who was organizing farm workers and how "*los chicanos*" were beginning to organize. Farm workers were the poorest, most recently arrived, least Americanized, most often targeted, abused, and deported people of our community, and they sure needed organizing, I thought. I'd like to meet this guy, I said. Chicanos organizing was equally intriguing. "Chicano" was a term to describe ourselves used by "*la plebe*," the plebeians, the working people, often crude common folks in the eyes of the Americanizers, accented and unsophisticated. When the pachucos declared themselves to be "chicanos," the word became favored by young Mexican Americans to distance themselves from the obliging public face expected of them. By the late 1950s and early '60s the term carried a tinge of rebelliousness and was used freely among the young, but rarely with one's elders and almost never with non-Latinos. It was a private rebellion. Young folks openly referring to themselves as Chicanos implied a challenge to the regimen of compliant behavior that had been drilled into us. That possibility was exciting.

I was discharged in late 1966 and headed back home. I was twenty, and the mines were hiring. I came back to a culture that held you tightly. My first job was punching. You stood on a narrow elevated platform wearing a leather apron and leather gloves that reached your elbows, face wrapped in cloth under a helmet and goggles. Your weapon was a long steel pole and when you were given the signal you tapped into a cauldron of boiling lava and pushed open a relief valve so that the vessel across from you would not explode. When the valve was pushed open, fire and molten metal would spit violently, directly at the guy with the Union job, health care, pension plan, and two days off a week. A Union job was a good job.

As soon as I could I became a mucker. Muck is the rock that has been beaten into an endless sea of stones forced from the earth's innards onto conveyor belts that carry it to furnaces and acid baths. Mucker crews were young guys; the weapons of muckers are picks and shovels. It was a job you did not get old at. But there was a lot of overtime. And it was here that the culture tightened its embrace even more. Most often we worked swing shift, three to eleven p.m. On Fridays when the last whistle blew we ran to the baths, washed our faces, piled into cars, and roared out in a caravan down the sinewy mine road to the bottom of the hill, where the first bar was waiting to cash the check and ply you with beer. By one in the morning we would be carrying cases of beer to the creek banks where workers sat on fenders or boulders and sang those norteño ballads of love, pain, and betrayal until the sunrise brought some sanity. One night it didn't.

My friend Alex came back from combat in Vietnam and got hired at the mine straight away. We mucked the same crew and headed down the hill together. When we got to the creek bank Alex's father was leaning on a fender, belting out a corrido. Cruz was on the guitar. Cruz was a fellow from Mexico with a young wife who didn't speak a word of English. He had two little kids and seemed to know every corrido ever sung in these hills. Alex's arrival bothered his old man; he pulled him aside and we could hear a pretty heated argument. A few cases of beer and songs of betrayal often conjure up heated arguments. After a moment Alex stormed into the old man's pickup truck and roared away. Cruz began another corrido, the guys sang *"Por si acaso quisieras volver / Olvidando tu viejo rencor / Me hallarás frente a un trago de vino . . ."* and I grabbed another Coors. Suddenly the pickup truck was there, the singing stopped, Alex was in army

64

camouflage, carrying a hunting rifle with another strapped on his back, looking like he had smeared Shinola on his face. He didn't say a word . . . just shot. Cruz got it first, right through the head. He shot the old man's leg off as he ran toward the highway. Chicho didn't make it far, but the shot only ripped an arm. I hit the ground and crawled at the lowest profile, attracting the least attention and getting the hell out of the line of fire as fast as I could. I made it across the creek, but he saw me and started shooting. I'd volunteered for war and never saw combat, never got shot at outside of training, and now a madman's flashbacking and screaming "You fuckin' gook" and aiming to kill me. I figured then that it was time to head down the hill and go to college on the GI Bill.

CHAPTER 4

The Chicano Movement

The Chicano Movement seized the stage in the Latino community from approximately 1965 to 1975. It was a movement led by young people, primarily college students, overwhelmingly US-born, and raised in the stifling conformism of the 1950s and early '60s. Gregory Rodriguez, in his important account of the Mexican experience in America, *Mongrels, Bastards, Orphans, and Vagabonds*, found that according to the opinion surveys,

> the term "Chicano," and presumably its attendant ideology, had not actually filtered down to many average Mexican Americans. One 1979 survey . . . found that only 7 percent of respondents called themselves Chicanos. Another survey of US Citizens of Mexican descent conducted three years later in California and Texas also found that 7 percent of respondents referred to themselves as Chicanos, 1 percent higher than the number who called themselves as Hispanics. Not surprisingly given its origins in an ethnic American movement, 0 percent of Spanish monolingual respondents labeled themselves Chicanos. Two-thirds of those who used the term were younger than thirty-six years old. Yet another survey published in 1981 echoed the findings that the term "Chicano" was most popular among the young and US-born. Significantly, the survey also found that those who called themselves Chicanos were more likely to have had attended or graduated from college than those who preferred other ethnic labels.[1]

We were the privileged few who had the opportunity to go to college. Many of us were the first persons in the family who had ever ventured so far. We were our family's hope and, we believed, our community's hope as well. As important to the formation of the Chicano generation as our resentment of being raised in an era of relentless pressure to be "American" was the fact that any discussion of a rational immigration policy had virtually disappeared. The Chicano generation grew up at a time when hate and prejudice against immigrants was a constant.

Immigration was not.

In 1930, when repatriation destroyed much of the Mexican-American community, the foreign-born population of the United States was 12 percent of the total. By 1950 that population had shrunk to 7 percent. By 1970 it was 5 percent, the lowest proportion ever recorded then or since by the US Census.[2] This is perhaps why the immigration reform debates that had cast liberals in Congress against conservatives could rage for a decade with relatively little notice by the Mexican-American leadership or the nascent Chicano Movement. President Johnson signed the Hart-Celler Immigration Reform Act of 1965 into law with a symbolic ceremony at the base of the Statue of Liberty. The bill was sponsored by two of Congress's leading liberals, Senator Philip Hart and Representative Emanuel Celler. Its key provision abolished national origin quotas whose repeal the president described as "repairing a deep and painful flaw in the fabric of American justice. It corrects a cruel and enduring wrong in the conduct of the American nation. . . . From this day forth those wishing to emigrate to America shall be admitted on the basis of their skills and their close relationship to those already here . . ." The law, added the president, "values and rewards each man on the basis of his merit as a man."[3] In order to end discriminatory quotas against southern and eastern European sending countries, which were important to the eastern European and Jewish constituencies, the liberal reformers agreed to an annual ceiling of immigrants of 290,000. They also agreed for the first time to a Western Hemisphere quota of 120,000.

Attempts to limit Mexico's quota to 20,000 failed. The 120,000 quota represented a 40 percent reduction from pre-1965 levels. In Mexico's case the problem was greatly exacerbated by the cancellation of the Bracero Program just one year earlier. "Legal" Mexican immigration pre-1965 consisted of upwards of 200,000 braceros and 35,000 regular admissions for permanent residency. In 1976 the Congress finally conceded the quota that the nativists had demanded. Mexico's quota was set at 20,000. In addition, the provision that allowed an undocumented parent of US-citizen children to legalize his or her status was repealed. The absurd outcome was that Mexico, with a shared border thousands of miles long with the United States, a history of war and conquest, and a complex symbiotic employment history, has exactly the same quota as Outer Mongolia or the Principality of Liechtenstein.[4] In 1968, after the liberal immigration reform went into effect, INS enjoyed a 40 percent increase in deportations; in 1976, after the quota of 20,000 was imposed, INS deported 781,000 Mexicans.[5] By legislative action, while Chicano and Mexican-American activists were focused elsewhere, the Congress created the coming "crisis of illegal immigration." There were exceptions to the silence. Governor Pat Brown appointed Bert Corona to the California Civil Rights Commission in 1964. The Commission's primary role was to report the status of California's civil rights to the United States Commission on Civil Rights. Father Theodore Hesburgh, president of the University of Notre Dame and a hero of liberal Democrats, chaired the US Commission. Corona viewed hearings held in San Francisco by the joint commissions as an opportunity to raise issues that affected the Latino community. But Hesburgh rejected all of the issues proposed by Corona and the California commission; he was not even willing to allow testimony "about the gross violations against Mexican immigrants by the Immigration and Naturalization Service." With characteristic frankness, Corona dismissed Hesburgh as a "racist and a jingoist" who was "willing to weep crocodile tears for the poor but not willing to help them do something about their victimization." In protest, Corona resigned from the Commission.

So by the time I got down the hill from Miami and enrolled at Arizona State University, the demographic composition of the Mexican-American community was in a process of major change.

Most young Latino college students' concerns had little to do with demography, however. The urgent question of the day was, "When will the war touch me?" Vietnam, unlike later wars, could not be relegated to the poor and the willing. The draft would not end until 1972. Unlike mining town Latinos, who were volunteering or waiting for the letter from the draft board that opened with that dreaded phrase, "Greetings and Salutations," the college Latinos were fearful that the call would change their lives—perhaps end their lives—and suffered through a moral blur. To not embrace the war was a rejection of the very ethos inculcated into our upbringing.

The other great question of the day was, "What the hell is the matter with those guys at LULAC, anyway?" We declared ourselves Chicanos, inviting immediate repulsion by the conservatives in the Mexican-American leadership, we discovered our Aztec roots and proud mestizo heritage, we made Che our heroic icon (at least the image on the poster and the guy on the T-shirt), we dabbled in Marxist rhetoric, we referred to the old Americanizers as *vendidos*, sell-outs, and sought to humiliate them at every opportunity, we embraced our humble brothers and sisters who had just arrived to make a life for themselves in America, and we spent seemingly endless hours discussing our unique moment in history and the special responsibilities it placed on our shoulders. Those were heady times. We debated Frantz Fanon and José Vasconcelos, excoriated Octavio Paz's *Labyrinth of Solitude* and his disdainful description of the pachucos, but were overwhelmed by Paulo Freire's *Pedagogy of the Oppressed*; we questioned whether the one-dimensional man posited by Herbert Marcuse was our inevitable future, argued whether the Chinese barefoot-doctor figure was appropriate to our community and if Ho Chi Minh was an acceptable role model, and speculated whether Oscar Lewis's *Children of Sanchez* could possibly be an accurate picture of poverty and desperation; we wondered whether Eric Hoffer's description of the True Believers, the fanatics who are necessary to launch a mass movement, fit us, or were we different? Yes, of course we were. And we organized. Nationally, this was a time of extraordinary activism in the Latino community. My own awakening to action and my own discovery of purpose was inextricably tied to Cesar.

Shortly after arriving at ASU, I began hearing that the Cesar whose stories of bravery and dedication had spread halfway around the world was organizing a few miles away in Tolleson and Yuma. The admiration, even veneration in which Cesar was held by the young men and women of the Chicano generation is perhaps incomprehensible to someone born years later. José Angel Gutiérrez, the enfant terrible of the movement and a leader of the Mexican American Youth Organization, MAYO, described Cesar as "the embodiment of a Chicano. Chicanos see themselves in Cesar: clothes, personal style, demeanor and commitment."[6] Luis Valdez, the playwright and director of Teatro Campesino, approached Christian symbolism in relating Cesar's importance to the movement: "Without realizing it we already had the leader we were waiting for. It was Cesar Chavez, and he was there slowly burning, poor like us and telling us, suggesting to us what we should do—never ordering us—and little by little we began to organize around him . . . a man, in short, who had suffered in his very being the trials of all Mexican people in the United States."[7]

The poet Ricardo C. Perez took a step further and fully embraced the iconography of Christ:

> With a book of Gandhi in his hand,
> Like a hero in a decadent world
> Searching for justice in a contract
> The Chicano walks proudly
>
> He suffers like a heretic
> Suffers martyrdom like Christ
> Suffers for suffering which is the price
> For he who loves the flame of love, the lily
>
> But he is great in his humility
> And in all he truly believes
> Because his is the only way
> That is touched by redeeming faith.[8]

By the time I went to see him, Cesar was talked about more like a saintly mystic than a union organizer. We students had heard of house meetings with workers and the rumors of a coming strike. Finally, we came upon a mimeographed flyer announcing a meeting where Cesar would speak. A bunch of us rustled up a car and drove ourselves to the shabby union hall at the very margins of Phoenix. The place was packed with women and men and a mob of kids. By our clothes and demeanor we were clearly not farm workers, and we were stared at suspiciously but otherwise treated politely. After a while, a short fellow stood at the front of the hall and began to speak. The room quieted. This is an important guy, I thought; he's probably going to introduce Cesar. I waited for Cesar. I expected a Chicano Martin Luther King, Jr., who would rivet us with a preacher's soaring oratory. My mother had dragged me into plenty of evangelical church meetings, so I knew a good hell-and-brimstone sermon, in Spanish or English, when I heard one. After a moment I realized this was Cesar. He was unremarkable. He was humble, certainly not dressed like a preacher or a priest, indistinguishable from the men who listened to him reverently. His voice was not powerful; it quivered and was often delicate. I was not impressed. But over the next few days his words, the serenity that seemed to surround him and the obvious impact he had on everyone in that room kept coming back to me. It was not long before I was volunteering and organizing in the fields.

It was a calling. It was missionary work. It was a journey into understanding yourself. My father, the Union guy, didn't care if it was for the Union. He was skeptical of religious charlatans and Christ-like figures with messianic callings. He suspected a bit of both in Cesar. More importantly, he wanted me out of the picket line and back into the classroom. I remember the picket that particularly bothered him. The *huelguistas*, strikers, were lined up along the dirt road in front of the farmer's field, the scab workers were picking onions, and the sheriff's deputies were leaning against the farmer's fence armed with guns and a court order that prohibited the Union from approaching the scabs. The farmer had outfitted a sound truck with loud country music aimed at the picketers, rendering our bullhorns useless. One morning, which promised to be like every other, Cesar and the important organizers were talking near me. Cesar speculated that a guy who was a runner and maybe really, really fast, who trained daily, could probably jump over the ditch, hurdle the fence, get the leaflets to the workers, then jump back out and disappear into the crowd of picketers before the overweight, out-of-shape deputies could respond. Astonishing as it may seem, I just happened to be a really, really fast runner who trained every day.

The first time I jumped the fence I sprinted wildly, thrusting leaflets into the workers' hands. The deputies were shocked and frankly useless. They were indeed overweight and out of shape. The workers were laughing, some even cheering. When I jumped over the fence again and out of the field, the union picketers were waiting to surround me, change my shirt, stick a hat on my head and disappear me into the line. By the third time, a couple of days later, the deputies were ready, the trap was set, the wagon waiting, and off to jail I went. Even jail was a spiritual experience.

But my father prevailed. I had to get back to school.

My time at ASU ended badly. Cesar's good friend Bill Soltero was president of Laborer's Local 383, the largest local in the state. Local 383 had launched a campaign to organize industrial laundries. The workers were mostly undocumented Mexican women. In 1968 the minimum wage was $1.60 an hour. By paying piece work and manipulating hours, Phoenix Linen and Towel Supply Company was actually paying the women working for it an average of $1.15 an hour. The union also documented incidents of sexual harassment and abuse perpetrated by the all-male supervisory staff. The case against the company was compelling. Bill and his lead organizer, Ted Caldes, came to see me to ask for an intervention by ASU students. I had helped organize the Mexican American Students Organization, MASO, and was one of its co-chairmen. The company's largest single contract, they told me, was with Arizona State University, and the mere threat that they might lose the contract would cause the company to reach a unionization agreement. They wanted MASO to pressure the university administration.

Along with Ted, we presented the case to MASO, and the response in support was overwhelming. We took our case to every student organization that would hear us, asking them to join a coalition in support of the workers. We were surprised by the immediate and broad support we received, and naively assumed that the ASU president would quickly meet with us. He refused. Rhetoric escalated and to the ramparts we went. In November of 1968 a mass of students, led by MASO, stormed the administration building and took over the president's office. We held it for two days. President Durham finally met with us and, to our shock, announced the appointment of a commission to review the allegations against the Linen and Towel Supply Company. If proven true, they would have to be rectified, or the university would cancel the contract. We had won. The company quickly agreed to a corrective plan, but unfortunately the Laborers never persuaded the majority of the workers to sign a union card.

The Arizona Legislature and the Board of Regents were apoplectic. Someone had to pay, and I was the public face of the egregious insult. It's often been said that I was thrown out of ASU, but in fact it was a bit more subtle. The university adopted a new Code of Conduct that allowed it to harass me into leaving. I was forced out before I could graduate. Years later I would be awarded an honorary doctorate degree. Justice delayed.

That final semester at ASU was troubled from the beginning. During the summer of '68, Cesar had committed to taking part in a get-out-the-vote campaign on behalf of Bobby Kennedy in Los Angeles. The California presidential primary was scheduled for June 5. Weeks before the election, Gustavo Gutierrez (the Union's lead organizer in Arizona), the Union's Arizona attorney, and I headed to East L.A. to participate in that final push. It was a remarkable experience. I was in awe of the characters who marched through that campaign: Cesar and Dolores, Bert Corona, Herman Gallegos, Julian Nava, Fred Dutton the national campaign manager, Ted Kennedy,

Ethel Kennedy, and of course the candidate, Senator Robert Kennedy. After the polls closed, Gustavo rounded up me, the lawyer Jim Murkowski, and his wife Tina, and we all headed for a taco and a burro, then on to the Ambassador Hotel. We were part of a celebratory horn-honking, corrido-singing, whooping, and yelling caravan led by the car carrying Cesar, Dolores, and the Union's big mucks. Cesar and the mucks headed to the invitation-only main ballroom, and we to an overflow ballroom which was, as I recall, downstairs. It was a joyous event, and being part of Cesar's entourage we were treated as special guests. Beer ran freely and the food was plentiful. Exhausted, Gustavo, Jim, and I ended up sitting on the floor at the far end of the ballroom.

It was the perfect place to witness the pandemonium that soon struck. The police secured the room, kept us there for perhaps an hour or two, and then released us into the night. Jim drove all the way to Delano, the Union's headquarters, that night. We weren't sure why we were going there, but we needed to go somewhere we would be embraced. All night we listened to the radio, hoping for a miracle. It didn't come. Senator Kennedy was declared dead as we drove northward in the dark. Somehow, I forget exactly how or when, I made my way back to Phoenix. I felt something was stolen from America that night, but I also felt that something irreplaceable had been taken from me.

My life without the GI Bill and ousted from the university was made easier by being named a recipient of the Robert F. Kennedy Memorial Fellowship in its inaugural year. It provided a stipend for the next year, and the freedom to organize. Along with Joe Eddie Lopez, his wife Rosie, and a small group of activists, we founded a neighborhood membership-based advocacy organization we named— capturing the spirit of the times—*Chicanos Por La Causa*, CPLC. Though Joe Eddie and I and a small group of activists are credited with the founding of CPLC, in reality it was an idea first proposed by Mac Barraza, Herman Gallegos, and Ernesto Galarza. Herman, Ernesto, and Julian Samora were the most respected and best-known intellectuals and social scientists in the Latino community. The three were commissioned by the Ford Foundation to survey the Latino community and propose a strategy for the Foundation's future involvement with the community.

The choice of these three scholars was prescient. Ernesto Galarza was a Mexican-born immigrant who had overcome poverty to become a graduate of Stanford and to receive his doctorate from Columbia in economics in 1947. After a distinguished career in Latin America with the Pan American Union, he became the director of research for the National Farm Workers Union. For the rest of his life Galarza would be a tireless advocate and organizer for farm workers, stridently opposing the Bracero Program and speaking out on behalf of Latino workers' rights. Galarza was a prolific author of polemic works that left little doubt of his activist worldview. Julian Samora was a pioneering Latino anthropologist and sociologist who devoted his life to the betterment of the Latino community. Herman Gallegos was also a noted scholar, a graduate of the University of California at Berkeley; since graduation he had been the lead organizer with Community Services Organization and ultimately became its national president. Cesar Chavez would become the CSO's executive director and Dolores Huerta an organizer. CSO, along with MAPA, was active throughout California, fighting discrimination and registering voters. It was changing the political landscape of California by organizing communities to take control of their own destiny.

Not surprisingly, the three experts would recommend that the Ford Foundation become actively involved in funding community-based organizations. The direct result of the report was the founding of the Southwest Council of La Raza by dedicated Mexican-American activists, trained and nurtured by the progressive union movement, MAPA, and CSO. SWCLR saw itself as the repository of organizational skills and leadership that would assist local communities in building their unique organizations to respond to the challenges each faced. The phrase those early organizers often used to describe their mission was "capacity building" for barrio organizations. Years later, Herman wrote to me, in response to my inquiries about the formation of the Council, saying that its original mission was

> To close the social, economic and political gap that exists between the greater majority group and the Spanish-speaking community, generally, and the Mexican-American barrios, specifically. . . . Programs included local community cooperative action projects to be formulated and controlled by recipient neighborhood organizations, including voter registration and region-wide social action; to establish leadership training programs for developing and giving technical/organizing assistance to community workers in Mexican American neighborhoods; to organize and maintain research and information related to securing public and private resources in support of local efforts.[9]

That, of course, is foundation-speak for "its mission was to raise hell." SWCLR was a reembodiment of the defunct Asociación Nacional México-Americana, and a means of making the CSO and MAPA's philosophies of local political empowerment a national reality. Mac became the Council's first chairman, Herman its executive director, and Ernesto and Julian joined the board of directors along with Bert Corona, Judge Alberto Peña of San Antonio, and a group of the most distinguished men and women activists in the southwest. Mac and the trio of activist intellectuals persuaded Ford, the Office of Economic Opportunity, the UAW, and a smattering of religious groups to provide initial funding for a network of activist organizations in Phoenix, Los Angeles, San Antonio, Albuquerque, San Francisco, and Denver, to begin with. In Phoenix, Chicanos Por La Causa was organized before the deal was done with Ford. CPLC was the means to organize health-care forums demanding that Arizona, the only state still refusing to provide Medicaid services, finally provide decent care for the poor; it was organized too late to stop the encroachment by the airport into the city's oldest barrio, Golden Gate, but CPLC fought the city ruthlessly and negotiated fair compensation to the families that were forced to move. It took on the Phoenix Union High School system and ultimately organized a two-week walkout of Phoenix Union High School, providing an alternative high school, with the parents of the protesting students enforcing attendance; and it organized voter registration drives with local parishes and churches. CPLC was officially non-partisan, but its very large membership enthusiastically endorsed and actively supported the candidacy of Joe Eddie Lopez for the Phoenix Union School Board. We lost that election, but we learned. Like CSO with Ed Roybal in Los Angeles, we would be back. The magic of CPLC was that the lessons of ANMA, CSO, and MAPA were put into effect. It was barrio residents that were discussing the issues, sometimes for hours, and setting the agenda for action. CPLC provided the forum, the tools, expertise on occasion—but the fire and passion came from folks who were taking control of their schools and their neighborhoods.

The dream of Southwest Council's founders, to organize Mexican Americans nationally "from the bottom up" (as Ernesto Galarza described it, the only way for the Mexican-American community to achieve political power),[10] took root in every major city of the southwest in which the Council was active. SWCLR launched major voter registration initiatives in each of the communities. The effort was named the Political Research and Education Project, or PREP, and modeled on CSO's and MAPA's successful organizing campaigns in California. Finally, it seemed the community would define its own needs, articulate its own ambitions, and create for itself its own identity in America. The tension between being an American or an American of Mexican descent or even a Chicano, and the contempt with which the "Americanizers" had regarded recent arrivals, documented or not, would be relegated to the past. In this new era of a powerful Mexican-American community, citizens, legal residents, and undocumented workers would work toward the American dream as equals.

SWCLR was part of the larger War on Poverty. Herman, Mac, and Ernesto had seized the historic moment to craft an organization that would uniquely respond to the Mexican-American community. The founding philosophy of the War on Poverty was to empower the poor to resolve their own problems. Often that took the form of the poor challenging their congressmen, mayors, and councilmen (there were very few women in political office in the late 1960s) to either produce results or get out of the way. Sixties-era good old boy politicians were not accustomed to being confronted by the poor, be they black, Mexican, or Appalachian white, and the poor were not schooled in the niceties of lobbying. Getting lambasted in public by a farm worker or a city sanitation worker was not pleasing to the powers that be. The politicians demanded that this business of empowering the poor be stopped.

To understand how Mac, Herman, and Ernesto's dream was strangled and finally transmogrified, it is important to understand the conflicting philosophies that wrestled for control of the War on Poverty.

This administration today, here and now, declares uncondi-
tional war on poverty in America. I urge this Congress and all
Americans to join with me in that effort. It will not be a short
or easy struggle, no single weapon or strategy will suffice, but
we shall not rest until that war is won. The richest nation on
earth can afford to win it. We cannot afford to lose it.[11]

With those words President Lyndon Johnson launched the
War on Poverty during the State of the Union address in January of 1964. Hundreds of millions of dollars would soon
begin to flow into the inner cities of America. The generals of
the war were the social scientists that, beginning with the
Kennedy Administration, had debated the root causes of
poverty and delved deeply into the science of community and
human development for the keys that would transform stub-
bornly poor communities into model middle-class enclaves.

The precursor to the War on Poverty was the so-called
Delinquency Commission appointed by President Kennedy
early in his administration. Focused on eradicating youth
crime, the Commission relied heavily on two prominent
Columbia University social work professors, Lloyd Ohlin and
Richard Cloward. Their influential work, *Delinquency and
Opportunity*, contended that delinquents had mainstream
values but were surrounded by an urban environment that
blocked their aspirations. Organized crime, political machines,
decaying schools, and corrupt governmental institutions
worked together to corrode normal social controls and to
effectively frustrate any attempt to achieve those mainstream
aspirations. The authors argued that the appropriate path
toward resolving the delinquency problem was to restore order
in the urban environment and provide opportunities for
advancement.[12] Proponents of opportunity theory's approach
clearly believed that the problem to be corrected lay with society, not in the community that had suffered at the hands of

that society—a view that was about to be upended by other influential social scientists. This became the operating philosophy of the Commission. By the time of President Johnson's State of the Union speech, poverty was both racialized and criminalized in the eyes of most Americans. The March on Washington for Jobs and Freedom, where Martin Luther King, Jr., delivered his historic "I have a dream" speech, took place in 1963. The march intended to awaken the country to the disproportionate share of poverty that was borne by the African-American community. A long season of racial unrest began soon afterwards with the Harlem riot of 1964. Throughout the presidential campaign, Senator Barry Goldwater had criticized the Johnson and Kennedy Administration's failure to control street violence. Michael Flamm's *Law and Order* is perhaps the most intensive study of the era. Flamm describes Goldwater's campaign code language as follows:

> Behind this breakdown in civic order . . . was the welfare state, which promoted paternalism and dependence at the expense of opportunity and responsibility. "Government seeks to be parent, teacher, leader, doctor, and even minister," he charged, exploiting the increasing association of welfare, like crime, with black Americans. "And its failures are strewn about us in the rubble of rising crime rates." By targeting liberalism as the ultimate source of these problems, Goldwater implicitly downplayed the differences between urban riots, political demonstrations, street crime, and juvenile delinquency. Instead, he explicitly combined these distinct phenomena into a common threat to a society of decency, security, harmony— in short, to a society of law and order.[13]

President Johnson initially ignored Goldwater, but by late October the continued conflation of race, crime, and urban riots had apparently taken their toll. The president responded

by expressing his belief that the War on Poverty would complement the War on Crime by bettering conditions that bred
violence. Perhaps in his frustration the president contributed
to further linking the two in the public's eyes.

Johnson won an overwhelming victory. During the entire
campaign, his own social scientists toiled away in corners of
the federal bureaucracy, and they, not surprisingly, were not
enamored with the Kennedyesque Opportunity Theory.

Daniel Patrick Moynihan, destined for a distinguished
career as ambassador and US senator, prepared a report on
behalf of the Department of Labor. The report was leaked
to the public shortly after Johnson's historic defeat of Goldwater. It proved to be simultaneously explosive and
influential. *The Negro Family* argues that having endured
years of poverty, discrimination, and continued unemployment, black families had been rendered "a tangle of
pathology" that served to continue "the cycle of poverty and
deprivation." The cause of this pathology was the absence
of the male role model, and without role models young men
could not learn responsible behavior. Matriarchy was
branded deeply dysfunctional. After leaked excerpts were
met with uproarious protest, *The Negro Family* was made
public by the Department of Labor. Moynihan immediately
became the target of a venomous backlash, but the controversy that followed contributed to solidifying the public's
view that poverty was racial, and that the War on Poverty
targeted a specific group: blacks.[14]

The most direct route to resolving poverty is of course
jobs. In those days, before the Internet and e-mail, simply
adding a second mail delivery a day would have created an
estimated 50,000 jobs. But resolving poverty by providing
jobs was rejected by the administration. The social scientists had successfully convinced the administration, as well
as the public, that the problem of poverty was not lack of

cash but lack of character. Providing jobs would not be enough to defeat the enemy, and providing cash assistance would only perpetuate "the tangle of pathology." The War on Poverty was sliding into a war to fix the poor, rather than to fix poverty. So when Sargent Shriver assumed the generalship of the war, the enemy was clear: the pathological poor (mostly black).

Latinos, poor though they were, were left out of the discussion of poverty, race, and pathology. There was great concern among the Latino leadership that unless something was done, Latinos would also be left out of the federal largesse promised by the War on Poverty.

The intellectual fashion of the 1960s among Chicano activists was delving into the psychological and sociological status of the Mexican American. Social science, we believed, could be a path to understanding our powerlessness. Max Weber's *The Protestant Ethic: The Spirit of Capitalism*, proposing an archetype for success in a capitalist world that valued above all else the acquisition of wealth, was a highly influential work. Wealth was a temporal sign of Calvinist salvation, it seemed. Building on Weber, Talcott Parsons developed a typology, "pattern variables," to distinguish the modern from the traditional. The noted Chicano intellectual David Hayes-Bautista describes the impact of Parsons' theory thus: "It seemed clear that modern values had to be substituted for the dysfunctional traditional ones if a society were to develop modern, capitalistic structures. 'Improving' traditional cultural traits became a policy imperative."[15]

Parsons' typology has served as the paradigm for sociological and anthropological research ever since. Latinos, more specifically Mexican Americans in the southwest, were traditional folk whose cultural values were "diametrically opposed to the modern set: passivity, fatalism, present-time orientation, emotionality, superstition, and inability to defer gratification."[16] Hayes-Bautista quotes another influential social scientist of the era, William Madsen, describing Mexican Americans in south Texas as holding "a fatalistic philosophy [which] produces an attitude of resignation which often convinces the Anglo that the Latin lacks drive and determination. What the Anglo tries to overcome the Latin views as fate."[17]

I spent many hours during my undergraduate years devouring the social scientists of the time and discussing with other Latinos the meaning of it all. Arguing, for example, whether common salutations and sayings like "*si Dios quiere*" or "*Dios sabrá*" or "*era la voluntad de Dios*" were independent verification of the scholarly findings of those brilliant intellectuals. The other possibility was that the so-called intellectuals were simply offering up the same claptrap as the obviously racist pseudoscientists of the 1930s. They just talked more pretty.

In any event, we may not have been a "tangle of pathology," but social science could demonstrate that we were certainly dysfunctional and obviously needed some federal money to fix ourselves. In the pursuit of federal dollars, many were prepared to embrace the theories of dysfunction. We would soon regret it.

There was one more hurdle between the money and us. The War on Poverty was clearly a response to the civil rights movement, and it was made even more urgent by the urban riots in black communities across America. Latinos had, conforming to the pattern proposed by the social scientists, mostly been passive observers. Not much urgency there. The Chicano movement provided what urgency did exist, but the movement itself was regionalized to the southwest, and its only national figure, Cesar Chavez, was focused specifically on the plight of farm workers. The two largest and oldest Latino organizations, LULAC and the GI Forum, which had spent their entire existence aspiring to be white in the eyes of their tormentors, were hardly credible—in fact, they were laughable when they strutted their militant stuff and demanded, to quote the phrase of the day, "our piece of the pie and not the crumbs that are left over."

In 1965, during his commencement address to the graduates of Howard University, President Johnson announced a White House Conference on Civil Rights, to be held the following year. The president said in his call that "its object will be to help the American Negro fulfill the rights which, after the long time of injustice, he is finally about to secure."[18] (Mexican Americans, their supposed dysfunctions and their indisputable poverty notwithstanding, were completely left out of the president's call.) The howls of protest from Mexican American and Chicano organizations were predictably loud and angry. The White House quickly responded by whipping out a rabbit from the bureaucratic hat, called the Interagency Committee on Mexican American Affairs. Vicente T. Ximenes, a past president of the GI Forum, was appointed director of the Interagency Committee. The Committee, moving at bureaucratic breakneck speed, called a White House Conference on Mexican American Affairs to be held in El Paso in October 1967. The conference was in fact a gathering of second-tier cabinet officials to hear the lamentations of the invitees, primarily social service professionals. Cesar was invited but declined. Bert Corona, the fiery leader of MAPA, was invited but pointedly chose to boycott the hearing, as did Rodolfo "Corky" Gonzáles, a former boxer and community organizer whose poem "I Am Joaquin" became the anthem of the Chicano movement. Both would take part in the rival conference, convened a mile away in El Paso's poorest barrio.

Herman Gallegos recalls that the organizers of the

as-yet-unformed SWCLR decided that the White House Conference on Mexican American Affairs deserved to be confronted. Unlike the earlier White House Conference on Civil Rights, this conference was neither in the White House nor in Washington, and also unlike the earlier conference, cabinet members were absent. There was little glamour and no pomp. President Johnson and President Adolfo López Mateos of Mexico were scheduled to be in El Paso during the time of the conference to ceremoniously end a long-standing land dispute known as El Chamizal. Neither would attend the White House Conference on Mexican American Affairs, and both would hog what little interest the press had about Mexicans, Mexican Americans, or their affairs.

The distinguished group of radicals that would form SWCLR held the anti-conference in El Paso. It was Ernesto Galarza, along with a United Auto Workers organizer and Chicano activist, Henry Santiestevan, who wrote the announcement for the conference, Proclamation for La Raza Unida. Herman was given the task of organizing the conference. It was held in the gym of St. Mary's parish in the center of barrio El Segundo. Ernesto was the honorary chair, and hundreds of people, mostly college students, attended two days of fiery speeches and angry confrontations with the "*vendidos*" that attended the White House conference.

Playing a major role in the alternative conference was José Angel Gutiérrez and the Mexican American Youth Organization. Gutiérrez was by then a well-known firebrand orator and organizer in south Texas, and MAYO was one of the most outspoken and militant Chicano organizations. MAYO was the driving force behind La Raza Unida Party, the separatist political party that would upend south Texas politics a few months later. MAYO picketed the White House Conference and the hotel where some of the official attendees were staying. José Angel led a loud, defiant march of students and young people through the streets of downtown El Paso. Maclovio Barraza, the union organizer who had only a few years before been hauled before a congressional committee and declared a secret subversive and communist, was selected as La Raza Unida's ambassador to downtown El Paso. Mac's summation to the bored bureaucrats was angry and emotional: "The Mexican American is growing more and more restless. He's patient but it's running out. He may soon be forced to seek dramatic alternatives to his patience—alternatives that seem to bring more generous responses from government than obedient restraint in the face of adversity and injustice."[19]

Between the options of Opportunity Theory, organizing communities to empower themselves and craft their own future, and the theories of underclass social dysfunction, the organizers of SWCLR defiantly chose empowerment. The week in El Paso strengthened Mac, Herman, Ernesto, and Bert's resolve to launch the council. SWCLR was officially formed and headquartered in Phoenix shortly thereafter. Funding was received from the Office of Economic Opportunity, the UAW, and religious denominations; the majority of funds to launch and maintain the community organizing effort throughout the southwest came from the Ford Foundation. But the Southwest Council of La Raza, like the Asociación Nacional México-Americana barely two decades earlier, would not withstand the political forces arrayed against it.

By the time of Richard Nixon's presidential victory in November of 1968, local elected officials had flooded Congress and the White House with complaints about Community Action Programs and the War on Poverty. Empowering poor folk, often black and brown, to demand services and justice was intolerable. Local politicians demanded control of the federal dollars pouring into their communities.

President Nixon, even before being sworn in, began preparing legislation that would repeal the Office of Economic Opportunity, provide for local political control, and drastically limit the ability of foundations to engage in voter registration or other political activity. According to Herman Gallegos, then executive director of SWCLR, the pressure to cease community organizing was intense. Soon there was a directive from the Ford Foundation, the single major funder of SWCLR, ordering the closing of PREP, the voter registration initiative. (It would resurface in 1974 as the independent organization Southwest Voters Registration Project.)

The second directive was more drastic still, as Herman recalls it. "The terms from Ford were clear: adopt hard programming or face termination of support." "Hard programming" was the term of art for the myriad of federal and foundation programs that had been devised to cure the social dysfunctions that plagued the poor, particularly minorities. The ultimatum, stripped of the foundation code talk of the time, meant: Stop empowering the Mexican-American community to speak for themselves. Whatever opportunity there may have been to enter into discussions with Ford and the other grantors ended abruptly when José Angel Gutiérrez, representing MAYO— which at the time had a small grant from a SWCLR affiliate—held an unfortunate press conference. The *San Antonio Evening News*, probably to dispel any suspicion that they had misrepresented José Angel's responses, printed the transcript of the press conference on April 11, 1969.

> **Reporter**: What is meant by the phrase "eliminate the gringo" in the MAYO statement?
> **Gutiérrez**: You can eliminate an individual in various ways. You can certainly kill him, but that is not our intent at this moment. You can remove the basis of support that he operates from, be it political, economic or social.

88

That is what we intend to do.

Reporter: If nothing else works you are going to kill all the gringos?

Gutiérrez: We will have to find out if nothing else will work.

(later in the interview)

Reporter: If worse comes to worst will you kill gringos?

Gutiérrez: If worse comes to worst and we have to resort to that means it would be self-defense.

Reporter: Do you hate gringos?

Gutiérrez: Yes I do.

(later in the interview)

Reporter: Why have 500,000 Mexican nationals immigrated to the US in the last 15 years despite the charges of the misery and the degradation they faced?

Gutiérrez: Maybe they don't know any better. You will find an equal number going back.[20]

The reporters were left wondering when the gringo killing would begin, and the immigrants were upset to discover they didn't know any better.

The ensuing uproar overwhelmed SWCLR. Congressman Henry B. Gonzalez of San Antonio, a long-standing critic of MAYO and the Chicano Movement, immediately demanded that the Ford Foundation stop funding SWCLR. Former Executive Director Gallegos laments, "In the end, a hostile Nixon administration, the broadly negative and punitive overtones of Congress's 1969 Tax Reform Act, the arrogant and provocative racist comments by a young Chicano militant, an upset and angry Congress member, led not only to the humbling of a preeminent foundation but abruptly put an end to the original Council's progressive agenda aimed at empowering

Mexican Americans for responsible social change. What became the National Council of La Raza is an entirely different organization."[21]

On July 17, 1969, Mac Barraza convened the board of directors of SWCLR and led a divided board to accede to all of the demands made by the Ford Foundation and the other funders. Herman resigned soon thereafter. Henry Santiestevan, the old UAW organizer, was named his successor. Mac was convinced, he told me, that he and Henry would be able to maneuver through the crisis, limit the welfare programs, as he termed them, and get back to creating a politically powerful Mexican-American community. It was not to be. Henry too was forced out; the organizers that composed the staff were ousted as well. More passive administrators and technicians were recruited, familiar with the desires of the funders and expert at the jargon of social dysfunction. Docile board members replaced the warhorses, and the scene was set for the transmogrification.

The noose tightened at first imperceptibly. Once the new speech and behavioral norms pleasing to the government and the foundations were imposed, the money flowed quickly. The original member agencies of SWCLR grew in dramatic fashion. The agencies began administering social programs to treat every conceivable malady that besets a dysfunctional people, and boy did we have them. Chicano activists were hired by the thousands across the country to assist in curing the poor. We were young, we were hungry, we were idealistic; but we believed ourselves to be incorruptible, and so we readily accepted the temptations of government and the foundations. And the noose tightened. Thousands of activists were reminded subtly and not so subtly of the new standard for job security: "don't bite the hand that feeds you . . . and don't criticize it either." It turns out that with enough money, boiling the frog really isn't that difficult.

It was not long before Mac saw it coming. He was instrumental in forming the Mexican-American Legal Defense and Education Fund, and the Southwest Voters Registration and Education Project, just as the Chicano movement was hollowed out and the bureaucrats began to dominate what was left. Mac paid a terrible price for his selfless idealism. He was accused by the Congress of the United States of subverting the country he loved and of being a communist, at a time when such an accusation could ruin a life. Mac was too strong to be destroyed, and the union families would not abandon him. He was embraced rather than rejected by the mining towns he had so often fought for. But it hurt. I recall a meeting with young Chicano activists where he recounted those events as tears streamed down his cheeks. His idealism survived to witness its resurgence in the Chicano Movement. Mac was there to mentor many activists of the 1960s. But Mac's idealism could not survive the maze of money and bureaucratic restrictions that spread across the movement. He foresaw the silence that would follow the money. Of this time he was proudest of MALDEF and Southwest Voters. He believed that those two agencies had the potential to truly challenge the status quo and change the condition of the Latino community.

In 1973 the Southwest Council of La Raza renamed itself the National Council of La Raza. NCLR is an enormous force for good. But NCLR has brokered and distributed billions of dollars from foundations and the federal government by successfully defining Latinos as a perennially poor minority in need of governmental assistance to make it in America. The economic success of NCLR and much of the existing Mexican-American leadership structure depends on the continued depiction of Mexican Americans as dysfunctional. Community organizations across America have received funding for low-income housing, teen pregnancy, mental health, rural clinics, abused women's shelters, alcoholism and drug abuse intervention, dropout prevention programs, and every other conceivable program to intervene in whatever tangle of pathology ails the community. NCLR and its affiliates employ thousands of Latinos. It has developed a highly respected public policy research and advocacy division that analyzes social ills and advocates for corrective legislation and further funding to treat them. Its celebrity galas and fandangos are unquestionably the most prestigious events in the Latino community. It no longer confronts the establishment; it mingles with it, embraces it, and seeks its approval. It may indeed be a powerful force for good. No one will ever confuse it, however, with the idealistic, impassioned instrument of empowerment that Mac, Herman, Bert, and Ernesto envisioned.

In the first decade of the twenty-first century, under new leadership, NCLR would clumsily initiate attempts to become relevant in the struggle for immigrant justice and rediscover the roots of its founding.

By May of 1972, CPLC was tame, compliant, awash with money, and pleasing to the foundations and the feds. I too was enjoying the benefits: I was executive director of a non-profit organization focused on gangs, high-school dropouts, and youth summer programs called the Barrio Youth Project. My office was a cell-like concrete cube in Santa Rita Hall, a forlorn church property belonging to Sacred Heart Parish in El Campito barrio. Santa Rita Hall was also the epicenter of Chicano political activity in Phoenix. The Arizona Legislature, a few miles away, was busily writing legislation that would make union organizing of farm workers virtually impossible by criminally prohibiting strikes during the harvest season and also criminalizing boycotts of agricultural products. Allowing strikes when there is no harvest is of course allowing them when there are no workers to strike.[22] On May 11 the bill passed the legislature. Cesar, who had been personally coordinating the lobbying against the bill, asked Governor Jack Williams for a meeting to argue his case for a veto. The governor never acknowledged the request and signed the bill forty-five minutes after its passage. The union responded by angrily demanding a recall of Governor Jack Williams that was doomed to fail. Cesar announced he would begin a fast. It was Father Frank Yoldi, the parish pastor, who told me that Cesar was appropriating my tiny office at Santa Rita as his home for the ordeal. For the next twenty-four days Cesar fasted and Santa Rita Hall became a shrine, with crowded masses every evening and daily pilgrimages by famous folk to kneel beside the weakening Cesar. He would end his fast with a mass in an uptown hotel ballroom large enough to accommodate the worshipers. Robert Kennedy's son Joseph would break bread with him, as had his father in an earlier fast at Delano.

While the holy paused and reflected, we heathen were busy registering and organizing. Joe Eddie Lopez, our past candidate for the Phoenix Union School Board, would be the candidate for a newly created Maricopa County Supervisor's seat. I would be a candidate for the state senate, against an incumbent, Cloves Campbell, who had an abysmal record of service to the poor. Campbell was, however, a Democrat in a Democratic district and an African American in a district whose largest plurality was African American. He was widely perceived as invincible, and since the senatorial district was wholly within the boundaries of the supervisor district, my candidacy was seen as merely an organizing ploy to get out the Mexican-American vote for Joe Eddie. But in fact my candidacy was a direct result of many meetings with Campbell, in which he derided each of our requests that he become involved in demanding decent health care for the poor. At the time, Maricopa County Hospital was a collection of surplus World War II army hospital units, barracks, and Quonset huts. Admission to care was controlled by a commission which, in the opinion of advocates for the poor, acted callously, arbitrarily, often in response to personal prejudices, and seemingly always to cruel effect. The senator had little interest in the health of the poor, and little time for brash poor folks and community organizers. He felt himself in an invincible sinecure, being both a senator and community relations executive for the state's largest utility. Months earlier I had been awarded a Ford Fellowship to complete my bachelor's degree at the University of Maine and to continue with graduate studies in philosophy, but the incumbent's supreme disregard for the poor—and the district was perhaps the poorest in urban Arizona—grated inside me. I finally persuaded myself that beating an African-American incumbent in a district with an African-American plurality and more than a decade of public service was probably impossible. What was possible, I concluded, is that a campaign of hundreds of volunteers would ultimately disclose his miserable record to the religious leaders, the business folk, educators, and every voter in the district. It was that embarrassment and ensuing pressure that would force change. And then I could go on with my studies satisfied that a hard blow had been landed on behalf of the poor and against arrogant indifference.

Joe Eddie won his seat with ease. My candidacy caused a split in the African-American community, with a small number of significant members of the Black Ministerial Alliance choosing to support me or refusing to support my opponent. Nonetheless, I was expected to lose. After the ballots were counted on election night, my opponent was declared the victor by a narrow margin. I gave my concession speech, congratulated my opponent, and celebrated Joe Eddie's victory. The following evening, after absentee and questioned ballots were counted, an excited volunteer stormed into Santa Rita Hall to tell me that the final count had declared me the victor. I had won by seventy-six votes.

CHAPTER 5

Chicano Movement Ends,
Immigration Surges Once More

By the fall of 1972, when I was elected to the Arizona State Senate, the Chicano Movement reached the height of its inspiration and influence. In 1967 Rodolfo "Corky" Gonzáles had published the poem that electrified Chicano activists and quickly became the movement's anthem, "Yo Soy Joaquín" (I Am Joaquín).[1] The poem opens with lines that captured the cultural schizophrenia of Chicanos seeking an identity.

> I am Joaquín,
> lost in a world of confusion,
> caught up in the whirl of a gringo society,
> confused by the rules, scorned by attitudes,
> suppressed by manipulation, and destroyed by modern
>   society.

And its final lines expressed with uncompromising finality that Chicanos would not be blended away in that mythical melting pot that was perhaps that generation's greatest fear:

> I am the masses of my people and I refuse to be absorbed.
> I am Joaquín.
> The odds are great but my spirit is strong,
> My faith unbreakable,
> My blood is pure.
> I am Aztec prince and Christian Christ.
> I SHALL ENDURE!

Corky Gonzales, transformed into a cultural icon and an important revolutionary voice by the power of "I Am Joaquín," convened the National Chicano Youth Liberation Conference. The conference was the first time Chicano student leaders from California, Texas, Arizona, and Colorado had met. The rhetoric of revolution filled the air. Corky presented his *Plan Espiritual de Aztlán*, a hodgepodge of Marxist concepts and a call for the "liberation" of the Chicano people, filled with messianic notions of reclaiming Aztlán, the legendary ancestral home of the Aztec people. The plan was adopted by the conference but soon forgotten. What remained in popular discourse after the conference was the poetry of another Chicano bard, Alurista, whose poetry had opened the conference. It was Alurista's words that were insisted on by the conferees as the preamble to the Plan Espiritual de Aztlán that was finally adopted as the official proceedings of the conference.

> In the spirit of a new people that is conscious not only of its proud historical heritage but also of the brutal "gringo" invasion of our territories, we, the Chicano, Mexican, Latino, Indigenous inhabitants and civilizers of the northern land of Aztlán from whence came our forefathers, reclaiming the land of their birth and consecrating the determination of our people of the sun, declare that the call of our sangre is our power, our responsibility, and our inevitable destiny.[2]

Alurista became the poet of the moment. The students, moved by the rhetoric of revolution and the call for unity but resistant to Corky's odd assemblage of Aztec and Mayan belief, Marxist ideas, gringo hate, and mystical musings, decided to come up with a plan of their own. A national conference convened in Santa Barbara a few months later. The outcome

was the national student organization Movimiento Estudian-
til Chicano de Aztlán, best known still by its acronym MEChA.
It was a heady moment; students felt that with this act they
had taken a major step toward assuring Chicano cultural
survival.

José Angel Gutiérrez and Mario Compean, the student
leaders who founded the Mexican American Youth Organization, sought to influence the political future of south Texas
directly. They formed La Raza Unida Party in early 1970. The
party gained national recognition and ignited a heated debate
within the Latino community when it won rapid political
victories in Cotulla and Crystal City, Texas. Similar efforts
mushroomed throughout the southwest. They were just as
quickly met with fierce resistance by other Chicano leaders,
who vehemently criticized the party for being divisive, discriminatory, even racist. In retrospect, La Raza Unida Party was a
spectacular but momentary aberration.

Reies Tijerina and the armed followers he called *mis
valientes* stormed the Rio Arriba County Courthouse in New
Mexico on June 5, 1967. The charismatic leader of the effort
to reclaim the Spanish land grants from over a century of
encroachment and confiscation, Tijerina had been overcome
by an impulse to arrest the man who had been seeking to prosecute him. Upon hearing that District Attorney Alfonso
Sanchez would be at the courthouse, "my heart jumped and I
felt a magnetic wave course through my blood and my internal
organs. Like being stabbed with a knife. I was assaulted by the
idea I least expected, to go to Tierra Amarilla and arrest the
symbol of Anglo-Saxon justice: Alfonso Sanchez."[3] Tijerina
and the *valientes* took control of the courthouse for ninety
minutes; a state patrolman and a corrections officer were both
wounded in the assault. Upon realizing that Sanchez was not
in the courthouse after all, Tijerina and his men retreated to
the hills, taking a reporter for the *Albuquerque Journal* and a

deputy sheriff as hostages. The state responded aggressively by calling out the National Guard, armed with tanks and helicopters, to the hills surrounding Tierra Amarilla, and over 100 local police officers joined by Apache Tribal police to scout down the fugitive Tijerina and his band of *valientes*. The members of the Alianza were rounded up and held in sheep pens overnight.[4]

The manhunt, which lasted four days, fit so wonderfully into the narrative of the mythical Aztec homeland of Aztlán, and the fugitive protagonist so skillfully played the role of the victim/hero seeking only justice, bread, and land, that Tijerina was catapulted into the minds of some Chicano activists as the one–the One–to lead the revolution. My father, whose antennae for false prophets and religious charlatans were always alert, reminded me that we knew Tijerina. He was the itinerant evangelical madman whose visions had brought him and his followers to the desolate Arizona desert, down the hill from Miami, to build a utopian paradise and await further instructions from God. The community dug their homes into the ground and covered them with car hoods and doors. They were nothing more than filthy holes in the ground, my father recalled. There were few Mexican evangelicals in the desert or the copper hills in the mid-1950s. It was a small community that shared quickly the news that affected them. The wild-eyed, dirt-covered pastor who preached an odd, unforgiving gospel and lived with his flock like gophers in the ground was quite a curiosity. My father needed to suffer through only one of his sermons to conclude, "*Está más loco que la ching–*," he's crazier than hell. My father found the admiration Chicano activists felt for him uproariously funny. He assured me that as soon they met him, and heard in person about his bizarre encounters with angels who arrived in what sounded suspiciously like flying saucers, they would be cured of their romantic fantasies. Over the course of the following year, the activists who made their pilgrimage to hear the Che of northern New Mexico invariably returned confused and disappointed. Tijerina spent the next few years fighting court battles and serving prison sentences. He was quickly marginalized. Today his prominence is relegated to Chicano Studies Departments at colleges and universities, where he still plays a role in a favored narrative.

The East Los Angeles High School student walkouts of 1968 began in Roosevelt High School and quickly spread to encompass an estimated 20,000 students in the Los Angeles area. The contagion of students demanding recognition as Chicanos quickly spread across the country, and walkouts took place throughout California, Arizona, Texas, and even in Chicago.

The Chicano Moratorium was organized to protest the Vietnam War and particularly the inordinate number of deaths suffered by the Chicano soldiers. There were marches and demonstrations in various southwestern cities, but it is the demonstration on August 29, 1970 in Los Angeles that will be always remembered by the movement's generation. The rally was 30,000 strong. The police, for reasons still debated today, deployed units to break up the crowd. Violence ensued, and in the end 150 people were arrested and four were dead. Among the casualties was Ruben Salazar, a columnist for the *Los Angeles Times* and perhaps the only voice in support of the movement in a major news outlet. A comment often repeated at the time and attributed to the poet Alurista captured the mood of the moment: "the police called it a people's riot, the people called it a police riot."

Perhaps no mass movement can possibly span a decade without losing its energy. Perhaps the Chicano movement was destined to recede slowly at first and then fade into memory. The movement indeed lost its energy, but it also saw its greatest hero, the one constant light of hope and resistance, damaged and diminished. Perhaps it was this that signaled the end of Chicano idealism.

Cesar Chavez had as early as 1969 undertaken major public actions opposing "illegals"; that year he was joined by the Rev. Ralph Abernathy and Senator Walter Mondale on a march from Coachella to the Mexican border to protest the use of undocumented workers by California growers to break the strikes in the fields and to undermine the union agreements that had been reached. Still, the power, mystique, and charisma of the man were such that immigration justice advocates cringed but remained silent. Cesar continued to claim that the Union would have won more victories, and that those that were in place would not be in jeopardy, were it not for the "illegals." Some close to the Union would quietly comment to each other that most members of the Union were recently arrived from Mexico and undoubtedly many were undocumented. By the time of my election to the state senate it was becoming evident that Cesar and the Union were out of step with the consensus forged by Chicano organizations and even with the more conservative Mexican-American organizations who at one time shared his point of view. Cesar's isolation became even more pronounced in July of 1974, when Union officials were quoted in an AP story as saying: "Aliens were depriving farm workers of jobs and presenting a threat to all people."[5] At that point, a coalition of incensed Latino organizations answered with an unprecedented open letter, part of which declared that "all workers have the right to seek work in order to support themselves and their families . . . when we ask for the deportation of all workers who have no visas we are attacking good Union brothers and sisters who have no visa but would never break a strike." The letter's conclusion was particularly loaded: "The [employers'] traditional response was to deport not only the leaders of strikes but the workers themselves. Thus when a Union calls on the US

Immigration Service to help them it is calling upon a traditional tool of employers and the United States Government." There had been rumors among activists for years that the Union was calling *la migra* and reporting undocumented workers. By the time the coalition letter was sent they were no longer rumors. In the spring of 1974, Cesar launched the Campaign Against Illegal Aliens, urging organizers to find and report "illegals" and encouraging the government to ramp up deportations.

Then, when the situation seemingly could not get worse, the US Attorney General William B. Saxbe announced that the Justice Department would deport one million illegal aliens. Saxbe proudly added that the United Farm Workers fully supported the deportations. The announcement electrified the Chicano community. Calls for Saxbe's resignation were immediate, and the tactful phrasing and gentle rebuke that had hitherto characterized criticism of Cesar ended. The criticism was now public, direct, and unrestrained.[6]

By the fall of 1974, though not yet having completed my first term, I was elected majority leader of the senate by my colleagues. The honor also meant that I was immediately thrust into issues that until then I could choose to ignore. One issue that could not be ignored was the "wet line" that the Union had established at the Mexican border near Yuma, Arizona. As part of the Union's Campaign Against Illegal Aliens, Cesar appointed his cousin Manuel to establish observation points along the border where the undocumented were known to cross. The observers sought to actively persuade the crossers to go back; failing that, the observers were to call the Border Patrol to pick them up. The Border Patrol rarely showed up, I was told, and the consequence was that wet-line thugs would beat the undocumented and force them to return to Mexico. There were many reports of beatings from organizers and activists I trusted and had known for years. None would confront Cesar, but they wanted it stopped before it became a public relations nightmare, and they wanted it stopped because, though they loved Cesar, they bitterly opposed his policy. Over the years I have met with even more organizers who were in Coachella or Yuma at the time. All have repeatedly confirmed that the wet line was basically a bunch of paid, roaming thugs under Manuel's direction.

At my request, Cesar and I met in a mid-town Phoenix hotel restaurant to discuss the wet line and his growing public support for mass deportations of a magnitude not seen since the repatriations of the 1930s. I was the twenty-eight-year-old majority leader of the Arizona State Senate meeting with an icon, a legend, a spiritual leader, a mentor—a man I had been in awe of for over a decade. In a hesitant, halting manner, I argued that the wet line had to stop immediately and that Cesar should reconsider his support of mass deportations. I was the supplicant and he the master. The meeting was uncomfortably tense and brief. Cesar's answers were prac-ticed: those of us who were not in the fields could not understand what was at stake; once the Union established labor contracts even the illegals would benefit, thus his actions were for their own good. I never told Cesar how close I came at that moment to shouting over him. "For their own good?" I almost asked in disbelief and anger. But he was Cesar, and I fell silent. He confirmed the existence of the wet line, but he adamantly denied that beatings or violence of any kind were taking place. And with that, the meeting was over. Cesar got up and left, his close friend Bill Soltero, the leader of the Laborers' International local in Arizona who had accompa-nied Cesar, hurried after him. Lunch was left uneaten, and big cheese Majority Leader was stuck with the bill . . . but Cesar had made his point. He would not back down.

Or so I thought.

On November 22, 1974, the *San Francisco Examiner*

published a letter to the editor from Cesar where he carefully danced back from his seemingly immovable position. The historian David Gutiérrez attributed the shift to Cesar's finally seeing his support weaken: "Aware that he desperately needed to maintain his base of support amongst urban Mexican Americans—particularly Chicano activists and students— Chavez was compelled to reassess his position on this explosive issue." In the letter Cesar flatly denies Attorney General Saxbe's claim that the Union supported the deportation of one million undocumented laborers. In fact, he goes on to charge the Justice Department itself for "the mass recruitment of undocumented workers for the specific purpose of breaking our strikes . . ." The Saxbe plan that the Union had, according to the Justice Department, supported was now "a ploy towards the reinstatement of a bracero program, which would give government sanction once more to the abuse of Mexican farm workers and, in turn, of farm workers who are citizens." And, perhaps most surprising of all, the letter's final paragraph began with a commitment that the Union "will support amnesty for illegal aliens and support their efforts to obtain legal documents and equal rights, including the right of collective bargaining," because, he concluded, "the illegals are our brothers and sisters."[7]

From "wets" deserving of deportation to "our brothers and sisters" deserving of amnesty was perhaps too great a distance to bridge in a letter to the editor. It was certainly intended to quell the anger, but to many activists the letter was insufficient and unconvincing. Although the criticism of Cesar did subside, the damage had been done. The Chicano Movement was already depleted by the War on Poverty's long reach and insidious effects. It may be that for the remaining idealists, to witness Cesar as a flawed human being espousing the discredited and shameful views of the 1950s Americanizers was too troubling to bear. Cesar personified the Union even as its membership shrank, its victories grew sparse, the young idealists drifted away, and the reverence in which he had once been held diminished. Only after his death would Cesar become once more the spiritual leader, the symbol of courage, idealism, sacrifice, selflessness, and quiet wisdom that inspired a generation.

And then the Chicano Movement, such as it was by the mid-1970s, simply deflated and died. The historian F. Arturo Rosales, in his history of the Mexican-American civil rights movement, observes that "none of the Chicano Movement cultural or political pronouncements became part of an unchangeable dogma."[8] That is true. It is also true that the decade of the Chicano Movement dramatically redefined the self-image of the Mexican-American community. The acceptance of ourselves as flawed and inferior, and having to be forced to be white or at least white-like in order to be proud Americans, is permanently extinguished. Assimilation continues without impediment, but it does so on our terms. That is the legacy of the Chicano Movement.

The year of 1974 saw the election of Latinos in historic numbers throughout the southwest, but perhaps the most extraordinary and unexpected victory was the election of Raul Castro as governor of Arizona. He was the first and only Mexican-American governor in the history of the state, and given Arizona's particularly strong enchantment with the Confederate south, the Ku Klux Klan, armed patriot and Aryan militias, this was and remains a remarkable achievement. Raul Castro was born in Cananea, Sonora, in 1916, number thirteen in a family of fourteen kids. The family migrated to the border mining town of Douglas, Arizona, where he was raised. Castro overcame all of the obstacles of his generation to become an attorney and one of the state's earliest Mexican-American superior court judges. He was named by President Johnson as ambassador to El Salvador in

1964 and ambassador to Bolivia in 1968. Many Tucson-based Chicano activists had hesitated to support Castro in his first campaign for governor in 1970. His reputation as a juvenile court judge held that he was particularly harsh on Chicano youth, and it was also widely rumored that while in Bolivia he had been involved in the assassination of Che Guevara and the subsequent scandalous public display of his corpse by the Bolivian military. He lost the campaign of 1970, but in the intervening years he reached a delicate peace with his young detractors. He ran again in 1974. The campaign against him was predictably marred by racial innuendo. Billboards throughout the state featured a huge photograph of the Republican candidate, Russ Williams, with one, simple, bold phrase below his shiny white face: "He looks like a Governor." Despite it all, the unlikely-looking Raul Castro won.

The political columnist for the *Phoenix Gazette*, John Kolbe, described the euphoria at Governor Castro's inaugural: "For Mexican Americans it was Christmas, Fourth of July and Cinco de Mayo all rolled into one. Easily half the well-wishers on hand to christen the Castro administration were of Latin heritage. The mood at the noon inaugural reflected the easy-going and ebullient enthusiasm of the Latin temperament."[9]

Castro's tenure as governor was short-lived and troubled. Even before his inauguration, the press broke the story that he insisted on a "governor's mansion." Shortly after being named majority leader, I met with his staff and discovered that indeed the press stories were true. He wanted a house. The fact that Arizona had never had a governor's mansion was irrelevant. The staff had it all worked out. A wealthy friend would donate a luxury home in a gated community in the elite enclave of Paradise Valley. Arizona would accept the gift, provide the friend with a tax benefit, and the legislature would pass an emergency appropriation to furnish the house, build security quarters, and plant a really tall flagpole in front. It was politically absurd and the subject of great humor. Castro would not back down. He wanted that big house. So we gave him one. He never quite overcame the ridicule.

As the Democratic majority leader, I was expected to carry out his legislative program. After I repeatedly requested to meet and discuss their proposed legislation, Governor Castro's staff presented me with a single bill for the session. It was massive in size. The governor requested that we pass a bill that changed the term "peace officer" to "police officer" each and every time it appeared in the entire legal code of Arizona. I asked, that's it? They said, yes, that's it. This is it, the entire legislative program? Yep, that's it, they answered. No more peace officers? Governor feels that the state would be safer if they were police officers instead. You gotta be kidding me! Nope, this is it. Okay, then . . . So I introduced the draft, assured its passage by the state senate as quickly as possible, and sent it to the Republican House, where it languished unheard and unseen until its merciful death from inattention. I think that was the last time I asked for a meeting on the governor's legislative program.

In the first year of his term, the governor caused something of a national scandal regarding immigrants and Vietnamese refugees. The Vietnam War was deteriorating toward its ultimate end. Saigon was lost by the South Vietnamese and the Americans in April of 1975. President Ford strongly supported Vietnamese immigration to the United States and proposed the Indochina Migration and Refugee Assistance Act, which was passed in 1975. The act gave Vietnamese refugees expedited immigration status. In May of 1975, Arizona was informed by the federal government that some of the refugees would be relocated to Arizona. Governor Castro, who along with his family had fled Mexico during the revolution and entered the country as a refugee, learned of the plan while visiting Mexico City, and shared his thoughts with an AP reporter:

> I'm not going to be that callous to them and uncharitable . . . but I intend to limit them. I intend to be rather strict, although you can't close the whole state to them . . . I recognize we are a country that always welcomed immigrants. I was a refugee too, and many people were . . . but I don't think we ought to welcome them anymore. I think we ought to put a limit on them. They've got children who have to be fed, people who have to have jobs . . . [10]

The governor of course had no authority to limit Vietnamese immigrants. There were fewer than 120,000 Vietnamese refugees nationally at the time. Most were being relocated to Texas and California without incident. The few who arrived in Arizona quietly blended into the community and have become part of the diverse fabric of the state. The comments, however, immediately sparked questions about Mexican immigration. The governor endorsed reestablishing a Bracero Program and questioned the efficacy of deportation. "Deportation is obviously not the answer . . . the problem with deportation is you take the illegal person out of the country and a few hours later he's back." With a breathtaking logical contortion, the AFL-CIO Central Labor Council's leader, Jim White, predictably criticized the governor for the bracero proposal: "There probably has been no other time in Arizona history when more citizens have agreed on the need for halting the importation of cheap Mexican labor—legal or illegal. . . . On the other hand, when Vietnam refugees want only to make their own way—with no handouts—our governor is opposed."[11] Cesar, too, noted that Castro "asked for Braceros the other day and that's not helping."[12]

An employer sanctions bill was endorsed by the AFL-CIO and quietly supported by the governor in 1975. The bill would have imposed a $1,000 fine and up to one year in prison for an employer who knowingly hired "illegal aliens." Most surprising to me was that Chicanos Por La Causa, now replete with federal and Ford Foundation money and obviously not listening to the community they purported to represent, hired an investigator, a former business agent for the Plumbers Union, to find undocumented workers. At the hearing of the Senate Agriculture Commerce and Labor Committee, this investigator testified in support of the bill that he had "found them on construction jobs, especially at McCormick Ranch [a large luxury community then under construction], and I even found two on an Air Force job in Yuma." To paraphrase Captain Renault in the movie classic *Casablanca*, I was shocked, shocked I tell you, to discover there were undocumented workers in Arizona.[13] The district director of INS, Don Brown, also spoke out in favor of the bill, opining that "the labor unions killed the Bracero Program and now it looks like they might have been short-sighted." He added, "We're just taking pressure off the Mexican government by letting them come here."[14] That was on March 4, 1976. As if to illustrate his point, on March 17, INS rounded up sixty-seven illegal aliens and held a press conference to announce that "at least 15,000 illegal aliens hold jobs" in Tucson.[15]

The bill passed the Agriculture Committee and was never heard of again.

Midway into Governor Castro's term, President Carter nominated him as ambassador to Argentina. The governor hurriedly accepted and resigned. Governor Castro was a Mexican American of his generation. He was always uncomfortable with the aggressive style of the Hispanic Caucus, particularly with my own unabashed championing of Latino issues. He would bristle at the use of the term "Chicano".

Castro never understood the ambiguous sharing of power between the legislative and the executive branches. He tended to dictate, and occasionally the legislative leadership did as he wished, but increasingly his edicts were politely ignored. His time as an ambassador and a judge had perhaps accustomed him to deference and a more formal protocol than the rambunctious relationship that existed between the legislature and the governor's office. Once, during a heated legislative debate, a compromise was hammered out that needed the governor's approval. I grabbed the documents that illustrated the deal, called the governor's staff and rushed up to the executive offices to explain it. I was escorted into the governor's private office, and while I waited I sat on a sofa, spreading out the documents on a small table in an order that best demonstrated the proposed changes. I did not realize he had stepped into the office until I heard his voice, unquestionably angry, saying: "You stand up when the governor walks into the room!" He then turned and walked out. Some staffers rushed after him, others stood and shrugged, and I walked back to the senate floor to explain that the deal was dead.

An incident that illustrates his growing contempt for the legislature occurred during his second and final year, at a time when a national malpractice insurance crisis for health-care providers had struck the country. The legislature was forced to respond to an issue that bitterly divided urban and rural interests, liberals and conservatives, and of course trial lawyers and medical professionals. What made things even more complicated was that to avoid the cancellation of insurance policies in rural Arizona, we were constitutionally required to declare an emergency. An emergency required a two-thirds vote of both houses of the legislature. The Republican House of Representatives Majority Leader Burton Barr counseled, and I agreed, that success required bipartisanship and transparency.

At the end of the harrowing session, the daily newspaper described it:

> Forced by the need for a two-thirds majority in each house to seek minority help, Majority Leaders Alfredo Gutierrez and Burton Barr decided early on to keep politics out of it—and they remained true to their word throughout the five-month ordeal. They dealt squarely and candidly with each other and their minority counterparts and not incidentally with the army of lobbyists who contributed so much energy to the exercise. [16]

But transparency was sacrificed as the deadline neared: "the major compromises which made the final agreement possible were hammered out in long hours of tough bargaining in Gutierrez's office with the doors firmly closed."

Every member rose to condemn the bill as punitive, excessive, poorly drafted, a product of hysteria driven by the press and greedy interests, and certainly unconstitutional—and then two-thirds of them voted aye.[17] One important pundit reflected on what happened next: "The way [Castro] handled the bill-signing incidentally told a lot about why Castro has trouble getting along with the Legislature. Only one legislator was on hand, and a Republican at that. Gutierrez wasn't informed about the ceremony until 20 minutes beforehand. It would have been a little goodwill and let everyone share in the glory."[18]

Governor Castro hated the cajoling, backslapping, often insincere praise and promises that fuel the process. His was a troubled term, but I would learn too well how extraordinary was his accomplishment. I write this nearly forty years later, and he remains the only Mexican American ever to be elected governor of Arizona.

My own tenure in the state senate began with a reputation

for "being a hot-blooded liberal" with "a keen street sense and intense persistence,"[19] which I take it meant that though I could not possibly understand complex public policy, I did have a hoodlum's penchant for ferreting out weakness and inflicting legislative pain thereupon. I was elected majority leader of the senate less than two years after being sworn in with that radical south Phoenix gangster image. Democrats gained the majority of the senate in the fall of 1974. My nemesis, minority leader of the senate Harold Giss—a legendary figure from Yuma who had dominated Democratic legislative policy for over twenty years—had died weeks earlier. Giss disapproved of me from the moment I arrived. It was reputation, brashness perhaps, and certainly it was my rejection of rural domination of state government. As a freshman I did not support him for minority leader, and that meant banishment from the committees of power and influence and, of course, the worst office in the building; but more importantly it also meant that my reelection was not in his interest. My more docile predecessor was his preference.

With Harold gone, the majority was evenly split between urban liberals and rural conservatives. I ran hard for the leadership, but in the end it came down to a scene from a Mel Brooks movie: after a few votes, the stalemate was evident. Coming as I did from a mining town and a union family, I understood and supported many rural proposals, but I represented an urban district and had been a tireless advocate for the urban poor. I imagine that at some point as the two sides realized that the stalemate was hardening, the invective growing acidic, and the insults more personal, someone said, "Hey, let's shoot the Mexican instead!" and a stampede of agreement followed. I was elected unanimously after my rural opponent withdrew. I assume that both sides felt that my tenure would be short-lived and that the leadership would transfer quickly. As it turned out, I remained the Democratic leader for the next twelve years, until I decided to leave the legislature. At the end of my first year as leader, the *Phoenix Gazette*'s political columnist, John Kolbe, wrote a parody conflating the Academy Awards with an imaginary Academy of Legislative Arts ceremony. The extraordinary Republican leader of the house, Burt Barr, was, of course, the star of the show:

> For best direction, production and parliamentary choreography, the award must go—as it has for the past seven or eight years—to the irrepressible majority leader of the lower chamber Burton Barr. Time after time he has demonstrated his total mastery of the fine art of leadership—wheedling, cajoling, twisting, pushing, pulling and eyebrow arching his way to completion on the bills that really counted . . . he combined three essential personal traits (a rollicking sense of humor, spaghetti-like flexibility and rhinoceros-like skin) to stand head and shoulders above the crowd for sheer ability.

Burt Barr was indeed irrepressible, "the only guy I ever met who could talk and listen at the same time," the wise, wily, and loveable old Senator Stan Turley once told me during a tough negotiation. But Kolbe also glimpsed in me, even with my short tenure as Barr's counterpart, the promise of real leadership and the potential for great entertainment.

> For most promising young director and greatest improvement in a year, the award easily goes to the Senate's Alfredo Gutierrez. As a hot-blooded liberal freshman Gutierrez showed promise as an adept orator, but his minority status gave no hint of his future. But with a majority behind him, and the leader's title on the door, he blossomed into a skilled conciliator, a quick study and a caustic humorist. Most of all he learned the First Law of Legislating—what's

possible and what isn't. The windmill tilters never master it.[20]

And in a more serious analysis of the end of that legislative session, Kolbe, in an article entitled "Strife Marked 1975 Legislature," wrote:

On the final day of the five-month legislative session, a hand lettered sign appeared on the office door of an angry House conservative.

Alfredo 11 ½ Barr ½

The reference was to Senate Majority leader Alfredo Gutierrez and his House counterpart, Burton Barr, and reflected the member's embittered conclusion that his Republican leaders had surrendered too much in the search for détente with the Democratic Senate. But in a larger sense, it also encapsulated the intensity of the most significant force shaping the record-long 1975 session—partisan maneuvering and philosophical head-butting. In a word, politics.[21]

Backhanded compliments from angry conservatives notwithstanding, I had little doubt that Barr had prevailed in most of what he sought. But I also had little doubt that I was really good at this, and that Barr knew I was good at this.

The article went on to describe how a consumer rights bill on unit pricing in grocery stores led to an angry liberal revolt in my caucus. Rural conservatives supported me and put it down. Barr and I encountered each other in the mall between the houses later that afternoon; he was bouncing across the mall barking orders at staff running to keep up with him when he saw me. His eyes sparkled, his eyebrows arched, he smiled and shouted out in passing, "They hate you don't they? Get used to it, kid, they're gonna hate you at the end of every session . . . if you're good." I must have been. Rancor, anger, disappointment, and exhaustion characterized the end of every session, but each year we accomplished what we set out to do. Responding to the strife in his own caucus, Burt, the decorated World War II combat colonel who commanded Allied troops at Anzio, declared: "When people leave here convinced the leadership sold them down the river, we probably got something done. . . . Once you get your program set you've got to move that baby down the road like a tank, and some people get run over." The private from another war and another era listened carefully.[22]

Jimmy Carter's 1976 campaign for president provided one last bit of drama between Governor Castro and myself. I became a Carter volunteer early in his campaign; Governor Castro remained neutral until Carter's nomination was evident. Immediately after the Democratic National Convention, Governor Castro was asked to be the Arizona chairman of the campaign, and I was asked to coordinate the Arizona campaign. For me it was a dubious honor. Polls showed that we would lose Arizona overwhelmingly. For Governor Castro my appointment was apparently an insult: he immediately objected, both privately to the campaign and publicly to whoever would listen. Hamilton Jordan, Carter's campaign manager, and Tim Kraft, his field director, both had to become involved, and both had the same reaction. Basically, "Jesus! Doesn't he know we're gonna lose Arizona?" I offered to resign, Jordan said forget about it—but you're not sitting at the head table when Governor Carter comes to his Phoenix fandango. Not a problem, I answered. In fact, I was relegated to some dark, cordoned-off corner of the ballroom next to where the Secret Service had insisted we stuff the press. The press complained bitterly, and I blamed our shared lot on Castro.

Carter was elected without Arizona's support, and Castro left Arizona for Argentina as soon as he could. Arizona's constitution designates the secretary of state as the successor to the governor. Wesley Bolin had served in that position for twenty-eight baby-kissing, glad-handing, uneventful, inoffensive, good ol'boy, big-hatted, cowboy-booted years. Thrust unexpectedly into the governorship, the stress was perhaps too much. Wes died of a heart attack five months after assuming the office. Succession fell to Arizona's attorney general who had, until the moment fate dealt Wes that fatal blow, been preparing to run for the United States Senate. Bruce Babbitt assumed the office on March 4, 1978. He would be elected to a full term in November and reelected a second time in 1982.

The Babbitt family, early pioneers and Indian traders in the Arizona territory, had amassed a fortune in land, car dealerships, Indian trading posts, and mercantile companies. They were the most influential family in northern Arizona. Bruce Babbitt was a graduate of Notre Dame and Harvard Law. After law school, he became a federal poverty lawyer, got involved in the civil rights movement, went on the historic Selma march, and was an administrator of the VISTA antipoverty program before returning to Arizona and joining a prestigious law firm. Babbitt's tenure as attorney general had been notable for his aggressive prosecution of land fraud— Arizona's white-collar crooks' favorite pastime—and for tenaciously prosecuting major cases of consumer protection. He was an equally activist governor.

Babbitt was the beneficiary of a massive reorganization of Arizona's state government that had occurred in the years immediately prior to his assumption of the office. Arizona, like many states, had had for years a governance architecture that reflected the federal government. Each of Arizona's fourteen counties had two senators. The House of Representatives was apportioned every four years by the secretary of state on the basis of voter turnout for the gubernatorial race. In 1964, the Supreme Court, in Reynolds v. Sims, ordered states to redistrict to reflect the doctrine of "one man, one vote." At the time, Mojave County's 7,700 people had two state senators; so did the 663,000 people of Maricopa County, a ratio of eighty-six to one. Arizona, long dominated by conservative cattle farming and mining interests predictably refused. A lawsuit followed, and in 1966 the federal court formulated its own redistricting plan to put in effect until the state legislature acted.[23] The court's plan transferred power from sparsely populated rural Arizona to Phoenix and Tucson. 1966 was a bad year for farmers, ranchers, mining companies, cows, cactus, and rural Democrats. Urban Republicans took over both houses of the legislature and broke the big-hatted, cowboy-booted stranglehold on Arizona politics.

The new Republicans were led by the extraordinary Burton Barr, who would dominate the house for the next twenty years (and of whom it was often quipped that the house was "fifty-nine members surrounded by Burt"), and Sandra Day O'Connor, my immediate predecessor as majority leader of the Arizona Senate. She was one of the idealists on a mission to modernize Arizona. Wanting to quickly institutionalize change, they launched a reorganization of government that would take a decade to complete but would guarantee that state government would no longer be controlled by a series of commissions, geographically composed, that tilted executive power to rural Arizona. There was a Labor Commission, a Welfare Commission, a Highway Commission, a Real Estate Commission . . . Hell, there was a commission for just about everything in state government. The governor's authority was limited to appointing commissioners for staggered terms, and these, once appointed, were free to oversee their fiefdoms pretty much as they pleased.

Over the course of the next few years, state government would be totally transformed, and executive power would be transferred to the governor. Urban Democrats, though in the minority until 1974, joined with Republicans to change the face of government. Babbitt assumed one of the most powerful executive offices in the country—and Babbitt would deftly exercise that power to help transform the state from the rural backwater it had been to the diverse, modern, urban pioneer it was to become.

The "Guv," as everyone seemed to refer to him, was a skillful and unstoppable torrent of activity. He was a passionate environmentalist and a ferocious steward of Arizona's huge holdings of public lands. He is singularly responsible for confronting Arizona's chronic water disparities and rewriting the entire water code. In a desert state, this is an achievement of gargantuan magnitude. He pushed major reforms in primary education and continuously advocated for higher education. Arizona's infrastructure was overwhelmingly modernized during his tenure.

For a fellow who had met his youthful patrician obligation serving as a poverty lawyer, the governor took remarkably little interest in social services, the poor, or poverty law. That, of course, was just fine with me. We developed a close relationship best characterized as a balance of our interests and the use of our individual points of power and leverage to achieve mutual ends. I made sure that the governor's ambitious environmental agenda became law, and he was always helpful to further my restructuring of social services in Arizona. Arizona was the only state or territory in the country to reject Medicaid. Though a bill authorizing the state to enter the program was pushed through by Barr in 1968, each year either the House Appropriations Committee or the Senate Appropriations Committee refused to fund the matching dollars required by the federal government. I was committed to changing that. I introduced my first bill mandating Medicaid in 1973. It failed, then failed again in 1974. In 1976, Barr and I constructed a new funding formula that transferred the amount county health departments would save by not providing care to indigents, who would now receive their care from the Medicaid program. It passed the senate but was never heard in the house. Burt, who had been struggling to pass Medicaid for nearly a decade, took me aside to tell me there was no way the bill in its current form could pass. It was far too liberal and Democratic.

We turned to the leading theorist on health-care management systems, Alain Enthoven, a widely published professor at Stanford, who spent a few days brainstorming with senate majority staff and myself. The product of those sessions was a skeletal outline for a prepaid capitated program with services provided by private health maintenance organizations. The bill I introduced in 1977 reflected the Enthoven principles, but it, too, failed. Babbitt was intrigued by Enthoven's innovative approach and joined the battle in the session of 1980. We reintroduced it in 1981. It was a contentious and controversial session, since hospitals opposed the bill, as did the Arizona Medical Association. Conservative Republicans, still a minority of the Republican Caucus, considered the bill a major step toward socialism. We prevailed only because Babbitt agreed to strategically threaten to veto the favored bills of our opponents in order to gain their silence or their votes.

Unfortunately, in order to cobble together the votes, we agreed that management of the program would be privatized—and perhaps the biggest mistake of all was my stubborn insistence that the program provide services fifteen months after passage of the bill. It was against all advice, but I was certain that if implementation took two to three years, conservative Republicans would block appropriations or seek a repeal. As I had been warned, both of those decisions were nearly fatal to the program. The private administrator proved to be a disastrous choice. The short time period I had insisted upon for service delivery made most experienced HMOs unwilling to participate. Hurriedly formed, poorly organized entities bid to provide services. Programs to detect and prevent fraud were untested and ineffective; the result, just as I had been warned, was scandalous corruption.

In 1984, after the record of mismanagement and scandal was threatening the very survival of the program, Babbitt, Burt Barr, and I agreed that the state had to take it over. Burt and I pushed through emergency legislation in a matter of days authorizing the governor to seize the program. Babbitt attracted immensely talented and experienced public servants to join his administration; administrators who, absent Babbitt's rising national stardom, would have certainly gone to a larger state, or perhaps to prestigious academic posts. Babbitt's emergency takeover team was composed of such folks. It was led by Bill Jamieson, a former top federal Department of Health and Welfare administrator and former director of Arizona's Department of Economic Security. The moment the governor signed the emergency legislation, the team moved in, physically removed the private provider, and declared themselves in charge. Lawsuits initiated by the state and lawsuits against the state followed; accusations, allegations, disclosure of even more incompetence and corruption marred the takeover for many months, but by the following year the program was a national model. Fee-for-service Medicaid would steadily be replaced by the Enthoven principles everywhere in America, and Babbitt—already considered a brilliantly innovative governor on the environment and public lands—would now become recognized as a social service innovator as well.

Douglas Patiño joined the Babbitt Administration in 1983, immediately after serving as California Governor Jerry Brown's Secretary of Health and Welfare. Brown's campaign for the presidency proved unsuccessful, but the campaign forged in the public's mind his reputation as perhaps the most creative and capable governor. Patiño was Latino, a nationally respected as a leader in social service delivery, blessed with unbounded energy and a mind that seemed to move untiringly at breakneck speed. In California, Patiño had been limited by the clumsy administrative design of the department he led. The California department allowed each of its divisions to be independent of the others, develop its own budget and programs, and report directly to the legislature. The secretary herded egos, cajoled, pleaded, and meted out discipline. By contrast, all lines of authority in Arizona's Department of Economic Security ultimately led to only one final decision maker, the director, and the director reported only to the governor. Governor Babbitt was no doubt hoping that Patiño would contribute creativity to the department, and Patiño was relishing the idea of launching new programs and reforms to the tired bureaucracy of welfare, unemployment insurance, food stamps, and a myriad of other social service programs that had been placed in the DES.

The concept of empowering welfare recipients, mostly single mothers with young children, with the resources they need—childcare, transportation subsidies, training, and clothing allowances so that they could join the workforce and leave welfare behind, hopefully permanently—requires that you consider welfare recipients as human beings who share your aspirations and your work ethic. In 1983 that was a tough sell (and it has only gotten tougher).

Ronald Reagan was elected in 1980, having traversed America for five years telling the story of the Chicago "welfare queen" who has "eighty names, thirty addresses, twelve Social

Security cards, and is collecting veteran's benefits on four non-existing deceased husbands. And she is collecting Social Security on her cards. She's got Medicaid, getting food stamps and she's collecting welfare on each of her names. Her tax-free cash income alone is over $150,000!"[24] I would recoil each time Reagan added that subtly race-baiting flourish, the "Cadillac Welfare Queen." But of course I was overreacting . . . Reagan muttering racial stereotypes? It wasn't because she was black, surely, it was because she was cheating. Reagan never mentioned a name, but the press concluded that there was only one case that even remotely approximated the Chicago Welfare Cadillac Queen. There was a "Miss Taylor" who was actually charged and convicted for using two separate aliases to falsely collect $8,000. Even after his staff was confronted with the facts, Reagan kept spellbinding the crowds with his mendacity. Reagan would usually go on to brag about how as governor of California he had "lopped 400,000 off the welfare rolls"; the truth was that the lowest case load during his tenure, over 2 million recipients, meant a decline of only 232,000.[25] Reagan's story may not have been true, but it succeeded in victimizing welfare mothers for generations. Arizona's United States Senator Paul Fannin, concerned that in the southwest it was illegals who were defrauding the system, introduced federal legislation making the use of false documents a crime: "The problem of illegal aliens is especially serious in Arizona and is a matter of concern . . . by fraudulently obtaining passports, credit cards, Social Security cards . . . illegal immigrants are able to obtain social, health and welfare benefits . . . illegal aliens are a double drain on the taxpayers because they take jobs which go to unemployed US citizens and if they lose those jobs then they siphon off welfare benefits . . ."[26] Fannin did not offer even the pretense of credible evidence to bolster his arguments.

It was in that atmosphere that Douglas Patiño proposed empowering welfare mothers with a program that would prepare them for the workforce. His scheme entailed additional appropriations for enhanced childcare while mothers were in training, and a childcare subsidy if they obtained employment. It envisioned training programs funding for businesses to train mothers for specific jobs, plus funding for clothing allowances and public transportation. "Welfare to Work" had been discussed in the social service literature for some time, but Douglas proposed to actually create such a program. All hell broke loose.

Arizona's welfare mothers were fat, illiterate Mexican women strolling into government offices trailed by five dirty kids eating popsicles and smearing the furniture. And of course there were also the Welfare Queens driving up in their purple Cadillacs, leaving their man behind only for a moment while they grabbed that free money. Stereotypes were tough to battle, but the welfare-to-work tax credit for employers was Douglas's key to organizing a major coalition of businesses to support the project. The design of DES had brought labor programs, unemployment insurance, and training primarily from the old Labor Commission into an integrated department to allow for streamlined service. The old labor stalwarts and the Federal Department of Labor wanted none of it: they serviced working people, they would sneer, not welfare mothers. Their bureaucratic opposition was formidable. At one point, a key senate staff person wrote a scathing but hilarious, and obviously absurd, letter repeating every ridiculous stereotype of welfare mothers and demanding that the DES cease and desist. The letter was sent on Federal Department of Labor letterhead to the deputy director of DES, Bette DeGraw, the former majority staff director in the senate, and was signed by "Deputy Regional Director, Department of Labor, Al Bondigas." As the story was recounted to me, the letter caused immediate concern: division heads were summoned to contemplate the appropriate response, and finally the letter and their recommendations were shared with Douglas. He was furious at the contents of the letter but suddenly burst out laughing. Al Bondigas . . . *albóndigas*, he kept repeating. albóndigas is the ubiquitous Mexican meatball soup . . . some meatball had written the letter that ultimately embarrassed the Labor rebellion into silence.

Throughout the controversy, Babbitt kept his distance. When it was clear that the program could be launched primarily with existing executive authority, a tax credit bill that the business community supported, and relatively small increases to the budget, Babbitt declared it his priority. Arizona was the first state to adopt a welfare-to-work program.

It was a great experiment that unfortunately would not last. Babbitt left office in 1986; his successor had little interest in treating welfare women with dignity. In 1996, Bill Clinton signed a bill often described as "welfare to work." This was the Personal Responsibility and Work Opportunity Reconciliation Act, sponsored by Representatives Clay Shaw and Lamar Smith. In an op-ed authored by both men, they offered their primary reason for the bill: "In fact, many aliens immigrate to America with the express intent of accessing welfare as soon as they are eligible." They went on to write, "American taxpayers are spending more than $8 billion a year providing welfare benefits to people who claimed they were coming to America for opportunity."[27] Clinton famously pledged during his second campaign to "end welfare as we know it," and the bill he signed was intended to force folks off welfare; but it was also a clear signal that the Mexican woman with the dirty kids and the strawberry popsicles had replaced the "welfare queen" as America's favored object of scorn.

Babbitt, however, basked in his growing reputation as the brilliant innovator of social policy. In 1985, now a true believer, he dedicated his entire State of the State address to children's issues. It was at that moment, contemplating the sheer radical departure from tradition, not a word about infrastructure or the budget or even Babbitt's passion, the environment and public lands, that I realized, "This dude's running for president!"

Babbitt sought the Democratic nomination for president in 1988. Intellectuals and policy wonks welcomed his candidacy. His initial public debate was a disaster. The *New York Times* described his appearance at that Houston debate as the candidate "who kept tilting out of camera range, eyes roving, long face jiggling like two tots on a trampoline."[28] Arizonans had grown accustomed to his volleys of ah-hahs and pauses between words and geeky squints. They found them endearing. The national press not so much. But even if it had gone spectacularly well and everyone had loved him, there was an issue in the wings that would still have denied him the Democratic nomination.

In the early hours of July 26, 1983, a single bullet pierced the wall of a company-owned home in the isolated Arizona mining town of Ajo, crashed into the bedroom of three-year-old Chandra Tallant, tore through her pink pillow, and shattered her skull. Chandra was hurriedly medevaced to a hospital in Phoenix. Governor Babbitt rushed to her bedside, and the Phelps Dodge Mining Corporation offered a $100,000 reward for information leading to the capture of the assailant. The *Arizona Republic* asked, "What did the child do to deserve the bullet? She has a father working to support her while other Ajo kids' dads are on strike against the copper mines."[29] No one has ever been charged with firing that bullet, but the *Arizona Republic*, Phelps Dodge, and the governor quickly confirmed the impression that it must have been a striking mine worker. Indeed the sheriff arrested one, but soon released him for lack of evidence. The image of a helpless child almost murdered by a vengeful striking miner would haunt the Union for months to come.

Chandra's father, Keith Tallant, was often called the first scab by striking miners in Ajo. Tallant was the first worker to respond to Phelps Dodge's call for workers to replace the striking miners in Ajo.

The strike against Phelps Dodge had officially begun at midnight on June 30, 1983. The United Steelworkers and the smaller crafts unions had negotiated agreements with all the major mining companies, except one. Since the merger of Steelworkers with Mine Mill, the Unions and the companies had engaged in what came to be known as pattern bargaining, whereby the Unions would reach one master agreement with the major producers, thus ensuring that no one company could wrangle a sweetheart deal. The specter of a walkout by every union in a mining operation meant a complete shut-down of the companies. It proved ample incentive to reach industry-wide agreements. Until 1983.

That was a bad year for copper. It was particularly bad for Phelps Dodge. In *Copper Crucible*, his definitive history of the Morenci strike and its consequences for organized labor, Jonathan Rosenblum described Phelps Dodge's situation:

> In 1982 the worst recession since the 1930s sent copper prices plunging. The construction and auto industries—copper's biggest customers after the power companies—were in the doldrums. Furthermore, crushing debt burdens led copper-producing countries like Zaire, Peru, and Chile to keep mining (and pushing down world prices) just when production curtailments were needed most. Finally, Phelps Dodge's diversification efforts had failed on all counts. Investments in uranium had gone sour—a public utility

had just breached all of its purchasing contracts when interest in nuclear power dropped. An aluminum investment failed to take off. Oil and natural gas purchases had simply gone nowhere . . . losses eventually mounted to $74 million.[30]

The declining fortunes of Phelps Dodge did not go unnoticed on Wall Street. *Business Week*'s cover on July 26, 1982 announced "Management Crisis at Phelps Dodge." The accompanying article said of the chairman, George Munroe, that "Munroe is considered a decent, intelligent man. But he is also known to be extremely cautious making hard decisions and has an aversion to hearing bad news." Munroe was a former professional basketball player with the Boston Celtics, a Rhodes scholar, a graduate of Harvard Law, and the primary instigator of Phelps Dodge's diversification away from its reliance on copper. That appeared to have been a failed strategy. Though the company moved its headquarters to Phoenix in 1982, Munroe kept his office and residence in New York, along with his board seat on the Metropolitan Museum of Art and on the Council of Foreign Affairs. When he did visit the hinterlands, "company officials treated Munroe's rare visits to Arizona like a tour of a head of state." As for visiting the isolated mining communities, "Munroe arrived in the copper towns looking and sounding more like a copper czar than a negotiator seeking to find common cause with the workers."[31] While Chairman Munroe was aloof and lordly, Phelps Dodge's president, Richard Moolick, was an angry engineer that had come up the company ranks running mining operations, including those at Clifton and Morenci in Arizona. Moolick was mostly angry at unions:

> You're naive if you think it's good to operate with a union. It's no way to work for the company, for the employees, or for anyone . . . Mine Mill was an old and militant union.

The first time I sat at a bargaining table there were some card-carrying commies on their side. To me it was an affront to sit across from a goddamned commie. And those people remained in the Steelworkers, too, you know. It was the same crowd.[32]

The pattern agreement the Union had arrived at with the other major copper producers included a wage freeze, a variety of cost-saving measures, and a Cost of Living Adjustment, or COLA. The item that Phelps Dodge would not accept in the pattern master agreement was the COLA, an integral part of pattern agreements since 1967. Phelps Dodge proposed reverting to the "Miami scale" that was used in the Miami mines through the 1930s, wherein miners' pay would float with the price of copper and the profitability of the company. It was one of the first provisions that the increasingly powerful Mine Mill had fought hard to do away with, since the mining executives would always be able to ride out the lean years, but the hourly workers could not. The price of copper was $.70 a pound in 1983. Only when copper prices rose to $1.20 a pound would workers get any increase at all under the Phelps Dodge proposal. And Phelps Dodge president Moolick was in no mood to compromise. He ordered each of the mining operations to sidestep the Union and offer work to all of the striking workers. Fewer than 500 of the more than 2,400 miners accepted.[33] Five hundred was insufficient to operate any mine and, more importantly, insufficient to win an election decertifying the union.

On August 5, the Corporation declared war. It announced it was hiring outside replacement workers, beginning immediately. Offering jobs to striking miners was offensive, but anyone who accepted was still a worker within the brotherhood, a neighbor, perhaps a friend. Recruiting replacement workers was declaring the company's intent to kill the Union. The following day, the *Arizona Daily Star*, Tucson's major newspaper, headlined "In Morenci, Tension Builds on Picket Lines." The story quoted the Union spokesman, Cass Alvin, as saying that if the company hired outside replacement workers it "was inviting trouble . . . it would take an army to protect the mines."[34] On August 8, Governor Babbitt went to Clifton to attempt mediation. It was a fool's errand. Phelps Dodge intended to break the unions, and they expected Babbitt to side with the company. Pattern agreement negotiations required a coordinated national strategy, since decisions on favorable changes at Morenci would have to be incorporated into every other agreement. Pattern agreement negotiations also meant that the local authority that had made Mine Mill so effective was no longer in local hands. President Angel Rodriguez, his board, and his members had ceded final decisions to the Steelworkers national office. Phelps Dodge did offer a ten-day moratorium, but during the few discussions that took place during the pause, the Corporation refused to budge, and on the tenth day the confrontation at the gate resumed.

Morenci was a company town. Phelps Dodge responded with termination notices, eviction demands from company houses, and cancellation of health insurance, while the county sheriff took care of arrests: twenty-four miners were arrested for "rioting" in the days that followed. The press continued the demonizing of the Union that began with the shooting of little Chandra. In her book on the conflict, *Holding the Line*, Barbara Kingsolver depicted the sacrifices and courage of the women of Morenci during the strike and described the press coverage in harsh terms.

> The press . . . portrayed the strikers as a bloodthirsty, immoral mob. In their coverage of the early weeks of the

strike, the state's newspapers seemed to go out of their way to provide photos of strikers drinking beer on the picket line. After the shutdown on August 8, the editorial pages fairly rang with bestial adjectives. "Mobs seem to be in control," proclaimed an editorial in the *Arizona Republic* on August 11. "The ultimate capitulation came when Phelps Dodge closed its Morenci plant when 1,000 wild-eyed strikers and their supporters—most armed with baseball bats—delivered an ultimatum: if the company doesn't close the plant, the herd-like mob, baseball bats and all, would." And a day later, in the same newspaper: "If the union leadership cannot be depended on to assert control over the rabble on the picket line . . . can the public rely on law enforcement authorities to prevent mob rule from compromising public safety? Whether mob or law prevails in this ugly dispute will be tested again next week, when Phelps Dodge plans to reopen the Morenci operation, and the bat-swinging strikers, some slurping beer for courage, plan to close it by force." This observation was printed beside a large cartoon featuring beer-slurping, bat-swinging, ape-shaped men in union caps, with the caption: "S.C.A.B.S. (Striking Copperworkers Anxious to Bash Skulls)."[35]

On August 9, thousands of strikers and sympathizers successfully shut down operations at Morenci once more. On August 10, the governor secretly activated the National Guard. On the 17th, Babbitt met with a group of union leaders and, according to Angel Rodriguez, president of the Morenci Steelworkers Union local, told them that he was under enormous pressure to enforce the law and that it was his duty to do so. Angel concluded the governor had gone to the other side, and that he would soon deploy the National Guard. He intended to keep Phelps Dodge operating and let them bust the Union. Two days later, the largest military invasion in the state's history descended upon Morenci. That morning, August 19, 426 law enforcement officers convoyed up Route 666 followed by 325 National Guardsmen, over 100 military vehicles, tanks, Huey helicopters, SWAT teams, and a general to coordinate the occupation of Morenci and safeguard Phelps Dodge. The picket line was dismantled. Phelps Dodge declared victory. In the course of the next year, Phelps Dodge would decertify over thirty local unions. These were the unions, led by the old Mine Mill, that had fought for equal work for equal pay for Mexicans, that had bravely fought against injustice and discrimination against Mexican workers. Our unions were gone.

Companies ranging from Continental and Eastern Airlines to Caterpillar and Holsum Bread would quickly adopt Moolick's template for union busting.

By the time Babbitt made his announcement for president, his campaign was guardedly touting his decisions at Morenci as evidence of moderation. Along with Governor Bill Clinton, Babbitt had formed the Democratic Leadership Council to formulate the new, centrist path for the Democratic Party. But there was one more shoe yet to drop—one whose thud would have surely brought his dream crashing down, had his own geeky idiosyncrasies not done it for him. The Arizona State Criminal Intelligence Systems Agency, or ASCISA, was created by the legislature in the early 1970s at the request of then Pima County Attorney (later US Senator) Dennis DeConcini as a secretive independent police agency whose mission was to gather intelligence for the prosecution of organized crime and drug smuggling. From the beginning, it was controversial, with the traditional law enforcement agencies that both envied and resented its extraordinary budget, access to sophisticated spying equipment, statewide jurisdiction, and secretive culture. The constant criticism had taken its toll, and the agency was facing complete repeal by the early 1980s. Perhaps the director, Frank Navarrete, saw an opportunity to please the Republican leadership of the legislature, or perhaps he was seeking to please the governor . . . but at someone's behest, the agency (known by its critics as the Arizona CIA) involved itself in the strike squarely on the side of the Corporation. In the years immediately after the strike, it became evident that the operation had been massive and had gone far beyond normal police work. The agents who took part began to brag about their roles and describe how they would go into the mine manager's office and brief him and his head of security on the Union's plans. The agency maintained a book of photographs of strikers they termed "likely troublemakers" which they shared with the company. Navarrete confirmed that he sent daily reports to the governor's office. The sophisticated George Munroe wanted not to be identified with the ruthless tactics of Moolick. Moolick and his team of thugs were forced into retirement shortly after the strike ended, and soon the rumors of state government complicity began seeping out. ASCISA was scheduled for its "Sunset Review" the year following the strike, 1984. Sunset Review is a statutory requirement that each state agency periodically justify its existence to the legislature. ASCISA had few friends among law enforcement. Its very survival was at stake. Its investigations were secret and could not be shared with the public, but its role in the strike and the degree to which Governor Babbitt was aware of or directed the stings, the spying, and the briefings to Phelps Dodge management all became the stuff of speculation as the director and his agents tried desperately to save themselves. ASCISA was repealed in 1984, and the agents who participated felt less inhibited over time from talking about their role in the strike.

Had the Babbitt campaign caught fire, the reporters and opposition researchers who would have swarmed into the state to find the "true Babbitt" would have surely surfaced the real extent of Babbitt's complicity with Phelps Dodge, and reopened wounds with Labor that had barely begun to heal.

During the governor's ten-day moratorium, while both sides were supposed to be negotiating in good faith, Moolick was bragging: "I had twenty shotguns smuggled into [the mine] with a bunch of ammunition . . . I was going for double-aught shot and another guy was for number seven . . . they won that one."[36] Number seven is birdshot, double-aught is at least four times as deadly. Babbitt's CIA was almost certainly aware of the weapons, and the information would have been contained in their daily reports that Agency Director Frank Navarrete delivered personally to Babbitt.[37] That information would have provided Babbitt with more than sufficient reason to intervene in the dispute. The reports, however, have since conveniently disappeared from state archives. Perhaps deep in Phelps Dodge's corporate files . . .

I doubt whether the Guv could have survived the scrutiny.

Nor was the Morenci strike my finest hour. Babbitt aides and supporters asked me early on to organize support among the Latino community, especially in mining country, for the governor. I refused, but I did make smarmy statements acknowledging the potential for violence. I was often quoted along the lines of, "'I don't know if I would've made the same decision as Babbitt,' Gutierrez says. 'But I can tell you the threat of violence was real. The danger of bloodshed was real.'"[38] The Union leadership, many of them old friends, asked me to organize support for the strikers. More specifically, they wanted me to criticize Babbitt and to warn him against calling out the National Guard, and once he had done so to condemn him for that action. I refused again. I admired and respected Babbitt, and frankly I needed him for my ambitious campaign to modernize social services in Arizona . . . but he was wrong. From the moment he responded to Chandra Tallant's shooting, the governor began parroting the Phelps Dodge narrative of a good corporate citizen facing mobs of strikers trying to impose their will by force and terror. The law was on Phelps Dodge's side, he repeated. He may have even convinced himself—but he was wrong. He chose a side. Babbitt chose the popular path being drawn for him by the daily press, and I, for reasons of misplaced loyalty and self-interest, refused to call him on it. Perhaps it would not have made a difference in the outcome, but it would have made a difference in how I perceive myself.

CHAPTER 6

Torture at the Border
and Immigration Reform

Throughout the years I spent in the legislature, Arizona and the rest of the country continued to see historic levels of apprehensions of the undocumented. Apprehensions are the basis for estimating the number of undocumented in the country. In 1954, at the height of Operation Wetback, the number of apprehensions of undocumented migrants exceeded one million, as compared to less than 100,000 in postwar 1946. In 1955, immediately after the end of Operation Wetback, the number of apprehensions fell to 254,096. They would continue to drop to a historic postwar low of 45,000 in 1959. As anti-immigrant hysteria increased thereafter, so did the numbers of apprehensions. By 1977, after the full implementation of Hart-Celler and after the Mexican quota was imposed, the number would once more exceed one million.[1] Apprehensions are primarily the fruit of the INS effort to capture the crossers at the Mexican border. The other major category of undocumented people are those who have entered the country legally and simply overstayed their visa authorization. The State Department did not have a means of knowing the number of overstays. In 1993, following the World Trade Center bombing in New York, the State Department received funding to institute such a program. It was still not in place on September 11, 2001, when terrorists destroyed the twin towers of the World Trade Center. Mexicans were the focus of enforcement and America's growing animosity.

The "push-pull" economic process is a simplistic

but popular explanation, subscribed to by both Marxists and capitalists, for undocumented immigration on the Mexican border. The "push" is the dire, often hopeless, economic conditions in the sending country; the "pull" is the attractive economic conditions in the target country. In the era since the repeal of the Bracero Program and the imposition of the Mexican quota, the "pull" from American farmers drawing in the migrant streams that traversed the country continued as strong as ever, but the workers who had once satisfied that inexorable demand, mostly braceros with a smattering of "wets," were now all illegal "wets." They were, of course, the same people, picking the same beets and strawberries along the same migrant streams, but Congress had created a crisis and transformed hundreds of thousands of workers into targets of scorn. During the Ford Administration, William Saxbe, the US attorney general, called the presence of the undocumented "a severe national crisis." Citing jobs, crime, and welfare costs, Saxbe called for the deportation of one million "illegal aliens" whom he claimed were mostly Mexicans. Saxbe's claim in 1974 that the United Farm Workers had endorsed his massive deportation plan is what of course led to Cesar's infamous letter of denial.[2] CIA Director William Colby warned that undocumented Mexican immigration was a greater future threat to the United States than the Soviet Union: "The most obvious threat is the fact that . . . there are going to be 120 million Mexicans by the end of the century . . . [the Border Patrol] will not have enough bullets to stop them."[3]

President Ford himself attributed America's economic woes to unwanted foreigners: "The main problem is how to get rid of those six to eight million aliens who are interfering with our economic prosperity."[4] A former Commandant of the Marine Corps, General Leonard Chapman, was named INS Commissioner in 1972. Chapman proved to be as simplistically jingoistic as his predecessor, General Swing. In 1973,

when General Chapman was asked by a congressional committee to explain his methodology for estimating the number of
undocumented immigrants as 4 to 5 million, he obliged as
follows: "It is just a mid-point between the two extremes. I
have heard one or two million at one end of the scale and eight
or ten million at the other. So, I am selecting a mid-point—
just a guess, that's all. Nobody knows." One year later, in the
INS Annual Report for 1974, Chapman had doubled his
guess. "It is estimated that the number illegally in the United
States totals six to eight million persons and is possibly as
great as ten or twelve million."5 In Congressional testimony,
Chapman would claim that he could open up "a million jobs
virtually overnight," and in an article he authored for the
Reader's Digest he wrote, "If we could locate and deport three
to four million illegal aliens who currently hold jobs in the
United States, replacing them with citizens and legal residents,
we could reduce our own unemployment rate dramatically—
as much as 50%." Chapman went on to claim that as many as
90 percent of "illegals" were Mexican.6 As he admitted in his
Congressional testimony, Chapman didn't have a clue, but he
did have the perfect pulpit for distorting, exaggerating, and
outright lying. Thankfully, President Carter replaced him
quickly with the first Mexican American to hold the post of
INS Commissioner, Leonel Castillo.

It seems that every generation of race-baiting politicians
and policy makers has a favored academic to lend the appropriate intellectual heft to their spurious arguments. In the
1920s and '30s, it had been the offensive theories of eugenics
and "race suicide" propagated by the likes of Edward Alsworth
Ross, a distinguished sociologist and nationally known
lecturer. In the 1970s the charlatan of the day was Arthur F.
Corwin. Corwin was a "Latin Americanist" whose early work
focused on the Spanish governance of Cuba. His later work
consisted primarily of alarmist hyperbole about Mexican

immigrants. One typical essay, co-authored by Corwin, entitled "Wetbackism since 1964," is a Chicken Little litany of the impending doom that threatens America from the "new wetback invasion." In 1975 the Mexican press published a letter Corwin had sent to Henry Kissinger, demanding that immediate steps be taken to halt "illegal immigration" lest the United States become a "welfare reservation." If nothing was done, the southwest would become a Mexican "Quebec." Corwin went on to recommend construction of an electrified fence along the southern border, the mobilization of the US Army, and a billion dollars so that the INS could deploy an additional 50,000 agents to the border.[7] Corwin's hysterics were rewarded with grants to carry on his "research" from the National Endowment for the Humanities and an appointment as a consultant to the House Judiciary Committee in 1981.

President Carter's newly named Director of Central Intelligence, Admiral Stansfield Turner, joined the chorus depicting undocumented workers as a greater threat to this country than the nuclear-armed military might of the Communist Soviet Union.[8] *Time* magazine, arguably still the establishment's most powerful voice, featured articles quoting anonymous INS sources: "the invaders came by land, sea and air . . ." and, according to INS, cost US taxpayers $13 billion in welfare and sent another $13 billion out of the United States to their home country.[9] The cacophony could no longer be ignored. In response, President Carter set into motion a chain of events intended to resolve the "crisis." That chain of events would ultimately culminate in the Reagan Amnesty and a seemingly ever-worsening situation.

As the mighty imaginary hordes massed in the desert, it is reasonable to expect that someone would be inspired to repel the invaders. When the head of the CIA describes immigrants armed at best with a hoe, a shovel, or a mop as more dangerous to America's wellbeing than the massive Soviet Army, it is reasonable to expect that his pronouncements will be taken seriously. The first major scandalous case of abuse of undocumented migrants happened just outside of Douglas, on the Arizona border. Douglas sits on the desert floor below the Mule Mountains of southern Arizona; Bisbee sits at the top of those mountains. Historically, Bisbee was the tough mining town at the top of the hill. Douglas was the cultured, dignified one where the mine owners lived. The ore was transported by rail from Bisbee to the smelters outside of Douglas to be converted into copper and shipped to points east. The desert floor is cattle country. Until the Gadsden Purchase of 1854, the San Bernardino ranch sprawled from northern Mexico into what is now the southeastern Arizona desert. The newly imposed border divided the ranch, with a third residing on the US side. Most of the northern third was purchased from the Pérez family of Agua Prieta, Sonora, by the legendary Sheriff John Slaughter in 1884. Over time, the Slaughter ranch was subdivided and sold by his heirs. George Hannigan's slice of that historic Mexican ranch abutted the border. On the Hannigan ranch's southern edge, State Route 80 runs parallel to the border.

It's on that route that in 1976 George's son Thomas spotted three young Mexican men who had stopped to refill a water jug. Thomas pulled his pickup truck over, pointed a hunting rifle at the three, accused them of being thieves, and forced them into his truck at gunpoint. Thomas summoned his father George and brother Patrick, and together they carted off the Mexicans deep into the Hannigan ranch, where they were forced to strip, then tied up and beaten with pistols and a metal rod. They scorched the soles of one young fellow's feet with a hot poker, staged a mock hanging of another, and threatened to castrate all three. After hours of terror and torture, the Hannigans tired of their sport and freed the immigrants to hobble and limp their way back to Agua Prieta.

To Sin Against Hope

The Mexican Consulate paraded the three before the press the following day. Each told a harrowing story of sadistic torture suffered at the hands of the Hannigans. The response was outrage on both sides of the border. A national scandal in Mexico, the story was more modestly covered at first in the US but within weeks had attracted intense attention. Chicano activists mobilized almost immediately, demanding that the Hannigans be charged and jailed to await trial. I was one of many activists that joined press conferences demanding justice, but I was also the Democratic leader of the senate. I did not keep the hate mail that followed—this was before e-mail, so the letters were handwritten or typed, none were signed nor were there return addresses, and most threatened my life. I was to be thrown out of helicopters or planes, drowned in the San Pedro river, the desert stream that runs near Douglas, impaled with a variety of instruments through every orifice, shot, castrated, decapitated, and painfully killed in ways that were unimaginable and still unrepeatable. The Hannigans were charged and tried in Cochise County. An all-white jury (in a heavily Mexican-American community) and a half-hearted prosecution resulted in a unanimous verdict of not guilty. Many agreed with Raul Grijalva, the Chicano activist, Tucson School Board member, and future member of Congress, when he called this racist frontier justice. President José López Portillo of Mexico denounced the verdict, and Chicano activists nationally were both dumbfounded and angered by it. We organized quickly and asked the US Attorney General Griffin Bell to retry the Hannigans on charges of civil rights violations. The answer came just as quickly: undocumented immigrants don't have civil rights.

A fresh uproar ensued. A young law student, a native of Douglas who was a former member of Cesar's personal bodyguards, Antonio Bustamante, was incensed at the attorney general's cavalier dismissal of the pleas for justice. Fortunately,

Antonio was a student at Antioch School of Law in Washington, DC. A regrettably short-lived experiment in legal education, founded in 1972 by longtime advocates of poor and minority communities, Antioch was focused on training highly skilled attorneys dedicated to public interest advocacy. In practice, it was more than a law school; it was a public interest law firm with teacher-lawyers and student-advocates representing the poor and others who were unable to obtain representation. Antonio persuaded one of Antioch's senior and most respected attorney-professors, Burt Wechsler, to form a law clinic devoted to the case. The Hannigan clinic recruited five attorney-professors and seven law students to examine legal avenues for federal prosecution of the three ranchers. It was the clinic at Antioch that came up with an ingenious idea that apparently no one at the Justice Department had considered: prosecuting the Hannigans for violating the Hobbs Act. They prepared a legal brief proposing the idea and presented it to the Justice Department at a press conference at the National Press Club, to make sure that it wouldn't be scuttled away. It was both novel and a stretch.

The Hobbs Act was enacted in 1946 as an amendment to the Anti-Racketeering Act. It was intended as a weapon against organized crime. Hobbs made a felon of whoever "in any way or degree obstructs, delays, or affects commerce or the movement of any article or commodity in commerce, by robbery or extortion or attempts or conspires so to do," with a possible sentence of up to twenty years if convicted. The Hannigans, the Antioch brief argued, had obstructed commerce by robbery. They had stolen a few cents and a pile of worthless belongings from a trio of immigrants who were on their way to work. To everyone's amazement, the US attorney for Arizona was intrigued. The attorney general who had succeeded Griffin Bell, Benjamin Civiletti, agreed—but, reflecting the sensitivity of the case, he assigned a senior lawyer in the Justice Department to prosecute. George Hannigan died shortly after the state trial. The case against Patrick and Thomas Hannigan was tried in the federal courthouse in Tucson, where the judge, prosecutors, defense attorneys, and witnesses all had to cross daily demonstrations by Chicano activists to enter the courthouse. The case resulted in a hung jury. The jurors voted eleven to one for conviction, but the one saved the Hannigans from prison.

Despite continued pressure from the Chicano community and a strong argument for retrying the Hannigans from one of the disappointed prosecuting attorneys, José de Jesus Rivera, there was very little interest in the Justice Department. It is unlikely that the case would have gone forward were it not for the unbridled braggadocio of Patrick Hannigan. Patrick Hannigan's interview in the weekly alternative newspaper *Phoenix New Times* was as explosive as it was incredibly stupid. Hannigan admitted to everything and described it all in great detail, with obvious gusto, and pride that he had gotten away with it. With the interview in hand, Rivera and the US attorney for Arizona, Mike Hawkins, made one more plea to Attorney General Civiletti. To everyone's surprise, Civiletti approved going forward. The presiding federal judge was not pleased. He informed the attorneys that he had no stomach for more daily demonstrations and was changing venues to Yavapai County. Yavapai had the least Latino population of any county in Arizona. Rivera filed a motion objecting. The judge compromised and moved the trial to Phoenix.

In the two earlier trials, the Hannigans had all faced the same jury together. By the time of the third trial, new evidence that implicated only Patrick had come to light. The judge ordered that there be two juries, one for each of the brothers, and that both juries were to be sequestered. Judge Richard Bilby's reputation as being both fair and intelligent was soon put to the test. First he asked, but only of possible Latino jurors: "If you find the Hannigan brothers not guilty, will you be able to go back to your community without a problem? If the evidence so shows, can you find them not guilty?" When Rivera entered an angry objection and a motion against the inquiry, Judge Bilby agreed to ask the question of all jurors, irrespective of race or ethnicity. Next, the judge used the term "wetback" to refer to the undocumented during his questioning of jurors. There was an immediate objection by Rivera. The judge ordered the attorneys into chambers but permitted the press to witness the discussion. Rivera told the judge that the term "wetback" was as offensive to Mexican Americans as the "N" word was to blacks; Judge Bilby answered that surely Rivera exaggerated. Rivera responded that he had been born in Zacatecas, Mexico, and had come across at the age of six: he had been hearing that term all his life, and it was offensive and demeaning. Judge Bilby said that he had heard Mexican Americans use the term, and that he often used it in front of his Mexican-American bailiff, and his bailiff didn't mind. Rivera retorted that because black people use the "N" word among themselves does not make it any less offensive. Bilby finally relented and agreed not to use the term. The attorneys were dismissed, but before they could leave chambers the bailiff piped up: "For the record, I think that 'wetback' is offensive also!" Everyone but Bilby burst out laughing.[10]

The Hobbs Act requires that there be theft or extortion that interferes with interstate commerce. The act explicitly states that the obstruction can be of "any way or degree." In the Hannigan case, the robbery totaled twenty-three cents in cash and a few items of old clothing. The interstate commerce requirement was met because the three were employed picking apples in the nearby orchards in the town of Elfrida. The orchard owner testified that they were good, reliable workers. The federal agricultural agent for southern Arizona testified that such workers were essential to picking the apples, packing them, and shipping them throughout the United States and the world. At the end of the trial, the prosecution expected that the judge find the requirements of the Hobbs Act met as a matter of law. The judge punted, and referred whether the test of the Hobbs Act had been met to the jurors.

Thomas Hannigan was found not guilty. The jurors later explained that they never deliberated the facts of the case because they found that twenty-three cents, a pair of torn pants, a shoe with a hole in the sole, and some soiled underwear were of insufficient value to meet the requirements of the Hobbs Act. But Patrick Hannigan's jury concluded that the phrase "any way or degree" did include twenty-three cents and soiled underwear. They considered all the evidence of torture and perversion. Patrick was found guilty and sentenced to three years in a federal prison.

The hope of the Chicano activists was that the Hannigan prosecution would deter others along the border from more vigilante acts of abuse against undocumented immigrants. There is little doubt that it had some temporary effect . . . but hate is relentless and memories are short. Soon the violence at the border would return.

There was one more twist to the Hannigan case. Antonio Bustamante had devoted almost two years preparing the brief and lobbying the case for prosecution at the Justice Department. He had neglected his studies, ignored his tests, and generally violated the school's requirements. The dean of Antioch recommended that Antonio be expelled. At his hearing Antonio argued that his obsessive involvement in the Hannigan clinic had provided him with a unique legal education. The faculty committee members conducting his hearing were torn between the academic requirements expected of every student and the fact that many faculty members and students had been involved in and admired Antonio's tireless and unquestionably legally creative effort to insure justice in the Hannigan case. They too found a creative solution to their dilemma. Antonio was expelled, the precise motion reading: "separated for failure to meet academic standards." Antonio had offered an alternative motion, "separated for failure to meet academic standards while striving to make this law school nationally prominent in the field of civil rights." The committee then recommended and the Dean accepted that Antonio be reinstated on a probationary basis. Antonio became a proud graduate of Antioch. Years later, after he had pursued a splendid career and gained a reputation as an extraordinary lawyer and a relentless advocate for the poor, I asked him about that notation in his transcript. He replied, "I didn't mind being considered a disobedient rule-breaker, but I could not countenance these white professors trying to brand me as intellectually lacking. ¡Chinguen sus madres!"

In October 1977, President Carter introduced into the Congress the Alien Adjustment and Employment Act. Carter's immigration proposal would become the template for every comprehensive immigration reform bill since. It called for an adjustment of status for the undocumented within the country, a temporary guest worker program, enhanced security at the border, and employer sanctions. The response was immediate. The day after its formal unveiling, Congressman Ed Roybal met with labor and the few Hispanic organizations that had national offices in Washington to deplore the bill. Every major organization in the country criticized the bill, most focusing on the employer sanction provisions in the Carter plan. Employer sanctions had been talked about since the 1950s, but the Carter proposal was the first time an administration proposed them. In 1972 the California Legislature had passed an employer sanctions bill that provided that "no employer shall knowingly employ an alien who is not entitled to lawful residence in the United States if such employment would have an adverse effect on lawful resident workers." The penalty was from $200 to $500 for each offense. When the California Department of Labor appeared less than enthusiastic to apply the new law, the United Farm Workers brought an action to force it to do so. The action was opposed by the farmers, and the case went all the way to the Supreme Court. The ruling in the case, DeCanas v. Bica, reflected Cesar's views precisely:

> Employment of illegal aliens . . . deprives citizens and legally admitted aliens of jobs; acceptance by illegal aliens of jobs on substandard terms as wages and working conditions can seriously depress wage scales and working conditions of citizens and legally admitted aliens; employment of illegal aliens in such conditions can diminish the effectiveness of labor unions. These local problems are particularly acute in California in light of the significant influx into the state of illegal aliens from neighboring Mexico.

The Union won the case, but by the time the ruling was handed down in 1976 Cesar had had his epiphany. He now stood with every major Latino organization opposing employer sanctions and supporting amnesty.[11]

The Latino community came together to fight the Carter bill with historic unanimity. Opposition to employer sanctions and support of amnesty for the undocumented were the unifying themes. There were only four Hispanic members of Congress in 1977, and the chairman of the newly formed Hispanic Caucus, Ed Roybal, immediately criticized the Carter employer sanctions. Roybal would argue throughout the debate, which went on for almost a decade, that employer sanctions would lead to rampant discrimination against citizen and legal resident Latinos. As the debate neared its end,

Roybal would conjure up a surprise. An ad-hoc coalition that included LULAC, the GI Forum, NCLR, MALDEF, and La Raza Unida Party had been formed to oppose the legislation shortly after it was announced. The coalition called for a National Chicano/Latino Conference on Immigration and Public Policy to be held in San Antonio in October 1977. The response was overwhelming. Virtually every Latino organization across the country was represented, and almost every Latino elected official in the country attended. Perhaps 2,000 people demonstrated overwhelming opposition to the bill. To the astonishment of many of the attendees, LULAC—only recently the national organization most critical of "wetbacks"—released one of the toughest statements of the conference. LULAC's statement read that it would be "unconscionable and objectionable" to subject Mexican nationals to the "second-class citizenship" that would be the consequence of Carter's "amnesty" plan.[12]

An unexpected turn came from Bert Corona and Soledad Alatorre's Center for Autonomous Social Action-General Brotherhood of Workers, or simply CASA. Corona went far beyond the opposition to employer sanctions to proclaim that undocumented workers, particularly Mexicans, had earned the right to be in this country and the right to work. The undocumented had sacrificed more than any other worker and contributed inordinately to the country's economic success. Corona and Alatorre stressed that the undocumented were our brothers and sisters and that they should be welcomed, not punished. Those views may often be heard today among Latino activists, but in 1977 they were radical, controversial, and a dramatic departure from the cautious language in which the Washington-based, government-funded, non-profit organizations described their opposition to the bill. Indeed, they were a radical departure from perhaps 100 years of servile "Americanization" views espoused by most

147

Mexican-American organizations. Corona and Alatorre changed the course of the conference from simply opposing employer sanctions to forcing the delegates to become advocates for the undocumented.

Certainly, the near unanimous opposition from the Latino community contributed to the Carter plan's demise, but perhaps Carter's famously strained relationship with Congress was the greater cause of its quick death. What Carter did achieve was the establishment of a Select Commission on Immigration and Refugee Policy, the SCIRP. The SCIRP consisted of four members of the House of Representatives, Peter Rodino, Elizabeth Holtzman, Robert McClory, and Hamilton Fish; and four members of the Senate, Senators DeConcini, Simpson, Mathias, and Kennedy. The executive branch was represented by the secretary of State, the attorney general, the secretary of Labor, and the secretary of Health and Human Services. The public members were Judge Cruz Reynoso of the California Court of Appeals; Rose Ochi, executive assistant to the mayor of Los Angeles; and Joaquin Otero, vice president of the Brotherhood of Railway and Airline Clerks. As chairman, Carter appointed the Rev. Theodore Hesburgh, the president of Notre Dame University. Yes, it was one more study commission, but there was little doubt that this one had clout and the president's guarantee of all necessary resources for the task. The SCIRP completed its work and presented its report to President Carter's successor, Ronald Reagan, and to the Congress in March of 1981.

The SCIRP recommendations that were unanimously adopted followed the Carter template. There was an additional recommendation, supported by only a minority of the Commission, that sought to make legalization of the undocumented into an acknowledgement that the United States shared some responsibility for the presence of the undocumented in this country, and, given that shared responsibility, deportation was not an acceptable public policy.[13] Governor Bruce Babbitt was much more explicit in his criticism of the SCIRP report. To begin with, "it started off with an unexamined premise that there was a large problem of illegal immigration to the United States . . . those assumptions are wrong." He urged a "more cautious and pragmatic approach." Of employer sanctions, the governor said: "Such sanctions would force businessmen to become police agents and could jeopardize the Mexican American community in the United States." Regarding the enhanced border security provisions, Arizona's governor was downright scornful: "That is a policy at odds with a hundred years of history and economic reality. The concept of sealing up the border is badly mistaken . . . it is a delusion."[14] It is jarring to read those comments today. Courage, lucidity, thoughtfulness, and a fundamental belief in justice are in short supply in Arizona. Since the Guv's departure, every governor has steadily fueled anti-immigrant venom in Arizona until that state became the symbol of hate to Mexican Americans and immigrants the same way that Mississippi was to the civil rights movement.

President Reagan incorporated the majority of the SCIRP recommendations into his Immigration Reform Bill presented to Congress in July of 1981. The bill consisted of employer sanctions, adjustment of status for the undocumented already in the country, a temporary guest worker program, and enhanced border security. Details differed from the original Carter bill, but the basic structure was the same. For the next few years the legislative debate sought to balance the elements of the grand deal. What constituted a violation of employer sanctions was debated until the last moment. Was it a pattern of behavior by an employer, or a requirement that the employer have certain knowledge of the worker's immigration status? What documents would be required to satisfy immigration officials that a reasonable inquiry by the employer had been conducted? Everyone expected a cottage industry in false social security cards to arise immediately, and the debate veered to what level of responsibility the employer had to verify that the card presented was not false. Would a cardboard cut-out drawn with a blue crayon to resemble a social security card satisfy the requirement? Was a violation of the employer sanction provision a criminal or a civil offense, and how severe should the fines or the jail term be? A national ID card was considered only briefly, but quickly dismissed as totalitarian. The elements were constantly shifting.

A major issue was the date the "amnesty" would go into effect. The proposal for a triggered amnesty was favored in the early years of debate. A triggered amnesty would delay the legalization of the undocumented until a presidential commission certified that sufficient border enforcement was in place. Otherwise, it was argued, the promise of amnesty was an open invitation for even more hordes to rush the border. In the end the compromise adopted allowed anyone who had entered the country before January 1982 and had lived here continuously to apply for residency.

What form the guest worker program would take was also the subject of much debate. Would there be a separate program specifically for agricultural workers? This proposal, heavily favored by the industry, drove both labor and Chicano activists to despair. The abuses of the Bracero Program were recounted again and again; the vacuum left when it ended was ignored.

And of course welfare was an issue. The detractors of reform argued, with a passion that surprised me, that the hordes reform would legalize were only interested in welfare benefits. They challenged the notion that immigrants, especially Mexicans, were coming here to work. They argued that legalization was a magnet for the lazy and shiftless Mexicans who would cross the border to get their countless kids all fed by welfare dollars. Offering welfare benefits would invite millions to join the entrenched underclass of Mexican Americans who were inherently incapable of overcoming poverty. There were proposals to permanently deny welfare benefits to the undocumented who legalized, or to deny them for five or ten years. The visceral attack on Mexican immigrants as lazy, morally flawed, and culturally, if not genetically, incapable of improvement was shocking. Those same critics might concede that the Mexican immigrant will work long hours under demeaning conditions for very low pay at jobs no one else will do but the catch is that they do it in order to continue wallowing in the culture of poverty. At the end of the day, they are going home to get drunk, eat tamales, and make babies.

This stereotype has been around for a long time—long before the War on Poverty's social scientists embraced Talcott Parsons' typology of traditional and modern cultures, with Mexicans falling squarely into the traditional. But the War on Poverty promoted a leadership structure rooted in the "tangle of pathology" ideology above all else. Funding for non-profits was based on servicing the ills of the poor. After Nixon's election, the federal government and the Ford Foundation retreated from opportunity programs into the hard programming of welfare and dependence. Following the money, a multitude of non-profits developed across the country to teach the poor how to shine their shoes and tie their ties, along with the importance of showing up for work on time and the nuances of filling out a job application, determined to hammer into their culturally impaired heads the Protestant work ethic. David Hayes-Bautista's observation of the era bears repeating: "It seemed clear that modern values had to be substituted for the dysfunctional traditional ones if a society were to develop modern, capitalistic structures. 'Improving' traditional cultural traits became a policy imperative."[15] The new leadership structure was primarily a creation of the foundations and the federal government. The Southwest Council of La Raza, envisioned as a confederation of communities organizing themselves, defining their own needs, and empowering the people to achieve those needs, had transmogrified itself into the major procurer of funds for non-profit poverty programs. Gregory Rodriguez wrote of the era:

> After the social upheaval of the 1960s, the federal government established what amounted to a race-based spoils system in which minority groups were encouraged to highlight their oppression and dysfunction to qualify for assistance. As a result, an increasing number of Mexican-American politicians, as well as spokespeople for the inside-the-Beltway advocacy groups, the National Council of La Raza, often found themselves vying with African Americans for the dubious title of being the most downtrodden minority in America. In a perverse twist, under this regime, a minority's weaknesses became its most salient source of political power.[16]

Kenneth Prewitt, the noted demographer, social scientist, professor of public affairs at Columbia University, and past director of the United States Census, has noted that "more than any group in American political history, Hispanic Americans have turned to the national statistical system as an instrument for advancing their political and economic interests, by making visible the magnitude of social and economic problems they face."[17] Illustrating his point was a presentation made at the Latino Civil Rights Conference by Raul Yzaguirre and NCLR's senior vice president, Charles Kamasaki:

> A less well-known, but perhaps as important, area in which Latinos experience unequal treatment is in the distribution of federal means-tested assistance, benefits, and services. Given

that Hispanics in 1995 constituted more than 22% of all poor American families and about 28% of American children who are poor, one might expect that Latinos would constitute approximately these percentages of participants in major federal anti-poverty programs. Actual Hispanic participation in such programs, however, is almost uniformly lower than the expected participation, according to a summary issue brief compiled by the National Council of La Raza.[18]

I am reminded of a visit to my senate office during the time we were considering the necessary legislative changes to implement the welfare-to-work program in Arizona. The dean of the School of Social Work at Arizona State University, along with a small delegation of professors, made a thoughtful presentation precisely along the same lines argued by Yzaguirre and Kamasaki. Using Arizona Census data and Arizona's Department of Economic Security data for ethnic participation in Aid to Families with Dependent Children, commonly called welfare, food stamps, and other financial aid programs administered by the Department, they made the case of underutilization by Mexican Americans and implicitly a case of discrimination.

The dean's data was frankly irrefutable. Hispanics underutilized the social safety net, and I, by seeking to implement the nation's first welfare-to-work program, was about to make it worse! It's even worse than you think, I told the dean. Your data includes only the undocumented who responded to the census, but unquestionably there is a substantial percentage that won't respond to an INS subpoena, much less to the census, so that the actual number of Hispanics is greater than that officially recorded. Your numbers, however, are misleading, since the undocumented are ineligible for the programs you analyzed; but even if you adjust the data downwards, by the INS's estimate of undocumented in Arizona, the data will still show that Latinos underutilize the social safety net. Latinos, even generations from their family's crossing, maintain a strong work ethic. Mexicans came here to work, *no para pedir limosna*. Not to ask for charity.

Needless to say, we had hit upon an ideological chasm within the leadership of the Mexican-American community that began with the demise of the Southwest Council of La Raza and the birth of its successor. It was my view that the Mexican-American community was making extraordinary progress in this country; it was the repeated refrain of the poverty industry that we were losing ground. Yzaguirre, certainly the best known of the poverty advocates, is quoted as saying in response to findings from the most recent Census: "I can't look at any institution, I can't look at any aspect of America, and say, 'this is where we have made progress.'"[19] Quoting Gregory Ródriguez again,

> even though Mexican Americans experienced unprecedented mobility into the middle class in the 1980s, activists could say with a measure of truth that "by 1990 Latinos were collectively even worse off than they had been in 1980." While in 1980, 12 percent of Latino families lived below the poverty line, that number had risen to 16 percent by the end of the decade. What these activists rarely pointed out, however, was that one-half of the Latino population growth—which increased by 34 percent in the 1980s— resulted from the arrival of poor immigrants. High poverty rates for newcomers had the effect of . . . eclipsing the socioeconomic progress of long-established immigrants and latter-generation Mexican Americans.[20]

Even Thomas Sowell, the conservative economist, made a more nuanced analysis of the Mexican-American economic condition than would the poverty industry:

Meaningful income comparisons are difficult because Mexican Americans are a decade younger than other Americans and have lower levels of schooling in both quantitative and qualitative terms. In 1971 Mexican-American males age 25 and up had higher incomes than the US average . . . with educations up to eight years, and 90 percent of the US average for those who had attended or graduated from high school. These pre-college brackets include the great bulk (over 90 percent) of Mexican Americans."[21]

Sowell's economic analysis was intriguing at the time. At least economically, his data implies discrimination is most apparent not against the poor but against those entering the middle class: "It is not surprising that Mexican-American males who have attended college earned only 77 percent of the US average for all men who have attended college." It was not surprising to Sowell because, as he put it, "the accumulated educational deficiencies affect what kind of college or courses can be pursued by those few Mexican-American young people who get there."[22]

By the 1970s and '80s the Mexican-American poverty-business non-profits referred to themselves as "civil rights organizations." Thus NCLR described itself as "the largest national Hispanic civil rights and advocacy organization in the United States," but its agenda, like that of its affiliates, was set more often than not by the funding foundations and federal government programs and not the folks they were supposedly advocating for. Neither the foundations nor the feds had much interest in educational reform at the time. The money was in lumping together every recently arrived immigrant, legal or not, eligible for benefits or not, into that statistically impoverished and dysfunctional community that seemed incapable of escaping poverty.

By the time the Immigration Reform Act reached its final debate in Congress, the self-described Hispanic civil rights organizations had for two decades been making the case that we were an economic disaster, incapable of betterment, in need of steady infusions of cash and corrective programming, cheated out of our welfare dollars and demanding even more. In retrospect, the offensive vehemence against Mexican immigrants should not have come as a surprise. A brew of historic prejudices, racist stereotypes, and misleading statistical presentations by Hispanic "civil rights" organizations all made the case that legalizing Mexicans was tantamount to legalizing a permanent underclass.

The journey to find the right balance of all the elements would take five years. Reform legislation passed the Senate in 1982 and 1983, but the House failed to act on the bills. In 1984 a reform bill passed both chambers but died when the House-Senate Conference Committee failed to reach an agreement.

By 1986 the historic unity of the Latino community forged only a few years earlier had frayed. The most startling reversal came when Congressman Ed Roybal, the most vehement opponent of employer sanctions, introduced a bill in early January that read suspiciously similar to the Simpson-Mazzoli Immigration Reform bill that he had once scathingly criticized. Most surprising of all, it contained the same employer sanction provisions. Roybal had a reputation of being something of a legislative loner, but this tactic stunned even his longtime admirers. His staff defended the action by saying that Roybal was "calling the question." No one ever quite deciphered what that meant. MALDEF dismissed Roybal as having "included sanctions without consulting anyone and without getting anything in return."[23] Ed Roybal was chairman and founder of the National Association of Latino Elected and Appointed Officials, or NALEO, and I was on its founding board. I was with him at a board meeting, and I asked him what he was thinking when he introduced the bill.

He stared back at me blankly for a second or two then simply changed the subject. Senator Simpson was pleased with Ed's bill, though: "It took a lot of courage for Ed Roybal to put in a bill with employer sanctions in it . . . It showed me that he too wants to do something about immigration."[24] The Hispanic Caucus had grown to eleven voting members, and the younger members were confused by Roybal's tactics but less inclined to simply resist. Congressman Bill Richardson, who wanted a bill, described Simpson-Mazzoli as "the last gasp for legalization to take place in a humane way." Congressman Esteban Torres penned a congratulatory "Dear Colleague" letter to the fellow members of the Caucus who voted for the bill, saying that "public attitudes about the illegal immigration situation are becoming increasingly harsh. I am convinced that continued failure by Congress to address this problem would have resulted in a far more punitive measure in the future. The immigration bill you supported is probably the best legislation possible under current political conditions." The United Farm Workers reached a compromise on a Special Agricultural Workers legalization program with the Western Growers Association that was folded into the bill. NCLR, the GI Forum, LULAC, even Bert Corona approved. Of the major organizations only MALDEF continued to oppose the compromise of 1986.

On November 6, 1986, President Reagan signed the Immigration Reform and Control Act of 1986 into law. President Reagan's signing statement ended as follows:

> The act I am signing today is the product of one of the longest and most difficult legislative undertakings of recent memory. It has truly been a bipartisan effort, with this administration and the allies of immigration reform in the Congress, of both parties, working together to accomplish these critically important reforms. Future generations of

Americans will be thankful for our efforts to humanely regain control of our borders and thereby preserve the value of one of the most sacred possessions of our people: American citizenship. [25]

In 1986 there was great concern among Democrats that the newly legalized Americans would be especially thankful to President Reagan, so much so that they would become Republicans and break the Democratic Party's traditional hegemony over the Mexican-American vote. It might have happened. Democrats should be grateful to the ambitions of Republican Pete Wilson and his enthusiastic support for the rabidly anti-immigrant Proposition 187 in his quest to be reelected governor of California. Wilson's outrageous characterization of the parasitic, welfare-sucking Mexicans invading California made the language of anti-Latino hate respectable and routine. The rhetoric of the campaign on behalf of Proposition 187 quickly became the norm among Republicans. Wilson made it safe for Democrats to take Mexican-American voters for granted for a few more generations.

CHAPTER 7

Proposition 187 and its Consequences

It is hard to imagine a public policy, debated for over a decade, for which there were such divergent expectations and that would so uniformly disappoint its proponents. Such was the fate of the Immigration Reform and Control Act. IRCA was truly an exercise in self-deception. The immediate causes of the so-called crisis, the repeal of the Bracero Program and the subsequent illegalization of hundreds of thousands of formerly legal workers annually, the absurdly low Western Hemisphere quota imposed by Hart-Celler, and the subsequent quota for Mexico, were simply ignored. I guess that, for Congress, correcting the crisis they had created meant admitting that they had created the crisis in the first place. Politicians would rather rewrite history and scapegoat the innocent than admit a blunder. Liberals would not admit that repeal of the Bracero Program was a mistake, and nativists wanted no more Mexicans, legal or not. Economic conditions in Mexico and the spiraling impunity and corruption of its ruling class were ignored as well.

Much of the debate had a surreal quality about it, as if America were a pristine island state that had never shared with a southern neighbor a border 1,200 miles long, a history of war and conquest involving blatant discrimination against the conquered, and a border culture that for over a hundred years allowed families to move easily across unguarded sand in the desert. The debate was very American—as if America could by fiat turn on and off the aspirations and dreams of young folks who wanted a better life for themselves and their children.

The hope of the proponents was that IRCA's "comprehensive" approach would finally deter illegal immigrations. The newly legalized would step out of the netherworld they had been relegated to in the past and replenish the workforce. Employer sanctions would finally extinguish the so-called pull factor as these became the norm in the workplace. The Special Agricultural Workers program would provide a workforce in the fields that was legal and ready to join the Union. All this was of course to take place while assuring that the undocumented would not be excluded from mainstream labor protections.

The amnesty provisions of IRCA survived a challenge to delete them by a vote of 199 to 192, with 41 absent. A swing vote of only four members would have reversed the result. Even the author of IRCA in the Senate, Senator Alan Simpson, said that legalization "was probably the one thing in the bill—and there were plenty—that was least acceptable to the American people. Legalization only passed the US House by seven votes. I do not think people ought to forget that."[1] Indeed. The passage of IRCA permanently recast the word "amnesty" to evoke capitulation and failure.

The Congressional Budget Office estimated that 1.4 million undocumented immigrants would apply under the amnesty provisions. The Department of Health and Human Services estimated a range of 2.5 million to 3.3 million eligible for amnesty. The bill's principal sponsor in the Senate, Alan Simpson, estimated 4 to 7 million applicants. Senator Orrin Hatch estimated 6 to 16 million. Representative Hal Daub volunteered that "everyone is in agreement, you're going to have 10 to 20 million people legalized if only half of those people come forward and take advantage of general amnesty." Rep. James Sensenbrenner, apparently winding himself up for his future starring role as an oversized villain in the saga for immigration justice, predicted that one-third of all Mexicans would legalize themselves (the population of Mexico in 1986 was 77,016,416). Rep. Bill McCollum offered a fancy formula reduced to this: 2 million applicants a year, each one petitioning for an average of seven immediate family members (them Mexicans do make babies), over the course of a decade . . . and hey presto! 100 million![2]

In the end, 1.7 million persons applied under the general program and 1.2 million applied under the Special Agricultural Workers program.

Immigration officials turn to apprehensions to estimate the flow of undocumented from the southern border. In 1986 there were 1.693 million apprehensions. 1986 was the peak year for apprehensions, and most observers believe it was in anticipation of IRCA's passage. By 1989 the number had dropped to 890,000. There was that moment of hope . . . and then the numbers rose steeply again. In 1991 there were 1.13 million apprehensions. During the decade between 1996 and 2005, the annual number of apprehensions reached a high of 1.8 million in 2000 and a low of 1.0 million in 2003.[3] As apprehensions soared, the need for prison space to hold immigrants soared as well. Corrections Corporation of America opened its first facility for immigrant detainees in 1984. With that, Wall Street discovered that "enhanced border security" was a great business. The private prison industry now joined the anti-immigrant mobs, albeit in Gucci shoes, fancy suits, and carrying a high-yield investment prospectus.

As a legalization program, IRCA was unquestionably successful; as a comprehensive deterrent to further undocumented immigration, IRCA would only worsen the situation. Employer sanctions and IRCA's enhanced border security buildup were intended to prevent immigrants, primarily Mexicans, from entering the country without authorization. These were perverse incentives that did little to keep immigrants out but were effective in motivating undocumented immigrants, once here, to stay put. Undocumented workers are at greatest risk of apprehension when crossing the border. Enhanced enforcement succeeded in dismantling the years-old annual migrant stream. Mexican laborers had traveled north following the harvests from Yuma and Coachella, then followed ripening crops north to central Arizona and throughout California, to the strawberries of Yakima, the beets of Colorado, the cherries of Minnesota. When the harvests came to an end they headed south to Mexico, where their modest wages could assure economic survival until the following year. Fear of apprehension and deportation post-IRCA meant that workers stayed in the United States. Laborers were primarily young men, so soon enough they were sending for their families. Some family unification was directly related to IRCA's legalization. In 1992, 55,000 IRCA-related dependents were granted permanent residence and 34,000 in 1993. Estimates are that 300,000 unauthorized dependents entered the country each of those years. The Mexican Migration Project at Princeton and the University of Guadalajara has been collecting data on both documented and undocumented Mexican migration to the United States since 1982. On the likelihood of migrants returning annually to Mexico, the researchers conclude:

> We computed probabilities of returning to Mexico by following respondents year by year from the moment they entered the United States. We then counted up the number of return moves in each year and divided by the number of person-years spent in the United States. To smooth trends over time, we computed three-year moving averages . . . the likelihood of returning to home peaked in 1980, fell through 1986, and then plummeted to very low levels thereafter, remaining at historical lows . . . Throughout

the 1990s, the probability of return migration hovered at just about 10 percent to 11 percent.[4]

With misplaced incentives and fear, Mexican workers who would otherwise have spent most of the year outside the United States were forced, in order to survive, to compete with the recently legalized and low-income citizen workers for jobs. Predictably, employers would adjust wages downwards. Scholarly research published in the *International Migration Review*, *Journal of Labor Economics*, *Social Science Quarterly*, and *Demography*, summarized by Jorge Durand, Douglas Massey, and Emilio Parrado in their widely recognized, authoritative article, "The New Era of Mexican Migration," leaves little doubt that

> whereas before IRCA undocumented migrants earned the same wages as documented migrants, and rates of pay were determined largely by education, United States experience, and English language ability, afterward undocumented migrants earned wages 28% less than those earned by documented migrants . . . As wages deteriorated for undocumented migrants in the wake of IRCA, so did working conditions, with higher proportions earning wages below the legal minimum and larger numbers working under irregular circumstances . . . entry-level wages for undocumented Mexican workers averaged $4.81 during 1980–1986, rose temporarily to $5.14 during the transition period, and then fell to $4.44 during 1991–1996 (expressed in constant 1990 dollars). [5]

IRCA was clear in its intent to protect the existing rights of undocumented workers. The House Judiciary Committee report accompanying the bill, for example, states: "It is not the intention of the Committee that the employer sanctions provisions of the bill be used to undermine or diminish in any way labor protections in existing law, or to limit the powers of federal or state labor relations boards, labor standards agencies, or labor arbitrators to remedy unfair practices."[6]

But any pretense of labor protections disappeared with the Supreme Court decision in Hoffman Plastic Compounds, Inc. v. National Labor Relations Board. The court found that an employee who had provided false documents to meet the employer sanctions requirements under IRCA and was subsequently fired for union organizing was not eligible for either back pay or reinstatement. On behalf of the majority, Chief Justice Rehnquist wrote: "We hold that [that back pay] is foreclosed by federal immigration policy as expressed by Congress in the Immigration Reform and Control Act of 1986."[7] So much for Congressional legislative intent. Since then, state and federal agencies have simply cited Hoffman for justification of denial of rights and benefits to undocumented workers.

Notwithstanding all of its glaringly dubious history, at the end of the day nearly 3 million persons, 70 percent of them Mexican, are able to walk about today as residents and citizens, and many more have been reunited with them, because of that decade-long struggle launched by Jimmy Carter and finally signed into law by Ronald Reagan. I suspect that the number should have easily been twice that. I was on Spanish-language talk radio throughout much of this period and was also often asked to churches to speak about the process. It was a relatively simple and inexpensive application, $185 for adults, $50 for children, with a maximum of $420 for a family. Catholic Social Services and other non-profits were designated to help prepare the applications free of charge. There was one problem, however: a distinctly Mexicano attitude. A small percentage of folks rushed to fill out the applications, but most required convincing.

Fear of being duped by INS was certainly a factor, but the

primary cause of doubt and inaction was that for most folks life was just fine. The current wave of hate against immigrants was in a nascent state; local police rarely detained the undocumented; INS was seldom vigilant away from the border; many folks had been working with assumed names, and emerging from the fiction was problematic; false IDs were readily available, and as soon as Social Security cards were required you could buy them cheap in the parking lot of about any *carnicería* or mercadito in the country. For folks who had been working for cash, legalization would mean taxes; and in order to apply for legalization you had to collect all those documents: letters, receipts, bank statements, the kids' school records . . . in short it was just too damn inconvenient. The excuses mirrored the excuses that many legal residents still use not to become citizens, and that citizens use not to register to vote, and that registered voters use to skip the obligation. It's just, they said, a Mexican thing. At the time, Dean Martin had a hit that seemed to grace the moment, "Mañana Is Soon Enough for Me." It was Martin's heavy, cartoon-like accent that further lent the racist ditty its humor, and that was precisely, of course, what grated so deeply.

Mañana was not soon enough for me. In 1986 I decided it was time to leave the legislature. Governor Babbitt would end his term in 1986 and launch his campaign for the presidency. Burt Barr was leaving to run for governor. My extraordinary journey from radical to state senator of inordinate influence was over. Bill Jamieson had been Governor Babbitt's administrative utility player. He had headed the Department of Economic Security, the Department of Administration, headed the team appointed by the governor that had dramatically taken over Arizona's Medicaid program, and, of course, had served on the governor's staff. Bill had left state government early in 1966 and formed the Bill Jamieson Company. Bill was a deeply religious man, and inheritor of wealth that provided him with the freedom to develop his next steps slowly and carefully. Bill's primary role in his company was to serve as a kind of ethical, moral, and business guide to CEOs of Arizona's major corporations. I joined Bill in 1987, with the goal of transforming his very small company into a major player in public relations and crisis management, using the tools and skills we had learned in government and in politics: negotiations, polling, and advertising, for example. We were successful. Success was not always welcomed by my liberal friends. The *Phoenix New Times*, the alternative newspaper that in years to come would become the major owner of weekly newspapers in the country, ran an article entitled "The Price of Power," decrying that,

> Upon entering the private sector, Gutierrez traded in his baggy suits for a subdued, expensive look. Few begrudged him the desire to make some money. He'd made little enough as a state legislator . . . Considerably more people, however, have a serious beef with the direction of Alfredo's midlife change. Critics compare the causes he championed as a student leader and politician with those he now promotes, and claim the man has forsaken principle as well.

And one of the founders of the *Phoenix New Times* who had also served in the state House of Representatives, Renz Jennings, conceded, "I like Alfredo . . . but I worry about his soul." In fairness, Jennings was quite laudatory about my past:

> He was about empowerment . . . He insisted on access for other Hispanics once he was in a position of power, rather than setting himself up to be the one guy the establishment would deal with and who would deliver the community's

vote on something . . . He's brilliant, funny, quick on his feet and to think . . . It's a devastating combination . . . He's more than just a good talker; he could glance at a bill and grasp its essential meaning immediately... So he impressed his colleagues with his technical skill, his oratorical skills were equivalent, and he was funny to boot.[8]

But my soul . . . my soul was in jeopardy. What prompted the scathing feature article was Jamieson and Gutierrez's representation of an out-of-state utility in a corporate takeover battle of the hometown utility, Arizona Public Service. The utility was a subsidiary of Arizona's major corporation, Pinnacle West, known popularly as Pinwest. J&G designed the public relations strategy and the advertising that accompanied it. According to the same article,

> Less than a mile from the barrios, but light-years away in social and economic terms, executives from the giant Oregon-based utility PacifiCorp made a . . . determination . . . as they huddled in a Phoenix high-rise planning a takeover bid against Arizona Public Service Company. The PacifiCorp executives knew their campaign needed at least tacit support from the state's business and political mandarins.
>
> So they went looking for the man who could take them straight into the governor's office and every private club in town—Alfredo Gutierrez, the prince of Phoenix influence peddlers.

In an earlier article entitled "Checkmate: Pacificorp's Bold Ad Campaign Has Left Pinwest Looking Like a Dork," the author Kathleen Stanton quoted advertising executives and public relations professionals describing the advertising and public relations strategy as "brilliant," "effective," "innovative," but dismisses J&G's participation in the strategy in one single line: "Gutierrez's firm also designed the daring ad campaign that has made PacifiCorp a household word in the Valley."[9] Otherwise, I was merely an influence peddler. The tension between myself and traditional liberals (though I still refer to myself as an unreconstructed liberal) was the tension that still exists between jobs and the environment. I had been Babbitt's right-hand man in the senate, I had assured passage of his ambitious public lands and environmental agenda, but there were limits—and the limit was reached when jobs were at stake. The article, "The Price of Power," quotes "Priscilla Robinson, a veteran Tucson-based activist" as saying "Gutierrez gave tacit support to Phelps Dodge . . . when it was under attack by environmentalists . . . during the struggle to clean up copper-smelter pollution, we were trying to rally Democratic support to counter Republican support for Phelps Dodge, and Alfredo refused to support us." Robinson goes on, "In fact, he was the sole barrier, and he never did have a good reason." My response, "I can't stress enough how important job creation was to me, that government had a role to stimulate the economy, build roads, make sure the mines stayed open . . ." will never be a good enough reason for some people.

There was one infuriating accusation that would continue to worm its way periodically into public discussion. Ethnic advantage. It's exemplified by this description in the "Price of Power" article of my battle to keep a major employer in a small Latino town operating:

> Alfredo recast the issue as a matter of protecting jobs in a poor Hispanic community rather than protecting the environment, which attracted Hispanic Democrats to support BFI. "He changed the issue from a fairly clear one of bad public policy, that is to put landfills on riverbanks, to an economic argument for a small, minority-dominated

town," [Maricopa County Supervisor Carol] Carpenter says. "What was amazing was his ability to influence Democratic votes that otherwise would have been dependably pro-environment."

Gutierrez denies that he manipulated ethnic themes and says, "I find it silly, offensive, that this whole thing is being reduced to the fact I'm Mexican."

Fighting for jobs was a continuing struggle throughout my tenure in the legislature, and keeping a smelter open, even one owned by Phelps Dodge, I considered a primary responsibility. But my soul may have indeed been in jeopardy. Soon after I joined the firm I convinced Bill that he was charging way too little for the counseling sessions he was having with major CEOs. I persuaded him to reevaluate each and steeply increase fees. From time to time, Bill would report that one CEO or another had agreed to the increase or had requested greater services. One morning he informed me that the president of Phelps Dodge wanted to see me. What! Why? I asked. Well, the president is one of my counseling clients, he has agreed to the new fees and he wants to meet you, was Bill's answer.

Bill and I had reached an agreement when we formed the partnership: if either one of us objected to working with a client, that determination was final. The partnership would never represent a client that both of us had not agreed to. Period. No questions asked. At that moment I could have objected, but we were still struggling, Bill would be the primary contact, and, hell, it was only a meeting. I didn't object, and J&G continued consulting with Phelps Dodge for years to come. I benefited from Phelps Dodge's payments to the firm, and it was for that bit of treasure that I had set aside a matter of personal ethics. In retrospect, I would learn from that experience how easy it is to slither downward into an ethical morass.

Governor Pete Wilson of California found himself at an

ethical crossroads as he sought reelection in 1994. As mayor of San Diego he had gained a reputation for being sympathetic to Latino issues. As a US senator, Wilson had supported IRCA and its amnesty provisions. In fact, Wilson had argued for an even more lenient program for agricultural workers than that proposed by the Reagan Administration. Wilson had clashed with Reagan's commissioner of immigration, Alan Nelson, and ultimately won.[10] He was elected governor of California in 1990. In addition to the normal earthquakes, torrential storms, forest fires, and landslides, Wilson faced a state in crisis. According to the *Los Angeles Times*, "California, dazed and bloodied from its longest and deepest downturn since World War II, is acting like a punch-drunk boxer in a grueling bout with no end in sight . . . having run out of cash, California faces a mounting fiscal crisis as legislators and Gov. Pete Wilson conduct a partisan tug-of-war over the state budget's $10.7-billion deficit."[11]

Then, on March 3, 1991, the California Highway Patrol and the Los Angeles Police Department conducted a wild high-speed pursuit which had begun as a simple traffic stop. The chase exceed 115 miles per hour on freeways and through residential streets. The driver, Rodney King, was tasered, beaten mercilessly with batons, kicked in the face and the abdomen . . . and, unfortunately for the police, the beating was videotaped by a nearby resident and televised worldwide to stunned disbelief that gave way to anger. The police claimed that King was high on PCP, causing him to be violent and dangerous. The tape shows King offering no resistance and crawling on the ground while the beating goes on. A drug test for PCP was negative. Four white Los Angeles police officers were charged. On April 29, 1992, all four officers were found not guilty of assault. Los Angeles' African-American community exploded. Three days of rioting followed, fifty-two people died in the chaos, and an estimated one billion dollars of damage was incurred. Just hours after the rioting began, Wilson ordered 2,000 National Guardsmen into the besieged neighborhoods. Tragically, Wilson's California National Guard lacked basic equipment, flak jackets, ammunition, riot shields, and batons. It took the Guard over a day to scrounge enough equipment and finally respond. Unfortunately for Pete Wilson, the rioting and the absence of the Guard were also reported and televised worldwide.[12] Those were not good times for Pete Wilson. Six months after the riots, the *Los Angeles Times* reported that barely 28 percent of voters approved of Governor Wilson.[13] In March of 1993, a *Los Angeles Times* poll showed Wilson losing to California's state treasurer by 22 percentage points.[14] Wilson was drowning in disapproval.

His lifeline came in the form of a no-holds-barred anti-immigrant campaign. Wilson had been desperately searching for an issue that would reverse what seemed the inevitable. In late 1992 he launched a vitriolic attack on welfare recipients. Polls measured no discernible impact.[15] David Hayes-Bautista describes what happened next:

> A political consultant, holding focus groups for a governor in trouble, mentioned the topic of undocumented immigrants and their role in the state. Instantly, a focus group of non-Hispanic whites lit up. Angrily, they denounced the immigrants for ruining the state; they took away jobs, they crowded schools and hospitals, they sucked up government expenditures fueled by tax dollars, they overused welfare, they increased crime rates, they rioted and broke into stores. As wave after wave of invective poured out, the consultant realized he had found the governor's "red-meat" issue.[16]

The moderate pro-Latino Pete Wilson self-immolated on August 9, 1993, by sending a letter to President Bill Clinton asking that the federal government support a revision of the fourteenth amendment to the United States Constitution that would deny citizenship to children born in the United States to undocumented parents. He also asked for legislation requiring a residency card to prevent "illegal immigrants" from receiving welfare or from obtaining work, and denying a public education to the children of "illegal immigrants." Wilson even proposed that the undocumented be denied emergency health care. His closing left little doubt which "illegal aliens" threatened the republic. He asked that the federal government use its influence during the North American Free Trade Agreement negotiations "as a tool to secure the cooperation of the Mexican government in stopping massive illegal immigration on the Mexican side of the border."[17] To ensure the appropriate impact, the Wilson campaign published the letter as paid advertising in California's major newspapers and in the western editions of the *New York Times*, *USA Today*, and the *Washington Post*. The fall-out was immediate. On August 17, Democratic US Senator Barbara Boxer called for the National Guard to be sent to the Mexican border. On August 22, the *Los Angeles Times* editorial noted that illegal immigration had become a "front-burner issue" that loomed "as an explosive topic for debate in the 1994 elections." On September 29, State Treasurer Kathleen Brown, the Democratic candidate for governor, proposed that illegal aliens in state prisons be deported, and in October, Democratic Senator Diane Feinstein, facing a tough reelection campaign, called for a $1 toll on all border crossings, with the proceeds dedicated to enhancing border security. Even the liberal Assembly Speaker, Willie Brown, would not resist the temptation. Brown proposed that businesses that hired "illegal aliens" should have their assets seized.[18] Wilson was on to something, and he wasn't letting go.

Wilson launched three strategically timed lawsuits against the federal government, claiming California was owed a total of $2.5 billion in reimbursements for providing services to "illegal aliens." The first suit called for a reimbursement of $377 million spent on incarcerating "illegal alien felons"; the second was a $1.7-billion claim for the cost of a public education for "illegal immigrant children," and the third was a claim for providing limited health care to the undocumented as mandated by federal law under California's Medicaid program, known as Medi-Cal, for $370 million. Ironically, as US senator, Wilson had voted for that very mandate . . . but consistency, as the saying goes, is the hobgoblin of small minds.

In April of 1994, Wilson made a highly publicized visit to the Mexican border, announced that National Guard troops would be deployed along it, and reiterated in detail why he had sued the federal government. Immediately after his visit to the border he launched a million-dollar television ad campaign. The campaign was a single ad that ran repeatedly. It was a grainy, black-and-white, ciné-vérité production showing distinctly Latino men running between cars at the San Ysidro-Tijuana border crossing. The music was ominous, pulsating, evoking danger, while the deep baritone voice-over menacingly pronounced: "They keep coming. Two million illegal immigrants in California. The federal government won't stop them at the border, yet requires us to pay billions to take care of them." Lest you think otherwise, John Gorton, Wilson's campaign manager, said apparently with a straight face, in response to the uproar caused by the ad, that the governor "was not trying to scapegoat anyone or whip up anti-immigrant hysteria. You don't create problems in politics . . . picturing them is what you do."[19] Indeed.

The governor wasn't finished. In July, the Democratic legislature passed the budget. Wilson vetoed it. Wilson demanded that the legislature pass an additional bill removing authority for undocumented pregnant women to receive prenatal care.

Prenatal care, he claimed, attracted undocumented pregnant women to enter the country illegally and cost the state $50 million. The legislature capitulated.

Wilson was careful never to personally invoke ethnicity, race, or culture. He focused on the financial burden that California taxpayers were being forced to bear. Were it not for the illegals, California's miserable economic condition over which he presided—"the longest and deepest downturn since World War II," according to the *Los Angeles Times*—would surely be resolved. His hands were clean and his heart free of racism or personal rancor. Others were less careful. Wilson has always denied authoring or launching Proposition 187. He may not have conspired to place 187 on the ballot, but he certainly created the anti-immigrant hysteria that led to it. Less than two months after Wilson sent his letter, Proposition 187, legislating by initiative much of what Wilson had proposed, began circulating.

> Section 1: The People of California find and declare as follows: That they have suffered and are suffering economic hardship caused by the presence of illegal aliens in this state. That they have suffered and are suffering personal injury and damage caused by the criminal conduct of illegal aliens in this state. That they have a right to the protection of their government from any person or persons entering this country unlawfully.[20]

Thus began Proposition 187. All social services would be denied to the undocumented, and all publicly funded healthcare facilities were prohibited from providing any treatment except for emergency care, and even that only to the extent that those services were required by federal law. All school districts would be required to determine the legal status of each student and also of the parents. A school district would have to remove a child ninety days after they determined that a child was undocumented. The ninety days, according to the initiative, "shall be utilized to accomplish an orderly transition to a school in the child's country of origin." If a child's parents were "determined or reasonably suspected to be in violation of federal immigration laws," the district was required to report the undocumented parents to immigration, even if the child was a citizen. Undocumented students were to be removed from California's universities and colleges. Police were required to cooperate with Immigration. The use of false papers was declared a felony. Except for Wilson's call for a constitutional amendment denying citizenship to the children of the undocumented, Proposition 187 codified the governor's platform.

The authors of Proposition 187 were well aware that an undocumented child's right to a public education had been decided upon by the Supreme Court. The 1982 decision in Plyler v. Doe overturned a Texas law that banned undocumented children from a public education. The reasoning followed by that five-to-four majority was highly controversial among legal scholars; Proposition 187's authors hoped that the initiative would lead to a rehearing that would result in the Court overturning their earlier decision.

Governor Wilson formally endorsed the initiative at the Republican State Convention in September. "The Save Our State initiative is the 2-by-4 we need to . . . finally force Washington to accept its responsibility for illegal immigration," but from the beginning the governor's campaign and the Save Our State campaign had conflated into a seamless attack on the undocumented.[21]

The campaign for Proposition 187 quickly grew rancorous. The committee supporting the initiative, Save Our State, did not share the governor's careful use of language. Gregory Rodriguez comments: "As one *Los Angeles Times* reporter noted, among Proposition 187's 'grassroots supporters there was a barely concealed layer of antagonism toward illegal immigrants.'"²² At public rallies, Save Our State advocates were not shy about characterizing Mexican migrants as "violent and parasitic." Voices of Citizens Together (VCT), another southern California anti-immigrant group, sent a mailing addressed to "California taxpayers" that began "OUR BORDERS ARE OUT OF CONTROL." It charged that "every twenty-four hours, four to five thousand illegal aliens cross our southern border in California virtually unimpeded." In another pro-187 piece, VCT charged that "over two-thirds of births in county hospitals are to illegal aliens."²³ Even Democratic Senator Diane Feinstein joined the paranoid chorus. As the demographer Hayes-Bautista points out,

> If two thousand or more Mexican immigrants indeed crossed the border every night, as Senator Feinstein's ads stated so convincingly, there would have been by 1994 nearly 9 million undocumented Mexican immigrants in California alone. The California Coalition for Immigration rights figure of five thousand border crossings a night would have resulted in 21.9 million . . . Although these numbers are clearly untenable, many Californians were left with the impression that from 10 to 20 million undocumented immigrant Latinos resided in a state of 27.8 million. Once they were convinced that this large number of undocumented Latinos were living in the state . . . distinctions between US-born Latinos, immigrant Latinos and undocumented Latinos became lost in the popular discourse.²⁴

And Linda R. Hayes, "media director" for the California Coalition for Immigration Reform, the umbrella organization coordinating the campaign in support of Proposition 187, prophesied the full horror of the impending apocalypse:

By flooding the state with 2 million illegal aliens to date, and increasing that figure each of the following ten years, Mexicans in California would number 15 to 20 million by 2004. During those ten years about 5 to 8 million Californians would have emigrated to other states. If these trends continued, a Mexico-controlled California could vote to establish Spanish as the sole language of California, 10 million more Californians would flee, and there could be a state-wide vote to leave the union and annex California to Mexico.[25]

And once the numbers gain acceptance, terms like hordes, floods, and invasion seem reasonable. As do accusations that Latinos are responsible for about everything gone wrong in California, from overcrowded schools, overflowing emergency rooms, freeways paralyzed by traffic, crime, and of course the state of the economy. VCT sent a mailing late in the campaign, warning: "As illegal aliens flood in, schools are overwhelmed, wages fall, and **English becomes an unknown language in this city.** Seeing this **Americans are fleeing Los Angeles,** leaving a collapsing real-estate market and declining tax base behind them. We are importing poverty and exporting jobs."[26] The bold lettering was in the original.

In August of 1993, when Wilson sent his infamous letter, only 4 percent of southern Californians thought immigration was a major issue, far behind crime and unemployment.[27] It even trailed graffiti. By October of 1994, the *Los Angeles Times* poll found that southern Californians now perceived immigration as one of the top three problems facing the state.[28]

On November 8, 1994, Proposition 187 passed with 59 percent of the vote. Governor Pete Wilson was reelected with 55 percent. The following morning Wilson sent faxes to every school district, hospital, university and college, social service agency, and police department in California demanding immediate implementation. Just as quickly, MALDEF filed for an injunction. The injunction was granted. MALDEF faxed a copy of the injunction to every entity that had received the governor's demand. Only two provisions relating to false documents withstood the injunction.

The most egregious sections of Proposition 187 never went into effect. On November 15, 1997, Federal Judge Mariana Pfaelzer declared that "Proposition 187, as drafted, is not constitutional on its face." Ironically, Judge Pfaelzer based much of her opinion on Clinton's welfare reform act, the Personal Responsibility and Work Opportunity Reconciliation Act of 1996. It was that law's far-reaching restrictions on benefits for immigrants, those here legally as well as the undocumented, that "serves to reinforce" her view that immigration is a federal domain.[29] The proponents hoped to reach the Supreme Court and challenge once more an undocumented child's right to an education. That too was denied them. Gray Davis was elected governor following Pete Wilson. In 1999 Governor Davis directed that the case, then awaiting appeal, be mediated. It was. The appeal was averted and the law was dead.

The lesson—that immigrant Mexicans can be easily demonized and voters be turned into an electoral mob in an amazingly short time—was not lost on the Clinton campaign. The 1996 presidential election was approaching, and without California, Clinton would be a one-term president. Getting ahead of what Wilson had unleashed was imperative. But the campaign wanted it both ways: on the one hand, Clinton initiated the North American Free Trade Agreement in January of 1994, encouraging free trade and commerce of goods, and on the other (for Wilson had left them with little choice), they set in motion with dizzying speed a draconian scheme to block human beings from unauthorized entry.

Operation Gatekeeper was launched in October of 1994, one month before the mid-term elections. A confidant of the president, a friend from Yale and Oxford, was named to lead the initiative, and the press quickly gave him the sobriquet of Border Czar. It is he, Alan Bersin, that is credited with authoring the marvelously simple plan. In bureaucratic-speak, it was termed prevention through deterrence; in plain English it meant concentrating so much manpower and technology on the fourteen-mile stretch of the San Diego border beginning at the Pacific Ocean and moving eastward that no one would dare to try to cross . . . but if they did, they would be apprehended or worse. Other major urban crossings were similarly toughened. Thus, the argument went, immigrants would be finally deterred from entering the United States. Bersin oversaw an impressive transformation of the border. Miles of fencing marked the front line, an uninterrupted wall of corrugated steel panels, formerly used to build battlefield landing strips in Vietnam, contiguously welded together. Behind them stood a series of staggered concrete poles planted five inches apart, and in some sections fencing of shiny steel with open, sharp dimples, towers of strategically placed stadium lighting, buried sensors. Equipped with infrared goggles, the number of agents in the San Diego sector would more than double in the following four years; an immigration court was built on the border to streamline deportations; and a new electronic fingerprinting system that would store fingerprints and digital photographs was installed.[30] In order for Operation Gatekeeper to succeed, Mexican immigrants had to respond as its author had predicted. They had to admit defeat and return to wherever the hopelessness lay that sent them to the border in the first place. Only someone profoundly ignorant of the human spirit's will to survive, or a mother's drive to provide a better life for her children, could have dreamt up such a scheme. But Clinton had found just such a fellow in Bersin.

Apprehensions did not decline. The human spirit was not deterred. Between October 1994 and September 2000 there were 88,000 fewer apprehensions at the California border, 564,409 more at the Arizona border, and 188,168 more at the Texas border.[31] As a strategy of deterrence, Clinton and Bersin's plan proved itself a failure almost immediately. But it is in a macabre, no doubt unintended, consequence that it has excelled. The desert, the remote rugged mountains, the temperatures that soar in summer on the desert floor, the way crossings that in urban corridors would take perhaps a few hours would now take days through the most hostile landscape in North America: herein lay the magic deterrent. Surely no immigrant in her right mind would risk it. Bersin and his bureaucrats understood so very little. Almost instantly the corridors of crossing changed to precisely the most hostile landscape in North America, and predictably, death followed. The *Arizona Daily Star* began accounting for border deaths in 2001, six years after Gatekeeper was implemented. Between 2001 and 2010 it counted 1,750 deaths in the eastern Arizona desert alone.[32]

Thousands of men, women, and children have suffered horrible deaths in the desert, but the true number may never be known. How many were ravaged by desert animals and their skeletal remains scattered in some arroyo, how many have simply been covered over by the desert sand, how many are laying there today waiting to be found, and how many have turned to dust . . . we will never know.

Gatekeeper had one other consequence. Smuggling had always been a mom-and-pop business in Mexico's northern border cities, mostly young fellows who studied the Border Patrol's patterns and could guide the southern Mexican immigrants through the cat-and-mouse game that played out every night. The service was rewarded with a few hundred bucks. At Agua Prieta, across from Douglas, the cost was $150 to get to

Phoenix, at Tijuana it was $300 to be guided across the border. By 2001 the cost at Douglas had risen to $1,300 and at Tijuana to $1,200.[33] The cost of being smuggled continues to escalate as danger rises. The cartels had been smuggling marijuana and heroin across the desert trails for years. Imagine the entrepreneurial synchronicity: drug cartels had been paying human mules to carry their contraband, and now, with a little nudge from the American government, the human mules would pay the cartels thousands of dollars to follow the same routes and carry the contraband to boot. Gatekeeper enticed the most violent criminal gangs in Mexico into the human trafficking business by creating an extraordinarily lucrative opportunity. With dreary regularity, Mexican newspapers cover the murder of migrants who refused to carry out the whims of the narco-gangsters or pay the ever-increasing cost of the crossing. Bill Clinton's commissioner of immigration, Doris Meisner, claimed that "it is not our border strategy that creates dangers at the border, but instead it is the smuggling that does so."[34] It is evident, however, to anyone who has the slightest knowledge of how capitalism works, that our border strategy created the lucrative enterprise and continues to enable the drug cartel's smuggling monopoly to thrive.

At the end of the twentieth century, 164 years since the end of the Mexican War, Latinos, Hispanics, Mexican Americans, Chicanos, Mexicans, whatever we choose to call ourselves, faced the most virulent anti-Mexican, anti-immigrant climate since perhaps that war. Certainly in my lifetime, and I am old. For three decades, so-called government- and foundation-funded "civil rights" organizations have portrayed the Latino community as a dysfunctional people incapable of bettering itself. National immigration rights organizations, funded by liberal foundations, continue to peddle a comprehensive immigration reform plan based on Reagan's reviled and discredited one. As apprehensions climb, Wall Street and

Immigration and Customs Enforcement (ICE) have made investment opportunities out of human tragedy, and deportations have reached record levels and continue to stack high, especially under Democratic administrations. Families destroyed, children deported alone and abandoned in Mexican orphanages, and death at the border is the daily bread of our immigration policy. Perhaps it is time to reconsider our options and challenge those who claim to lead us.

CHAPTER 8

An Immigration Policy
without Moral Consideration

The new century was a time to reconsider. The firm had provided me with economic success and occasionally with extraordinary excitement and intellectual engagement. We oversaw a major land exchange involving massive land holdings in the Florida Everglades and urban acreage in downtown Phoenix. The exchange was years in the making and involved federal legislation, with attempts to block the exchange by Barry Goldwater and by at least one of the three mayors that were ultimately involved. We prevailed. We were involved in the complex public relations and politics to assure construction of a new downtown stadium for the Phoenix Suns, and after that for the even larger and more difficult downtown ballpark for the Arizona Diamondbacks. We oversaw public communications for America West Airlines as it endured bankruptcy and emerged successfully; we designed advertising campaigns for hostile takeovers, and campaigns to halt them. But after fourteen years, whatever excitement there had been was waning.

Simultaneously, the issues impacting the Mexican-American community seemed to be hurtling toward crisis. The legislature appeared to have abandoned any concern for the poor, inner-city education was in crisis, the universities were under attack—but it was the attack on immigrants that most concerned me. It seemed that if you just prefaced a scandalous falsehood or outrageous insult about Mexican Americans with the word "illegal," it became acceptable in the politest of

183

company. I began to speak out more and more, and as a consequence began to regain my reputation as a radical. The clients grew nervous. In January of 2000 my nephew Tony and I went off for a three-week bicycle ride from Hanoi to Saigon, by then renamed as Ho Chi Minh City. Tony is a highly decorated war veteran who had served four tours in Vietnam and who was perhaps trying to calm persistent demons. I had never seen combat, my demons sprang from elsewhere, but I was intensely curious about the third-world country that so consumed my generation. I also knew it was time to think about my future.

My own demons were not calmed. I knew I had to make a change. In the summer of 2001 I decided to run for governor of Arizona. I was not drafted; there was no great clamor for me to take on the task. It was a singular arrogance to think that I could change the course of the debate. I sold the firm and began the process of mounting a campaign. Then came September 11. That American tragedy left us reeling. It was a time that demanded stability, that demanded that law enforcement come to the forefront to protect us. The favored candidate for the Democratic nomination was Janet Napolitano, then the popular attorney general of Arizona and immediate past United States attorney for Arizona. In effect, Arizona's top cop (and the future secretary of Homeland Security). Of course that should have been the moment I reconsidered my decision and quietly withdrew . . . but arrogance being what it is . . .

I was an atrocious candidate for the Democratic nomination for governor, and I was deservedly trounced. I refused to do any polling from which to fashion my issues and carefully construct the message. I was exceedingly candid about the state of the State. It was lousy. I proposed closing specific tax loopholes that totaled billions of dollars and touched about every business and special interest in Arizona. At that, a local political pundit, Bob Robb, quipped, "Alfredo is running a campaign that he would have advised his clients against." And I took on the prevailing antagonism against immigrants; but even if I had not I would never have escaped it. Perhaps the very first question I was ever asked as a candidate was about immigration and the hordes that were crossing, and predictably, my answer was not pleasing to the majority of Arizonans.

I believed, however, that we had reached a tipping point in the Mexican-American community: the point at which Latinos finally conclude that they have had enough, that it's time to change the leadership that either victimizes them or ignores them. And I arrogantly thought I could be the one to galvanize that sentiment into a reality at the polls. Sometimes I allowed myself to think I could win, but my primary goal was to mobilize a historic turnout. Of course, none of it happened.

I did learn a lot, however. One constant inquiry was about immigration. What are you going to do about it? The question was most often personalized in my case. "As a Mexican, what are you going to do about it?" At some point in the campaign, when the predictable question was asked, "As a Mexican . . . ?" instead of the candid answer that rarely pleased an Anglo audience, this time I hurriedly looked behind me and around me and asked in exaggerated, surprised disbelief, "What Mexican? Where's the Mexican? There's a Mexican up here? I don't see no stinking Mexican!" Most in the crowd were terribly uncomfortable, a few snickered, the Mexicans broke out in guffaws, the questioner, embarrassed, clarified, "You know what I mean," and I responded that indeed I did. The audacious exchange had the effect of putting the questioner and those that agreed with him on the defensive. It was fun but, of course, politically suicidal.

The wide cleavages in the Latino community also became starkly evident to me. The notion of the "southern church," the fact that religion in the Southern Hemisphere, Latin

America and Africa, was fundamentalist, conservative, and hostile to the liberalizing and tolerant trend of the American and European faith community, became a constant reality. I had embraced gay rights, including gay marriage, and I supported a woman's right to choose. The recently arrived Spanish-language community was in shock. It was right there in my campaign material in Spanish and in English, and it provoked long theological discussions and long debates about the choices new citizens had to make in choosing whom to vote for. Whether Catholic or Protestant, the new citizens were far closer to the social agenda of the Republican Party than they were to me or to the Democratic Party. Only the hateful rhetoric of the majority of Republican politicians deflected them toward the Democrats. I doubt if most Democrats realize how tenuous a hold they have on the fastest growing portion of our community.

The second and third generation of middle-class Latinos appeared to have become Hispanics. For the most part, they would assiduously guard against using the term "Mexican," or even Mexican American. I suspected that soon enough the fancy class of our community would be eating in restaurants featuring Hispanic-American cuisine. They say if you live long enough . . .

I had run as a publicly financed Clean Elections candidate and had agreed to a schedule of debates and appearances. By late July, I had received the funds and had expended a major portion of them. It was then that I first realized that Rose's cough had become persistent and louder, and that her strength and energy were depleted. It was then that the doctors became very concerned about her condition. Rose and I had been together for fifteen years, we were inseparable, we worked together, traveled together, and shared every aspect of our lives. Rose had been Miami's first Mexican cheerleader and grew to be an extraordinarily talented and beautiful woman.

She was a model throughout her life. She was seven years my senior and left Miami long before I went to the Army. It was twenty-five years before we saw each other again, and once we did I never left her side. Rose was the campaign's tireless volunteer, but by August she did not have the strength to go on. Having spent the Clean Elections funds, I could no longer withdraw from the race and was required to make certain appearances. I was not with her every moment as her health declined. The primary election was the first week of September 2002, and as expected I was roundly defeated. Rose was in the Intensive Care Unit of Good Samaritan Hospital. She never left. Rose passed away on October 7, 2002. We buried her on the cemetery up on the hill in Miami, only a few steps away from her mother and father.

There is an often-counseled truism that one should always wait a few years before making important decisions after the death of someone you love deeply. I would learn the reasons, both personally and economically, why it is so often counseled . . . but whatever is to come now in my life, Rose, I will always love you.

Operation Gatekeeper and the policy of prevention through deterrence was by any measure a catastrophic failure. Bill Ong Hing, in his book *Defining America Through Immigration Policy*, comments that, like in Vietnam, the commanders of this war kept seeing a light at the end of the tunnel. More troops, more equipment, more technology, longer and higher fences—and victory would be ours. Macho men armed with weapons of war rarely have the wisdom to admit failure. Gatekeeper had succeeded in creating a deadly funnel that forced the undocumented to take the most dangerous journey north. The fruits of that funnel are venom-filled politics and death. The number of dead will never be known. Border Patrol releases numbers of corpses found in the desert that are widely criticized as undercounted by the Pima County medical examiner and human rights groups; the *Arizona Daily Star* maintains its own tally, while desert rescue groups like Derechos Humanos and No More Deaths publish their own counts. In Pima County the medical examiner doubled the morgue capacity in 2005 and continues to rent mobile storage units to hold the bodies. They are held for one year, allowing time for the families to find their loved ones; they are then turned over for a pauper's burial. In Yuma County the corpses are held for only thirty days, then buried. Families arrive from Mexico daily into Tucson or Yuma or Phoenix, pleading for help to find a daughter or a baby left behind in the desert.

I was a daily Spanish-language talk radio commentator after the election. There was a constant stream of crossers who would stop by, having found someone's ID in the desert, or a jacket with a name inside, or a wallet with pictures of a family; a father might plead that we announce that his daughter was last seen crossing near Altar and if anyone had any information about her to please call. Once I was given a purse that held lipstick, a few trinkets, and a picture of a beautiful young woman holding a baby, another child hugging her leg. There was no name. Only the picture to describe on the air, and hope that someone would know who she was and call to say that she was alive. Lucrecia Domínguez Luna's father came once. His daughter had collapsed and died in the desert near Sasabe. The coyotes and her fellow pilgrims said a prayer, covered her with sand and continued on, taking with them her young son; when they could, the coyotes called Lucrecia's father. Cesario Domínguez traveled to Tucson, gathered his grandchild in his arms, and took him home. But he returned to the desert. He spent weeks searching for his daughter. The Border Patrol helped him for a few hours one day; the human rights group No More Deaths, moved by his determination, guided him day after day through the desert. In the course of their search, they found two other bodies, as yet uneaten or scattered about by animals. One beautiful morning, Cesario saw a gleaming in the sun coming from a dry creek not far from where he stood. He walked toward it, and as he approached he realized that there was a desiccated human hand protruding through the sand. It was the rings on the hand that had captured the morning sun and sent the light toward him. As he came closer he recognized the rings and he fell to his knees. They were his daughter's rings. It was his daughter's hand.

By sealing off urban corridors and the less dangerous paths of crossing, the prevention through deterrence strategy did succeed in funneling unauthorized immigrants through Arizona and concentrating the ills of a foolish immigration system into a state already historically hostile toward Mexicans. On November 3, 2003, President Vicente Fox of Mexico arrived in Phoenix to meet his paisanos at the Phoenix Convention Center and gave a rousing speech of hope, reconciliation, and reform. As he spoke, another drama was playing out forty miles south of Phoenix. Valuable cargo—human beings—was being smuggled into the country by coyotes. Gangs that abduct the cargo and hold it hostage until payment is made from the family are known as *bajadores*. *Bajar*, to lower, is how you refer to flushing a toilet in Spanish. Bajadores are the most violent and ruthless of the gangs. A van containing four gunmen pulled into the lane next to a pickup heading toward Phoenix, carrying eighteen immigrants stacked one upon the other, and the gunmen began shooting indiscriminately. When it was over, four immigrants from Mexico lay dead, five others were injured, all were strewn across the freeway surrounding the overturned pickup, and the gunmen fled on foot into the desert. The Pinal County sheriff, ICE, and the Department of Public Safety responded with a massive force, including Blackhawk helicopters, to track them down. Traffic was stopped on the major corridor between Phoenix and Tucson for nine hours. The television cameras captured and reported every gory detail, interspersing their coverage with shots of the president of Mexico trying to reassure Americans that Mexicans were honest, hardworking, good for the American economy, and in need of immigration reform. The anger and disgust that seized Arizona was of course aimed at the Mexicans and their president, making little distinction between the smuggled, the smugglers, the gang of bajadores, or even the ones, washing plates or eating from them, that had nothing to do with the incident. Hordes of violent illegals were the problem. The public policies—beginning with Operation Gatekeeper and continuing with each succeeding and more draconian escalation of enforcement—that channeled the immigrants into Arizona and made them into a commodity valuable enough to induce the drug cartels into entering the smuggling business were ignored completely by the media and by Arizona's politicians.

This mounting anger against the hordes led in 2004 to the first major ballot initiative patterned after California's Proposition 187. Proposition 200 passed easily. Yes, there is a reason Arizona's Democratic governor called for the National Guard at the border, and signed the toughest employer sanctions bill in the country and a bill that makes the smuggled victim a criminal equal to the smuggler, and that her Republican successor signed even more draconian legislation culminating in Arizona's notorious SB 1070. There is a revealing truth in SB 1070. Any pretense that the sponsors and the authors were aiming solely at illegals was dropped. SB 1070 required all police officers in the state of Arizona to stop anyone who appeared to be reasonably suspicious of being illegal and demand proof to the contrary. As originally passed and signed by the governor, an officer who chose not to do so could be sued and personally held liable. In the Pablo de la Guerra case in 1870s California, when he was prosecuted for attempting to exercise the rights of a white person, it was the court who took it upon themselves to determine who was sufficiently white; in 2004 Arizona, the legislature mandated that every cop on the beat determine who was not. The authors of SB 1070 are the same national organizations that are orchestrating a thus far successful campaign to sabotage any attempt at a reasonable immigration policy; the same organizations that are demanding ever more dragnets to identify, apprehend, and deport the undocumented, and the same that preach enforcement by attrition. Arizona has become their laboratory to determine the public's tolerance for increasingly mean-spirited legislation against the undocumented. The underlying purpose of SB 1070 is to test the public's tolerance for targeting all brown-skinned people. This should come as no surprise. These organizations are merely the current manifestations of the hate groups that have always existed in America against immigrants, especially Chinese, Mexicans, and other immigrants of color.

California's Proposition 187 was filed with the secretary of state, noting that the co-author was Alan Nelson—the same Alan Nelson who, as Reagan's immigration commissioner, had sparred with the then pro-immigration Pete Wilson. At the time Proposition 187 was filed, Nelson was a paid lobbyist for the Federation for American Immigration Reform. Late in the campaign, FAIR attempted to purchase advertising supporting the proposition, only to be met with severe criticism that the money for their furtherance of 187 was coming from the Pioneer Fund.[1] In the course of the coverage, it was revealed that since its founding FAIR had received $1.2 million from an organization that espoused eugenics theories that had been dismissed by serious scientists as nonsense. Dan Stein, FAIR's director, performed a public relations minuet that first defended the Pioneer Fund and then abruptly disavowed it, pledging to accept no more money from that quarter. The

Pioneer Fund was founded in 1937 at the height of the eugenics craze both in America and in Nazi Germany. Its incorporation documents state that its chief mission was to encourage the propagation of those "descended predominantly from white persons who settled in the original thirteen states prior to the adoption of the Constitution of the United States and/or from related stocks, or to classes of children, the majority of whom are deemed to be so descended." Its second purpose was to support academic research and the "dissemination of information into the 'problem of heredity and eugenics'" and "the problems of race betterment."[2]

The Pioneer Fund is only a bit more politic today: it is all about "restoring the Darwinian-Galtonian perspective to the mainstream."[3] The view of Sir Francis Galton, the founder of eugenics, was that "if a twentieth part of the cost and pains were spent in measures for the improvement of the human race that is spent on the improvement of the breed of horses and cattle, what a galaxy of genius might we not create! We might introduce prophets and high priests of civilization into the world, as surely as we can propagate idiots by mating *crétins*. Men and women of the present day are, to those we might hope to bring into existence, what the pariah dogs of the streets of an Eastern town are to our own highly-bred varieties."[4]

Mexicans were never the favored breeding stock of race-obsessed eugenicists.

FAIR would go on to financially support Proposition 200 in Arizona in 2004. The principal organization pushing Proposition 200 was Protect Arizona Now, better known by the acronym PAN. FAIR even sent its western field director, Rick Oltman, to assist in signature collection and sent over $300,000 to buy signatures for the effort. When the *Arizona Republic* reported that PAN had named a nationally known, self-proclaimed "separatist" as chairperson of its national board, a

IMMIGRATION POLICY WITHOUT MORAL . . .

mini-scandal ensued.⁵ Virginia Abernethy declared herself an "ethnic separatist" and not a racist; she was on the editorial board of the *Occidental Review*, whose statement of principle reads in part: "The European identity of the United States and its people should be maintained. Immigration into the United States should be restricted to selected people of European ancestry." Titles of some articles include "The Question of Jewish Influence," "Eugenics: Past, Present and Future," "Is Race a Valid Taxonomic Construct?" "Bioculture: A New Paradigm for the Evolution of Western Populations," "Two Models of White Racialism: A Preliminary Exploration of a Changing Morality," and "Understanding Jewish Influence I: Background Traits for Jewish Activism." Abernethy was also on the editorial board of the *Citizens Informer*, the journal of the openly segregationist Council of Conservative Citizens. The CCC is the inheritor to the notorious White Citizens Councils of the pre-civil rights segregated South.⁶

When the scandal blew open in August of 2004, FAIR was quick to distance itself and quick to condemn her—strangely never mentioning that their guy in Arizona, Rick Oltman, was also a prominent member of the CCC.⁷ That this was merely a good, albeit insincere, public relations ploy was made clear in the director's blog two months later on October 4, when the *Stein Report* objected to criticism by the media of Proposition 200. Stein announced simply, "Kathy McKee and Virginia Abernathy fire back at the *Washington Times* editors in separate letters over the weekend." There is a link to their letters, but no hint of condemnation. Kathy McKee was the chairperson of PAN who once during a debate told me that immigrants, and I have no doubt she meant Mexicans, represented "a stain on the purity of American culture." Abernethy's letter states, "I am not a 'racial' anything. I am an ethnic separatist, European-American to be exact, responding to the current national obsession with multiculturalism. Separatism is merely going with the flow. Multiculturalism was originated, ironically, by the same people who advocate open borders and mass immigration. Both are harmful to America, and I am the first to admit it."[8]

FAIR has learned that most Americans won't countenance their pseudoscientific racial nonsense, so they've developed a smoothly run public relations strategy to hide their true beliefs. John Tanton, the founder of FAIR, also founded the Center for Immigration Studies and Numbers USA. Like FAIR, they studiously avoid the language of race. Tanton is a fascinating fellow. He has created quite an anti-immigrant empire. It is well funded and extraordinarily effective, and all the while Tanton seeks to avoid the limelight. The one public gaffe that revealed an inkling of his true resentments came in a memo leaked to the *Arizona Republic* back in 1968. Tanton had formed another group concerned with Latinos, US English, opposing bilingual education and the use of Spanish by government. Addressed to key supporters of US English, the memo asked: "Will Latin American migrants bring with them the tradition of the *mordida* [bribe]? As whites see their power and control over their lives declining, will they simply go quietly into the night? Or will there be an explosion?" And Tanton crudely raised the issue that eugenicists and racists have been pondering since the Mexican War. "On the demographic question: perhaps this is the first time that those with their pants up are going to get caught by those with their pants down!"[9]

With that spectacular exception, Tanton's voice was rarely heard in the increasingly vitriolic debate. In 2009 Tanton donated his collected papers to the University of Michigan. According to a *New York Times* article, he did it "to show that he and colleagues 'are not the unsavory types sometimes alleged.' They include hundreds of private letters, some outlining his interest in genetic differences between the races and concerns about the country's changing ethnic mix."[10] The Tanton archives are still being studied by scholars and reporters, but what is clear is that Tanton has been in correspondence with about every racial kook and eugenicist in the country, and it is evident that their great preoccupation is not with immigration policy, but with race: "One of my prime concerns," he wrote to a large donor, "is about the decline of folks who look like you and me." He warned a friend, "for European-American society and culture to persist requires a European-American majority, and a clear one at that."[11] He corresponded with a lawyer for the Ku Klux Klan and also promoted the work of Jared Taylor, whose magazine, *American Renaissance*, warned: "America is an increasingly dangerous and disagreeable place because of growing numbers of blacks and Hispanics." Tanton wrote to Taylor, "You are saying a lot of things that need to be said." Tanton also maintained close contact with the chairman of the Pioneer Fund, Harry Weyher. Another Tanton-founded organization is the Social Contract Press, which publishes both a quarterly journal and anti-immigrant books. One of its first book titles was the lurid racist screed *Camp of the Saints*, which describes the end of Western civilization at the hands of a filthy, deformed horde of impoverished Hindus and other dark-skinned heathen that invade Europe with the help of complicit, white, softhearted liberals.

It is important to underscore that the question of immigration, documented and undocumented, is an important and controversial subject for America. We need to resolve it. Most Americans do not subscribe to the views that Tanton and his coterie of confederates hold, but Tanton has brilliantly overseen the hijacking of the debate by kooks, racists, pseudoscientific eugenicists, and Holocaust deniers. FAIR, Numbers USA, and the Center for Immigration Studies constitute the leadership of the anti-immigrant movement, and it is clear that their primary concern is not immigrants, but people of color, particularly Mexicans. They have no interest in resolving the issue: they simply want us gone. Theirs is a remarkable achievement. In 1924 Harry Laughlin, superintendent of the Eugenic Record Office and soon to be president of the Pioneer Fund, appeared before the US House of Representatives Committee on Immigration and Naturalization to successfully persuade Congress to pass legislation that kept the door closed on Asian immigration and would severely limit "dysgenic" Italians and European Jews. Using data from the US Census and from a specious survey of jails and prisons, he argued that the American gene pool was being polluted by a rising tide of intellectually and morally defective immigrants.[12] More than eighty years later the Pioneer Fund, through the front organizations it has helped launch—FAIR, CIS, and Numbers USA—still appears before the Congress to argue that America is in danger of being overwhelmed by perennially poor, socially inadequate, crime-ridden immigrants who threaten the American way of life.

When Jimmy Carter introduced his comprehensive immigration reform bill, Latinos were surprised and unprepared. As Senator Simpson gained influence, the scope of the proposed bill began to grow in breadth, and its punitive aspects grew sharper, costlier, and meaner. The opposition to the bill was on the defensive, disorganized and as wary of each other as they were of the Congressional forces that intended to pass the bill. The National Immigration Forum was formed in 1981 to coordinate the nascent coalition advocating for a humane immigration policy. Rick Swartz, NIF's founder and president, was the strategic force that created what he often called the "left-right coalition," an assemblage of big business and labor, libertarian think-tank intellectuals, big agriculture and the Farm Workers union, angry Latinos and more docile types, Asian-Americans guarding zealously

the advances made in the Hart-Celler act of 1965, and faith
leaders for amnesty but vehemently opposed to a renewed
Bracero Program. As flawed as it was, the Immigration
Reform and Control Act, the Reagan amnesty, was a much
better piece of legislation than its sponsors intended thanks
to Swartz and the left-right coalition.

Simpson would be back, with the Immigration Act of 1990,
intended to limit legal entrants and family unification. The
Swartz coalition would be instrumental in taking the offense
against the bill. When it was over, the bill's purpose had been
completely reversed, actually increasing family unification. Simpson came back once more to immigration in 1995: this time the
House was controlled by Republicans, and his lead co-sponsor
was Republican nativist Lamar Smith. To combat illegal immigration, the bill mandated a computerized national worker
registry, issuing national ID cards complete with biometric data
such as fingerprints and retina scans. It slashed family-based
immigration by a third, and cut refugee and asylum admissions
in half. Permanent employment-based visas were to be reduced
from 140,000 to 90,000. An immigrant tax of $10,000, or 10
percent of the worker's first-year salary, would be levied on firms.
Any foreign-born student would need two years' work experience outside the US before an American company could hire him
or her on a temporary visa, effectively prohibiting high-tech firms
from hiring students upon graduation.

The bill seemed unstoppable. Swartz quickly convened the
uneasy coalition with a new member, the tech industry, and
the lobbying began. Once more the coalition prevailed. What
seemed inevitable a few months before was dead. "It was, I
think, an astonishing victory," said Frank Sharry of the
National Immigration Forum. "Not only did we keep them
from getting everything they wanted on legal immigration, we
kept them from getting almost anything."[13] That victory
would mark the beginning of more than a decade of losses for

immigration advocates, and of the growing ascendancy of the Pioneer Fund, FAIR, Numbers USA, and CIS.

President George W. Bush assumed office in January 2001. President Vicente Fox of Mexico took office only months earlier, in July of 2000. The two had acted contemporaneously as governors; both had ranching backgrounds and an affinity for cowboy boots and Stetson hats. They understood the immediacy of the crisis in immigration on their shared border. Talks between the two began in February 2001 during a visit by President Bush to President Fox's family ranch in San Cristóbal, Guanajuato. For months, lawyers, diplomats, and academics met secretly, trying to agree on the specifics of a grand plan. *Time* magazine sketched in the outlines:

> The plan would take three giant steps. First, it would pave a road toward legal status for Mexicans who are already living and working in the US. Despite its name, "amnesty" for aliens has never been as simple as it is for draft dodgers or tax evaders. It isn't quick or easy; immigrants must earn it the old-fashioned way, through months and sometimes years of waiting and working. Both sides envision a new system in which Mexicans would spend several years in the amnesty program before getting their green cards. Eventually, that would allow millions of people to stop living in the shadows.
>
> The second step is arcane but crucial: remove Mexico and Canada from the annual US ceiling on immigration. Today Mexicans and Canadians have to stand in line with all other immigrants when applying to work in the States legally—and usually come up short. The US granted more than 100,000 work visas to foreigners in 2000; only 4,480 went to Mexicans. Bush and Fox believe that with Europe integrating and China becoming more competitive, the Americas can't afford such inflexibility anymore.

The third and perhaps most controversial part of the plan is a proposal to revise the US "guest-worker" program and allow as many as 300,000 Mexicans to work in industries like meat packing, construction and landscaping—and then return home.[14]

The plan was blessed with the sobriquet "the whole enchilada" when Jorge Castañeda, Mexico's foreign minister, told a gathering of labor Latino journalists that the plan could not be divided into only the pieces they found palatable. "It's the whole enchilada or nothing," he said.[15] The name stuck.

The whole enchilada was the first and last time that an administration seriously contemplated reversing the obvious policy blunders that created the immigration crisis in the first place: imposing a completely unrealistic quota on Mexico and repealing the Bracero Program without any thought to the consequences for the economy or for the workers. It was a welcome conversation that came to a tragic end on September 11, 2001. Unfortunately, with Bush gone to war, clarity and courage in immigration policy also came to an end. Every major immigration reform bill subsequently proposed follows the template invented by Carter, passed by Reagan, and denounced by almost everyone as failed policy ever since. Reflecting the growing vindictiveness of the times, each one is more punitive, creates higher hurdles, excludes more people, and causes more deaths at the border . . . and each one is endorsed, albeit cautiously, by the new assortment of Washington-based immigration advocacy organizations that have come into being or entered the fray since Rick Swartz formed the National Immigration Forum. And each one has failed to pass.

It is difficult to understand how the dogma of comprehensive immigration reform took such a fanatical hold. In time it was simply referred to by the letters CIR, and everyone involved in the issue, no matter how peripherally, would understand what was meant. It was not solely the Washington-based immigration advocacy organizations that sang the praises of and allowed no deviation from the dogma. The Congressional Hispanic Caucus would pay lip service to heresies like the Dream Act or AgJobs, but privately it was made clear they would only be considered if they were a part of CIR. (The Dream Act would legalize undocumented students if they completed high school and went on to college for at least two years or enlisted in the military; AgJobs was a compromise between the agricultural industry and the United Farm Workers that would legalize undocumented agricultural workers; both had substantial independent support.) The late Senator Edward Kennedy was of the faith and convinced his friend Senator John McCain to follow. McCain was never a true believer, but he was a pragmatist who recognized that the dogma would brook little dissent. The Kennedy-McCain bills strictly adhered to the trinity: legalization, guest worker program, enhanced enforcement. Anyone, like myself or even Rick Swartz, who apparently never drank of the holy water and advised against CIR and counseled taking steps more likely to pass, like the Dream Act, were quickly marginalized.

In May of 2005 Senators Kennedy and McCain introduced their comprehensive bill, followed a few months later by Senators Cornyn and Kyl's comprehensive bill. The following year Senator Arlen Specter's version passed the Senate but died in the House. In 2007 President George W. Bush finally made good on his promise and threw his full weight behind the Comprehensive Immigration Reform Act of 2007. There was greater hope, perhaps, for the so-called Bush bill than there had been since the Reagan bill of 1986, but not even the additional $4.4 billion for border security would satisfy the bipartisan opposition. Thirty-seven Republicans were joined by fifteen Democrats to kill the bill. The rhetorical bludgeon that destroyed Bush's bill was the argument given great currency by FAIR, CIS, and Numbers USA after 9/11: the immigration crisis was a threat to the rule of law; criminals and terrorists were gathering at the border and presented an imminent threat. The opponents of CIR did not adhere to any particular holistic dogma; they operated like an opportunistic disease, taking advantage of every fissure in the body politic and every vulnerable moment the legislative process provided. Their successes mounted quickly. Between the year 2000 and 2010 the budget for the Border Patrol tripled. In 2000 there were 8,580 Border Patrol agents on the southwest border, by 2010 there were 20,119.[16] The budget for US Immigration and Customs Enforcement grew from $3.7 billion in 2004 to $5.74 billion in 2010.[17] And the budget and manpower increases have served to confirm the picture of an invading brown horde. Since 2000, 98.7 percent of all apprehensions were made on the southwestern border.[18] So persuasive was the immigrants-as-criminals strategy that, in 2008, in preparation for the imminent election, Democrats introduced a bill to strengthen border security.

With the demise of the Bush bill, the Washington-based immigration advocacy organizations and the liberal foundations that maintain them found themselves reassessing their role in the future. By 2008 the other significant organizations included the Center for American Progress, a think tank that served as almost an adjunct to the Democratic Party and later as an extension of the Obama White House; America's Voice, a recently formed, richly funded organization whose role is to "conduct cutting-edge public opinion research, perform rapid response communications in English and Spanish"; the National Council of La Raza; the Center for Community Change, founded shortly after Robert Kennedy's assassination by old War on Poverty hands to assist local community groups; the Service Employees International Union, whose prominent role in the issue was almost certainly due to the singular passion for immigrant justice held by its vice president, Eliseo Medina; and of course NIF. The core group invited others to join them, but rarely those who questioned the wisdom of CIR. These were true believers.

Two of the core group's best-funded members, the Center for American Progress and America's Voice, commissioned a survey by the most prominent and respected research firms primarily used by Democrats: Lake Research Partners, Peter D. Hart Research Associates, and Greenberg Quinlan Rosner Research. These firms provided a report on July 24, 2008, entitled "Winning the Immigration Issue: Requiring Legal Status for Illegal Immigrants." It went on to say:

> Voters are looking for a realistic approach that will deal simultaneously with the border and the illegal immigrants already here. In developing such an approach, Democrats can unite rather than divide the party, as solutions that are most popular among the public overall also generate strong support from Hispanic citizens . . . Combining required legal status with conditionality makes for a very popular approach. The survey's strongest Democratic message acknowledges the problem of illegal immigration and focuses on requiring illegal immigrants to become legal with conditions, supplementing that with the popular idea of deporting illegal immigrants who have committed a crime.

The specific message of three of America's most experienced political research firms was that

> We must be tough and smart to get our immigration system under control. It is unacceptable to have twelve million people in our country living outside the legal system. We must secure the border but we must also require illegal immigrants to register and become legal, pay their taxes, learn English, and pass criminal background checks. Those who have a criminal record or refuse to register should be sent home.[19]

Tough, nicely crafted language that concedes to FAIR almost every point they had raised. It is unacceptable to have twelve million folks outside the law. It is urgent to secure the border. And, obviously, the freeloaders have not been paying their taxes, they can't speak English, and most importantly, there are criminals among them, so let's deport them. Chris Newman from National Day Laborers Organizing Network asked, "So, would you invite a criminal into your home? Would you invite twelve million of them?"

True believers flush with foundation money won't be deterred by naysayers, even those aghast at their message. When they distributed their polling report to significant Democratic Party officials, the Center for American Progress included a document entitled "Immigration Reform: Democratic Accomplishments 2008." It began with a quote from the speech Governor Napolitano gave when she called out the National Guard to the border: "This is a federal responsibility and they are not meeting it." That is of course precisely what FAIR and CIS were arguing. The document went on to outline those accomplishments. Each one further conceded that them immigrants were surely criminals:

- Directed $35 billion to the Department of Homeland Security for FY 2008—$3 billion more than the

Republicans in FY 2007—with $2.7 billion in emergency spending for border security.

- Implemented the complete recommendations of the 9/11 Commission, including improvements to aviation, infrastructure, and border security; providing the equipment and training first responders needed; beefing up efforts to prevent terrorists from obtaining weapons of mass destruction; and enhancing strategies to counter international terrorism.

- Funded an extra 3,000 Border Patrol agents (nearly 18,000 in total), as well as an additional 200 Customs and Border Protection agents, 4,500 detention beds, and border surveillance equipment.

- Dedicated $60 million to expanding the current employment eligibility verification system (E-Verify) and requiring Federal agencies and contractors to use the system.

- Supported state and local law enforcement through homeland security grant programs, assistance to agencies along the border, and the State Criminal Alien Assistance Program (SCAAP). In FY 2008 the Democratic Congress allocated $410 million for SCAAP, despite the Bush Administration's attempts to kill the program.

- Mandated the completion of an additional 370 miles of border fencing by the end of 2008.

- Strengthened the screening of visitors and immigrants by increasing funding for US-VISIT and for conducting criminal background checks on visa applicants.

- Made it a crime to construct a tunnel along the border.[20]

One would think that last point would not be necessary, but what the heck . . . Yes, the undocumented are costly criminals, but the Democrats will begrudge not a cent in defense of our country's borders. The DC advocates succeeded in having the Democratic platform reflect their new, tough FAIR-Lite statements. The Republicans of course needed no prompting from America's Voice; they had FAIR to push the real thing. I was one of those fellows aghast at what seemed the extraordinary stupidity and ahistorical ignorance of the act. In the 1950s, LULAC, the GI Forum, and the Americanizers never fought back: they adopted the language of hate, the assumptions of criminality and even terrorism in order to persuade the nativists that they and their followers weren't really like the "wetback" kind. I guess if you live long enough . . . However, this would not work either.

According to the polls, Latinos overwhelmingly supported Hilary Clinton in the primaries for the Democratic nomination for president. A few of us, most significantly Federico Peña, the former lawyer for the United Farm Workers, mayor of Denver and Secretary of Transportation and Energy under President Clinton, endorsed Barack Obama from the beginning. In a press conference in Phoenix, I explained that, yes, certainly, I supported many of his policy positions—but ultimately I was there because a man of color and the son of an immigrant ascending to the presidency of the United States would be like a bolt of hope striking the heart of the children of immigrants and the minorities in every community in America. The *Arizona Republic* reports that I said, "He's the son of an immigrant. There's a worldview—a whole world— captured in that statement that those of us who are immigrants and children of immigrants understand."[21] And I was even more certain of my decision when, as the nominee of the party, Obama spoke to the annual convention of NCLR in July. The speech, widely available online, is beautiful oratory that builds to a powerful crescendo demanding justice for immigrants. At these words, thunderously delivered, there were few who were not on their feet, cheering, clapping, crying:

> The system isn't working when twelve million people live in hiding, and hundreds of thousands cross our borders illegally each year; when companies hire undocumented immigrants instead of legal citizens to avoid paying overtime or to avoid a union; when communities are terrorized by ICE immigration raids—when nursing mothers are torn from their babies, when children come home from school to find their parents missing, when people are detained without access to legal counsel. When all that's happening, the system just isn't working.[22]

And when he made his promise, the crowd roared in approval, and there were few dry eyes; unquestionably, this son of an immigrant understood us.

> Well, I don't know about you, but I think it's time for a president who won't walk away from something as important as comprehensive reform when it becomes politically unpopular. And that's the commitment I'm making to you. I marched with you in the streets of Chicago. I fought with you in the Senate for comprehensive immigration reform. And I will make it a top priority in my first year as President of the United States of America. Not just because we need to secure our borders and get control of who comes into our country. And not just because we have to crack down on employers abusing undocumented immigrants. But because we have to finally bring those twelve million people out of the shadows.

That speech exemplified the power of words, the power of oratory to lift the human spirit. What has happened since exemplifies the power of words, the power of oratory to diminish it.

But we did not know that then.

It is difficult to overstate the ecstatic joy, the Obama swoon as I called it, that accompanied the election of Barack Obama. The Washington-based immigration advocacy groups were in love, and the object of their affection could do no wrong. The announcement that Congressman Rahm Emmanuel, a man with what can best be described as a troubled relationship with immigration reform, would be the chief of staff was met with reminders that Rahm Emmanuel worked for the man who made the final decision, and that man was committed to reform. The appointment of Janet Napolitano for Homeland Security was especially troubling to activists in Arizona, but we were reminded that she had once said that a fifty-foot fence could be overcome by a fifty-one-foot ladder. What she said was not the problem. The more serious matter of what she had done as governor—signing the most draconian employer sanctions bill in the country, making felons of smuggled human cargo, even calling out the National Guard—was airily waved away by the Washingtonians. After all, she supported CIR. This swoon was strong stuff. And when he named Cecilia Muñoz to the White House staff, the relationship was sealed. Cecilia was vice president of NCLR and had been for the past few years the most significant player in the quest for CIR. She was a true believer.

The inauguration ceremony of Barack Obama was the moment that hope became real. Justice was at hand. I don't recall what he said, and frankly it didn't matter, the point was that he was there to say it. The poet Elizabeth Alexander recited "Praise Song for the Day," in the bitter cold, buffeted by winter winds, and praised those who made this day possible:

Say it plain: that many have died for this day.
Sing the names of the dead who brought us here,
who laid the train tracks, raised the bridges,
picked the cotton and the lettuce, built
brick by brick the glittering edifices
they would then keep clean and work inside of.
Praise song for struggle, praise song for the day . . . [23]

"Praise song for struggle . . ." Something significant was happening in America, and even as we stood in awe of it all, a black man's hand was on the Bible, the son of an immigrant was assuming highest office, while the poet reminded us that many had died for this day and many more continued in the struggle. It was heady stuff, and it was now time for our brother Barack to deliver.

To the immigration advocacy groups and the liberal foundations that funded them, the certainty of CIR was unchallengeable. Obama was facing the worst financial crisis since the Great Depression: that phrase was the mantra of Obama's first year. It was the worst recession in fifty years, the banking system was at the point of collapse, millions of homes were insolvent and families faced foreclosure in unprecedented numbers, the American auto industry faced extinction unless the federal government provided massive financial assistance. In January of 2009 CNN reported that "the hemorrhaging of American jobs accelerated at a record pace at the end of 2008. . . . A growing number of workers seeking full-time jobs were able to find only part-time work. Those working part-time jobs . . . jumped by 715,000 people to 8 million, the highest since such records were first kept in 1955. The underemployment rate, which counts . . . those without jobs who have . . . stopped looking for work, rose to a record 13.5% from 12.6%."[24] These were not good times for the American economy, American workers, or their families. Not the best time to introduce legislation that encompassed all of CIR, but perhaps a good time to seek out the best opportunity for parts and pieces. Undoubtedly, the Dream Act was the most attractive piece of legislation, and AgJobs the best positioned with the business community. But the Washington-based immigration advocacy groups would not be deterred.

There were a few activists who raised objections, who suggested we focus on the Dream Act and AgJobs or that we try and revive 245.i—a provision in immigration law that allowed an undocumented person who married a United States citizen to legalize his or her status without being required to leave the country temporarily, and exempted workers who were petitioned by their employers and met certain criteria from the requirement to leave the country for years before being able to reenter legally. Advice from immigration lawyers, community organizations, from the old warhorses like Swartz, Tom Saenz of MALDEF, and Antonio Gonzalez of the Latino Congress was ignored. The dogma of CIR was never stronger. Cecilia Muñoz told the *New York Times* in early April that the president would begin addressing the issue by May 2009, in spite of the recession. The folks from the Tanton universe were ready to pounce: "It just doesn't seem rational that any political leader would say, let's give millions of foreign workers permanent access to US jobs when we have millions of Americans looking for jobs," said Roy Beck, executive director of Numbers USA, a group that favors reduced immigration. Mr. Beck predicted that Mr. Obama would face "an explosion" if he proceeded this year. "It's going to be, 'You're letting them keep that job, when I could have that job.'" And FAIR's Dan Stein added it would be "'politically disastrous' for Mr. Obama to begin an immigration initiative at this time."[25] Of course, Stein would consider it a disaster for the president to raise it at any time, but in this instance the White House would agree with him. There would be no

Comprehensive Immigration Reform bill coming from the White House.

Unbounded hope was not limited to the Washington immigration advocacy organizations. On my daily Spanish-language program in those early months of the Obama Administration, the callers were joyful, expecting real change. Some realized that it would take time to amend the law, but they believed the excesses of ICE and Sheriff Joe Arpaio would be rapidly curtailed. *El presidente de color, el hijo de inmigrantes*, was after all one of us.

The most hated tool in the local police arsenal against immigrants was 287(g). A section of the Immigration Act passed during the Clinton Administration contained a provision, 287(g), that authorized the federal government to assign federal immigration authority to local police agencies. In the view of most activists, and certainly most Latinos in Phoenix's barrios, it was 287(g) that licensed the worst abuses. Obama would surely suspend the sheriff's 287(g) agreement and stop the abuse going on in Phoenix.

Joe Arpaio, the Maricopa County sheriff, had applied for a 287(g) grant of federal authority twice, but the local director of ICE opposed his application each time. Arpaio turned to his friend Governor Janet Napolitano (whom he had endorsed for governor), and together they wrote a letter to ICE complaining about the local director. This director was duly replaced in January of 2006, and his successor developed a swimmingly good relationship with Arpaio and Napolitano.[26] Shortly thereafter, Arpaio received the largest grant of 287(g) authority in the country. Armed with that authority, the sheriff commandeered the parking lot of an abandoned big-box store in a central Phoenix, installed ten-foot-high chain link fencing, placed a portable command center in the middle of it, an interrogation center, a mobile holding cell, surrounded the compound with stadium lights, and deployed more than 200 armed deputies into the surrounding barrio in every conceivable kind of vehicle, determined to suppress crime. It was Good Friday, 2008.

Apparently, crime is suppressed by stopping every vehicle with what appears to be a Latino driver. The ostensible reason was the repetitive allegation that a taillight was not functioning. Within hours of launching the sweep (a sweep eerily reminiscent of the brown-uniformed troopers of another era in another country hunting down people of an inferior race and holding them on preposterously false charges), hundreds of protestors had gathered, and the holiest weekend in the Christian calendar was marred with anger, discrimination, hate, and so much pain. I witnessed ladies on their way to church paraded in front of a gauntlet of cameras and taken into custody, children in tears, workers, whole families humiliated for the pleasure and political benefit of a pathetic sheriff. In Maricopa County, hunting down the undocumented replaced the search for real criminals, and the "crime suppression sweeps" became routine.

Of course the sweeps were never stopped by the Obama administration. After immense pressure, DHS limited Arpaio's authority somewhat, but the sweeps continued and the hope of Latino activists that surely Obama would suspend 287(g) was met with an announcement that ICE would, on the contrary, expand the program.[27] At the end of the Bush Administration's eight years, there were sixty-four communities with agreements. Seven months into the Obama Administration there were seventy-one communities under 287(g) and another eighty were pending and awaiting approval.[28] The abuses by Maricopa County's caricature of a southern racist sheriff are well known, but such behavior is national in scope. The arrest rates in Davidson County, Tennessee, for Hispanic defendants driving without a license more than doubled after the county implemented 287(g). In

Alabama, Latinos constitute less than 2 percent of the population, yet 58 percent of motorists stopped by a deputized officer were Latino.[29] An analysis of the charges against persons detained under 287(g) across the south produced the following breakdown:

> In Gaston County, NC, 83 percent of the persons deputized officers detained in May 2008 were arrested for traffic violations. In Mecklenburg County, NC, of the 2,321 undocumented immigrants turned over to ICE in 2007, less than 5 percent were charged with felonies, while over sixteen percent were charged with traffic offenses. In 2008, the Cobb County, Georgia jail referred 3,180 inmates to ICE custody. Of those, 2,180 were initially detained for traffic offenses—almost 69 percent of the persons for whom ICE issued detainers. In Frederick, Maryland, of the 285 individuals referred to ICE in 2008, over 90 percent were initially arrested for misdemeanors and over 58 percent were initially detained for non-alcohol related traffic offenses. Less than 2 percent had a prior criminal conviction. According to OIG, less than 2 percent of the persons detained under the program nationwide were absconders—the original focus of the program.[30]

By summer of the Obama Administration's first year, community activists across America were beginning to openly criticize the president most had supported. The evidence was undeniable that 287(g) was not about absconders, felons, or violent criminals. Lying implies a conscious act, and perhaps the administration was merely ignorant of what local police departments were meticulously recording and the Department itself proudly hailing. In April 2009 Napolitano announced that Alan Bersin, the fellow who had authored and implemented Operation Gatekeeper and the policy of prevention through deterrence, the fellow whose policies, pursued in profound ignorance of the human spirit, have cost thousands of lives and millions of dollars and have never shown the slightest evidence of being effective, the fellow whose insensitivity to suffering and callousness toward death had made him the perfect border czar, was to be reappointed by the Obama Administration to carry on where he had left off. There could be little doubt now of what they intended.

Among the Washington-based immigration advocacy groups, the Obama swoon showed no sign of wearing off. In June the groups announced the formation of a multi-million dollar campaign "to help President Obama make good on his promise to pass comprehensive immigration reform in 2009 . . . to demonstrate broad national support for comprehensive immigration reform and a commitment to win the legislative battle expected later in the year."³¹ The millions provided by liberal foundations had made it possible to recruit over 200 community organizations to lend their name to the campaign and to host a pretty fancy fandango to launch it. All the leaders of all of the national organizations that had endorsed the new communications strategy conceding to FAIR's presumption of immigrant criminality were present. National Immigration Forum, Center for Community Change, the National Council of La Raza, Center for American Progress, America's Voice, together with members of Congress and compliant community leaders, but the star of the show was Cecilia Muñoz, bringing with her Obama's magic and his words of acknowledgement. The organization they formed, Reform Immigration for America (RIFA), would be the instrument the Washingtonians would use to attempt to control the message and the agenda of community organizations that were increasingly unhappy with the escalation of apprehensions and deportations. The campaign announced it was "deploying new technologies such as a national text messaging system and various on-line organizing strategies to direct messages from constituents directly to members of Congress. This is combined with a national campaign staff of organizers and policy experts."[32] It was a happy-faced campaign that hammered what they called "the new political reality for comprehensive immigration reform": a president committed to CIR and a Democratic-controlled Congress willing to pass it. They soon discovered that the president really didn't care all that much, and neither did the Democratic Congress.

A month after the conference, Roberto Lovato, an editor at New American Media, the former director of the largest immigrant organization, CARECEN in Los Angeles, and one of the most important voices in the Latino community, warned:

> In an environment in which visual, verbal and physical anti-migrant violence has gone viral, there should be a moratorium against ANY AND ALL LEGISLATION PREMISED ON DANGEROUSLY FALSE NOTIONS OF THE IMMIGRANT AS CRIMINAL NEEDING AND DESERVING PUNISHMENT FROM THE FEDERAL GOVERNMENT. Such notions only further legitimate similar notions proffered by pols—Republicans and Democrats—, mainstream media and the racial extremists whose ideas they give a platform to.
>
> We no longer need to give extremists and their ideas a platform by legitimating them thru "tradeoffs," "compromises" and with toxic talk of more enforcement and punishment. There has to be and is another way: stop.[33]

RIFA's happy-face campaign was precisely aimed at passing a comprehensive bill that further criminalized the undocumented. And the folks in the field ("the field" is how the

Washingtonians refer to the frontlines of the struggle) were getting restless. The RIFA message was beginning to chafe.

In March of 2008 ICE announced an initiative called "Secure Communities" that would complement 287(g). The program was deceptively benign. It was ostensibly voluntary, and unlike 287(g) it did not authorize local police to enforce federal immigration laws. A participating community police department forwards the fingerprints taken upon an individual's arrest to the Department of Homeland Security. DHS runs the fingerprints against a repository of over 91 million prints for travelers, immigration benefit applicants, immigration violators, suspected fugitives, criminals, sex offenders, military detainees, and other persons of interest. If there is a match, ICE then determines whether to issue a detainer, requesting the individual be held until ICE assumes custody. According to ICE, "The program takes a risk-based approach toward identifying and removing criminal aliens by focusing on those who pose the greatest threat to the public. In its initial phase, Secure Communities is targeting the worst of the worst, including criminals convicted of major drug crimes and/or violent offenses such as robbery, rape and murder."[34]

If removing murderers and rapists was the program's goal, it has been an astounding failure. Between October 2008 and April 24, 2011, there were 104,802 removals attributable to Secure Communities. Only 26 percent were for Level 1, or dangerous and aggravated crimes, and a mere 14 percent for level 2, violent felonies and three or more misdemeanors. The largest share, 31 percent of those removed, were for the lowest Level, and 29 percent were individuals without any criminal conviction. Sixty percent of those removed, in other words, were non-criminals or lowest-level criminal offenders. The claim by the Department of Homeland Security that it was targeting the "worst of the worst" was simply another lie.[35]

As Secure Communities spread, it became evident to local

activists that it was a digital dragnet aimed at indiscriminately apprehending and deporting the undocumented. The National Day Laborers Organizing Network (NDLON), the Center for Constitutional Rights, and the Cardozo Immigrant Justice Clinic sued ICE under the Freedom of Information Act, asking for full disclosure of the program. When a cache of documents was finally released, it showed that ICE was misleading local jurisdictions about the voluntary nature of Secure Communities. There was nothing voluntary about it. The administration had intended from the beginning to extend it to every jurisdiction in America by the end of Obama's term.

In Florida, four undocumented kids reached the end of their tether. The four had arrived here as children, each had excelled in school, all had dreams of graduating from university and starting professional careers; one had her home raided by ICE in the middle of the night, another had his entire family under a deportation order. All of them lived out their lives in fear of discovery and deportation, and all of them were active in the movement to secure immigration reform. For the four, Gaby Pacheco, Carlos Roa, Juan Rodriguez, and Felipe Matos, the moment came during a demonstration against a private ICE prison in Miami, Florida. The company was expanding the facility to accommodate even more immigrants, and along the march they joked darkly about ICE building their future cells. Then came the realization that there was too much truth in their playful banter.

That realization began a long conversation about how to confront the beast. Gaby recalls that they knew "that eventually they were going to deport us, they were going to take us out in the middle of the night, it came to us that we had to confront America and ask, 'Why do you want to deport us?'" Carlos added, "We were so fed up with being afraid, with knowing we could be deported at any moment, we were tired of hiding." It was Juan who said, "I'm tired of all this, I am putting my shoes on and walking to Washington." Felipe, a gifted student who had been accepted into a law school program but was forced out when the school discovered his immigration status, decided to join Juan on the walk to Washington. The four set out on January 1, 2010, on what they called the Trail of Dreams. They had three thousand dollars between them and the help of a few organizations, a mission to conquer their own fear, and a goal to inspire young people to take action to pass the Dream Act and to stop the deportations. Gaby: "We were stopped by the police every single day we marched . . . By South Carolina the fear was gone." "Courage," said Carlos, "is greater than fear." And the courage of these four dreamwalkers proved so inspiring that as they walked young people across the country started to come out of the fog of fear they had been hiding in. "Undocumented and unafraid": their rallying cry was heard across America.[36]

The Dream Act has been kicked about in Congress in some form or another for at least a dozen years. The Washington-based immigration advocacy groups and the Hispanic Caucus have supported it, but only as a section of the comprehensive immigration reform bill that had become their holy grail. Since the failure of CIR in 2007, many of us have been calling for a vote on the Dream Act without the baggage of CIR. The response had always been the same: If we pass the Dream Act, what do we tell the other twelve million left behind? "We saved your children from deportation" was not enough for them. And the second oft-cited reason was that the nativists would demand more repressive measures . . . but of course the nativists had been steadily winning that battle with bipartisan help. The real reason for the resistance to a stand-alone vote on the Dream Act was that the Dream students were the most attractive argument for passage of CIR; without them, the Washingtonians had concluded, CIR would be a hopeless cause. The four Floridians refused to be held hostage to CIR by the Washingtonians any longer. "The messaging was all wrong, it was top-down, we needed to tell our own story, I was tired of being pulled out of a hat to dance around for people and tell a sad story. It was not a sad story, it was a courageous story." It turns out that courage, like hate, is contagious.

The Washingtonians awash with millions of dollars in money for their RIFA campaign were undeterred. They organized a demonstration in Washington, paying community groups liberally to send delegations to the March 21, 2010 event. Two hundred thousand folks came to demand reform. The president, who was a block away from the crowd, did not bother to cross the street, instead sending a video endorsing what was known as the Schumer-Graham framework for immigration reform. This framework required the undocumented immigrant to admit to a crime before submitting him or herself to a harrowing legalization process. Worse still, the bill dumped more resources at the border and increased detention and deportations. So why would Obama sit out an opportunity to spellbind a crowd of folks who had overwhelmingly supported him in the last election? I suspect that by then the Washingtonians knew they could no longer control the crowd. Civil disobedience was growing throughout the country; if Obama appeared, there would be jeering and booing caught by the news cameras, for the anger at his campaign of repression, detention, and deportation would be uncontainable. The fiction that they spoke for the Latino community would be displayed for all to see. I suspect they advised the president to stay in the White House and send a tape instead, and they played it on a big screen.

The Schumer-Graham bill was never introduced. The campaign for a stand-alone vote on the Dream Act that the dreamwalkers had unleashed finally received a commitment from Congressional leaders, but the vote was delayed until the Washingtonians and the Hispanic Caucus were convinced that CIR was out of reach. On December 18, 2010, the Senate vote on the Dream Act failed by five votes to overcome the threat of a Republican filibuster. Five Democrats voted against ending the filibuster, effectively blocking consideration. The Dream Act was dead, but the courage that had been inspired by four undocumented kids who had conquered their fear and confronted the system was barely being born. Young "dreamers" committed themselves to a campaign of civil disobedience that would force the administration to halt the deportation of students who would meet the requirements of the Dream Act that had failed. President Obama's response to the escalating campaign of civil disobedience was to reject emphatically that he had the authority to act. "With respect to the notion that I can just suspend deportations through executive order, that's just not the case," Obama said at a March 28 town hall sponsored by the Univision television network. "There are laws on the books that Congress has passed."[37] The campaign continued unabated. The reelection campaign was of course always on the horizon, and there had never been doubt that the majority of Latinos would support President Obama. The nagging question among Democrats was—given the president's inaction on immigration reform—would Latinos vote? Dreamers undertaking major acts of civil disobedience in every major city in the country boldly reminded every Latino of the president's unfulfilled promises. With his reelection at risk, the administration was forced to revisit the legal question of the president's authority to defer deportations, and miraculously, they discovered that they had indeed had such authority all along. By mid-June, the pragmatists at the campaign apparently won out. The *New York Times* reported,

> Hundreds of thousands of illegal immigrants who came to the United States as children will be allowed to remain in the country without fear of deportation and able to work,

219

under an executive action the Obama administration announced on Friday.

Administration officials said the president used existing legal authority to make the broad policy change, which could temporarily benefit more than 800,000 young people. He did not consult with Congress, where Republicans have generally opposed measures to benefit illegal immigrants.

The policy, while not granting any permanent legal status, clears the way for young illegal immigrants to come out of the shadows, work legally and obtain driver's licenses and many other documents they have lacked.[38]

The Dream Act died, but hope still burned in thousands of kids across this country, and they took to the streets to teach the tepid Washington advocates about tactics and politics and to force the White House to reconsider its deportations and allow at least temporary sanctuary and safety in this country. Gaby Pacheco had told me that she "was tired of being pulled out of a hat to dance for other people and tell a sad story. It was not a sad story, it was a courageous story." Young dreamers were victims no more. They had found their voice.

Other notions should have died the day the Dream Act died. Foremost among them, the notion that four out of five Washington-based immigration advocacy organizations, only one of which is Latino-led, can speak for the Latino community on matters of immigration. The unifying cry of the Latino community is a demand to stop the catastrophic wave of repression and violence being perpetrated against us by the Obama Administration. There are very few among us who have the patience to hear more soaring oratory and obviously false platitudes. The Washingtonians and their funders have every right to keep swooning over Obama and to keep pushing their version of CIR, but it is increasingly clear that the Latino community is skeptical of their reverence for the Obama Administration or for a bill that further criminalizes the undocumented.

The practice of Latino poverty organizations of portraying Latinos as a failed people in order to persuade the government and private foundations to provide them with more money to cure our "tangle of pathology": that should die. It is not true, and conflating the rhetoric of the poverty industry with immigration reform is immensely damaging. NCLR, under new leadership after three decades, seems to be attempting to rediscover its roots in true community organizing, but it will be difficult. According to government filings, Chicanos Por La Causa, the first NCLR affiliate, pays its executive director more than a quarter of a million dollars. Its top executives combined make over $1,450,000. Folks that richly compensated rarely organize the poor to challenge the system.

The resistance by official Washington and many foundations to venture far from the comfort of the Washington-based advocacy organizations leads to distorted public policy positions. There are few outside of the favored four or five, for example, who would have endorsed the research-based message commissioned by America's Voice and the Center for American Progress. It was offensive and destined to fail. There are extraordinary arrays of community-based organizations that are truly involved with the community. The National Day Laborers Organizing Network, NDLON, represents immigrants and their families across America. Pablo Alvarado, its executive director, unfailingly speaks truth to power, and the powerful, if they want to hear the truth, should listen carefully. Latino Health Access in Santa Ana, California, is an increasingly powerful local force responding to community needs: diabetes, domestic violence, parks, crime, and education. LHA is a wonderful example of how people can organize themselves to help themselves meet their own challenges. Its executive director, America Bracho, is an inspirational figure.

The Consejo de Federaciones Mexicanas en Norteamérica, or COFEM, is an organization of Mexican immigrants and their children. COFEM brings together the recently arrived and those who have been here for years, and its membership ranges from the very humble to the wealthy entrepreneurs of Los Angeles. There are many, many more, of course, but you have to venture out and risk hearing unpleasant truths.

It's not enough to tiptoe daintily around FAIR, CIS, and Numbers USA's ugly relationship to the Pioneer Fund, eugenics, Holocaust deniers, anti-Semites, Conservative Citizens Council, ethnic separatists, and an assortment of other hate-mongers. They should be challenged at every opportunity.

The silence of the Mexican Americans in the Hispanic Congressional Caucus: this too should die. Across the country there is boundless appreciation for the leadership of Congressman Luis Gutierrez, a Puerto-Rican American, who has made immigration reform his life's passion. Unwilling to sit quietly as others run from the issue, his voice has been a beacon for the Latino community. But what about the Mexicans? The controversy over immigration reform is primarily about Mexicans, Mexican Americans, mestizos, and indigenous people of Mexico and Central America who cross at the southern border. In the 1950s Mexican Americans called themselves Spanish to curry favor with the majority. Today, "Hispanic" seems to serve the same purpose. Maybe there's only one admitted, outspoken Mexican American in the Hispanic Caucus, Raul Grijalva of Arizona; maybe the rest have become so self-important (and embarrassed at being Mexican) that they turned themselves into Hispanics instead. And maybe we should retire the Hispanics and elect a few folks who are proud of who they are and understand that this is our country, immigration reform is about our people, and we will not rest until we have a humane immigration policy that does not have as its underlying principle that immigrants are inherently criminals.

The same quota for Mexico as for the Principality of Liechtenstein or Outer Mongolia? Perhaps it's time to reconsider our leadership. Fear. Fear died that day. At an event in Arizona, I had occasion to introduce the young people who staged a sit-in at Senator John McCain's Tucson office on May 19, 2010. The five, Mohammad Abdollahi, Yahaira Carillo, Tania Unzueta, Raúl Alcaraz, and Lizbeth Mateo had requested to meet with the senator to persuade him to support the Dream Act. At the close of the business day they still refused to leave and were arrested by the Tucson police. They were heralded as the Tucson Five by their supporters and by the press. I was in awe of their courage. I said then that I had been arrested and jailed during the farm workers' fight for justice. I knew I would spend time in jail, but never once did I fear being deported, being separated from my children and my family forever, and being exiled because of my beliefs. It takes a special kind of courage to know that those are the risks and still step forward. That is what "undocumented and unafraid" means. What did not die that day are hope and the commitment to struggle on. We are here, we are staying, and we will ultimately transform America.

Arizona remains the flashpoint of violence and hate against immigrants, and I remain in the midst of the struggle. Richard de Uriarte in the *Arizona Republic* has described me as follows:

Three generations of Arizonans know him by his first name. Just "Alfredo." Not "Alfredo who?"

He's a singularly enduring, constantly evolving and complicated public figure, whose political career has spanned parts of five decades, crossing swords with Republicans from Sandra Day O'Connor to Russell Pearce.

Over the years, he's been a student protester, community organizer, legislative leader, businessman-consultant, bon vivant and Democratic gubernatorial candidate.[39]

And the syndicated columnist Ruben Navarrete wrote:

> One of Theodore Roosevelt's most memorable speeches praised "the man who is actually in the arena, whose face is marred by dust and sweat and blood; who strives valiantly . . . who spends himself in a worthy cause."
>
> The person who deserves even more praise is the one who climbs into the arena to take on a fight that doesn't impact him directly but who engages it anyway because it's the right thing to do.
>
> Alfredo Gutierrez has spent a lifetime in the arena, and now he's there again trying to slay Arizona's monstrous immigration law . . . He founded a Spanish-language news website that seeks to hold elected officials accountable, hosts Spanish-language radio shows and goes on cable TV to debate proponents of the law. At the grass roots, he also helps organize protests against the measure—and at one rally got arrested.[40]

They have the feel of obituaries, the pieces written about me now. An old warhorse, oddly not out grazing on some serene pasture. The battle for immigrant justice goes on unabated, and we must respond with the weapons available to us. There is such sadness in sitting with a child whose parents have been deported, or with a mother whose teenage daughter will be dropped off in the middle of the night in violence-torn Nogales by ICE agents; in seeing undocumented immigrants paraded about in pink underwear by Sheriff Arpaio; in seeing the hundreds of workers thrown onto the streets after ICE has conducted a worksite audit. That sadness turns into outrage, and outrage must turn into action against the government that perpetrates all of this. Recently, there was a story in the *Texas Observer* by Melissa del Bosque, exploring what happens to the thousands of children who are deported alone into Mexico. At one point she writes,

After I pester a DIF official in Reynosa for days, he finally opens up. He says he'll talk anonymously about organized crime. He furtively glances both ways down the hallway in front of his office, then gestures for me to come inside. He closes and locks both doors. "Look, I know what's happening," he says, mopping his brow with a tissue, "because we talk to the children." The man confirms that children are kidnapped at the bus station and that police are involved. "These are very well-known secrets," he says. "But we cannot talk about it openly because we live here, and it's very, very delicate. There are people in uniform and people without uniforms watching all the time." He means that if you say something publicly that might enrage organized crime, a group of armed men might show up at your door one morning, maybe with a police escort, march you to their SUV at gunpoint, and your family will never see you again.[41]

I had a very similar conversation with an official from Desarrollo Integral de la Familia, the DIF, the Mexican government agency that children are handed over to by ICE. She told me that the cartels send armed men to claim children who have been left behind, especially young girls. They claim to be a distant relative and provide obviously false documents. The DIF official was asking for my help to get a job in Phoenix: she could no longer live with herself, she told me, but speaking out meant torture and death at the hands of the gangs. Between January and August of 2010 there were 44,918 children deported alone to Mexico and Central America.[42] I wonder, what does Napolitano or Bersin or even Obama believe happens to the children who are taken by the cartels? Will they claim ignorance of it? Or simply wash their hands of it all, protesting that it is Mexico's problem? I sadly wonder whether there is room for the slightest moral consideration anywhere in our immigration policy.

To Sin Against Hope

The Obama Administration places all blame on the Republicans for the lack of reform. Republicans have indeed blocked any progress toward a humane immigration policy. But it is not the Republicans that have brought Bersin back to continue his deadly campaign against immigrants, nor is it the Republicans who have achieved record numbers of detentions and deportations, who continue deporting children alone into a country ravaged by drug violence. And it is solely the Obama Administration that is using the fiction of deporting criminals to spread a dragnet across the country known as Secure Communities. They intend to break apart more families than ever over the final years of his term.

They say that with age comes wisdom. I have seen little evidence of it, but perhaps this old warhorse, not yet pastured to await the inevitable, can offer this piece of wisdom I gleaned from the great Latin American writer Eduardo Galeano: "*Todos los pecados tienen redención menos uno: pecar contra la esperanza.*"

All sins can be forgiven save one: to sin against hope.

Endnotes

Chapter 1: To Sin Against Hope

1 Madison Grant, *The Passing of the Great Race*, Charles Scribner & Sons, 1916, p. 77.

2 This discussion and quotations draw on Jonathan Peter Spiro, *Defending the Master Race*, University of Vermont Press, 2008.

3 Ibid.

4 Francisco E. Balderrama and Raymond Rodríguez, *Decade of Betrayal*, University of New Mexico Press, 2006, p. 75.

5 Abraham Hoffman, *Unwanted Mexicans in the Great Depression*, University of Arizona Press, 1974, p. 51.

6 TK

7 TK

8 Christine Marin, "Always a Struggle: Mexican Americans in Miami, Arizona, 1909–1951," (PhD dissertation, Arizona State University, 2005.

Chapter 2: Return from Exile

1 D. H. Dinwoodie, "The Rise of the Mine Mill Union in Southwestern Copper," in James C. Foster (ed.), *American Labor in the Southwest*, University of Arizona Press, 1982, p. 54.

2 Quoted in Marin, "Always a Struggle."

3 Ibid.

4 David Hayes-Bautista, *La Nueva California: Latinos in the Golden State*, University of California Press, 2004, pp. 94–5.

5 Gregory Rodriguez, *Mongrels, Bastards, Orphans, and Vagabonds: Mexican Immigration and the Future of Race in America*, Pantheon, 2007, p. 194.

6 Juan Ramón García, *Operation Wetback: The Mass Deportation of Mexican Undocumented Workers in 1954*, Greenwood Press, 1980, p. 20.

7 Lawrence A. Cardoso, *Mexican Emigration to the United States, 1897–1931*, University of Arizona Press, 1980, pp. 100–1.

8 García, *Operation Wetback*, p. 19.

9 Ibid., 38–9

10 Ibid., p. 54.

11 David G. Gutiérrez, *Walls and Mirrors: Mexican Americans, Mexican Immigrants and the Politics of Ethnicity*, University of California Press, 2005 (1995), p. 162.

12 Ernesto Galarza, *Merchants of Labor: The Mexican Bracero Story*, McNally and Loftin, 1972, pp. 163–9.

13 García, *Operation Wetback*, p. 230.

14 Ibid., p. 172.

15 García, *Operation Wetback*, pp. 177–8.

16 Department of Justice, Border Patrol Management Report 1955, p. 53.

17 García, *Operation Wetback*, p. 183.

18 Ramos, pp. 176–7.

19 Ramos p. 227.

20 The official claim is that 1,300,000 left the country through "voluntary departure" or deportation. In California, INS reported a total 84,278 apprehensions. INS also reported that 540,000 "illegals" had been deported or voluntarily fled. On the safe assumption that you cannot be deported if you are not apprehended, that means that 455,722 "illegals" were scare-headed out. But the INS report also says that in California the number leaving voluntarily was so great "that it was impossible to count them." INS offers no further evidence for that very

precise number of 455,722. Applying the same logic to the west Texas campaign leaves over 700,000 persons unaccounted for. A "voluntary" exodus of the magnitude claimed by General Swing would have flooded northern Mexican cities, and certainly caused some press scrutiny and even diplomatic correspondence between Mexico City and Washington in response. The leading scholarly work on the subject, García's *Operation Wetback*, from which the data for this discussion is taken, concludes that there is simply no independent evidence to support INS and Swing's claims.

21 Mae M. Ngai, *Impossible Subjects: Illegal Aliens and the Making of America*, Princeton University Press, 2003, p. 164.

22 Patricia Sullivan, "Evan Mecham, 83; Was Removed As Arizona Governor," *Washington Post*, February 25, 2008.

23 Martha Menchaca, *Recovering History, Constructing Race: The Indian, Black, and White Roots of Mexican Americans*, University of Texas Press, 2001/2, p. 215.

24 Hayes-Bautista, *La Nueva California*, p. 26.

25 Gutiérrez, *Walls and Mirrors*, p. 143.

26 Rodriguez, *Mongrels*, p. 186.

27 Gutiérrez, *Walls and Mirrors*, p. 125.

28 Ibid., p. 126.

Chapter 3: War and Chicanos

1 David Hayes-Bautista, *El Cinco de Mayo: An American Tradition*, University of California Press, 2012.

2 Ralph Guzman, "Mexican-American Casualties in Vietnam," in Wayne Moquin (ed.), *A Documentary History of the Mexican Americans*, Praeger, 1971, p. 373.

3 Ibid., p. 171–2.

4 Menchaca, *Recovering History*, p. 222.

5 Hayes-Bautista, *La Nueva California*, p. 26.

6 Menchaca, *Recovering History*, p. 222.

7 Rodriguez, *Mongrels*, pp. 168–70.

8 Ibid., p. 123.

9 Ibid., p. 125.

10 Ibid., p. 157.

11 Ibid., p. 178.

12 Gutiérrez, *Walls and Mirrors*, p. 163.

13 Rodriguez, *Mongrels*, p. 188.

14 Ibid., p. 155.

15 Ibid., p. 162.

16 *Time*, February 27,1950.

17 Ellen R. Baker, *On Strike and on Film: Mexican American Families and Blacklisted Filmmakers in Cold War America*, University of North Carolina Press, 2007, p. 104.

18 García, *Operation Wetback*, p. 179.

19 Baker, *On Strike and on Film*, p. 46.

20 Ibid., p. 104.

21 Ibid., pp. 119–34.

22 Mario Garcia, *Life and Narrative of Bert Corona*, University of California Press, 1995, pp. 172–9.

23 James J. Lorence, *The Suppression of Salt of the Earth: How Hollywood, Big Labor, and Politicians Blacklisted a Movie in Cold War America*, University of New Mexico Press, 1999, pp. 77–9.

24 Ibid., p. 168.

25 Garcia, *Life and Narrative of Bert Corona*, pp. 179–82.

26 Gutiérrez, *Walls and Mirrors*, pp. 126–7.

27 Ibid., pp. 168–9.

28 García, *Operation Wetback*, p. 197.

Chapter 4: The Chicano Movement

1 Rodriguez, *Mongrels*, p. 220.

2 US Census Bureau, *Coming to America: A profile of the Nations's Foreign Born (2000 update)*, census.gov.

3 Ngai, *Impossible Subjects*, pp. 258–9.

4 Ibid.

5 US Census Bureau, *Coming to America: A Profile of the Nation's Foreign Born (2000 update)*, census.gov.

6 Rodriguez, *Mongrels*, p. 206.

7 George Mariscal, *Brown-Eyed Children of the Sun: Lessons from the Chicano Movement 1965–1975*, University of New Mexico, 2005, p. 154.

8 Ibid., p. 155.

9 Private correspondence via email to author, January 13, 2011.

10 Garcia, *Life and Narrative of Bert Corona*.

11 President Lyndon Johnson Annual Message To The Congress, January 8, 1964, Public Papers of the Presidents of the United States: Lyndon B. Johnson, *1963–64*, Volume I, Washington, DC: Government Printing Office, 1965, pp. 112–18.

12 Richard A. Cloward and Lloyd E. Ohlin. *Delinquency and Opportunity*, Free Press, 1960.

13 Michael W. Flamm, *Law and Order: Street Crime, Civil Unrest and the Crisis of Liberalism in the 1960s*, Columbia University Press, 2005, p. 33.

14 "The Negro Family: The Case for National Action," Office of Policy Planning and Research, US Department of Labor, March 1965.

15 Hayes-Bautista, *La Nueva California*, p. 34.

16 Ibid., p. 35.

17 Ibid., p. 35.

18 *Public Papers of the Presidents of the United States: Lyndon B. Johnson, 1965*. Volume II, Washington, DC: Government Printing Office, 1966, pp. 635–40.

19 George Mariscal, *Brown-Eyed Children of the Sun*, p. 35.

20 Available at http://24ahead.com/statements-jose-angel-gutierrez-san-antonio-evening-news-apr.

21 Herman Gallegos, private correspondence.

Chapter 5: The Chicano Movement Ends

1 Arizona Revised Statutes, Title 23, Chapter 8, Article 5.
2 Rodolfo Gonzáles, *I Am Joaquin: Yo Soy Joaquin; an epic poem. With a chronology of people and events in Mexican and Mexican American history*, Bantam pathfinder editions, English and Spanish Edition, 1972.
3 Menchaca, *Recovering History*, p. 23.
4 Rudy Busto, *The Religious Visions of Reies López Tijerina*, University of New Mexico Press, 2005, p. 60.
5 Ibid., pp. 60–1.
6 Gutiérrez, *Walls and Mirrors*, pp. 197–9.
7 Ibid.
8 Ibid.
9 F. Arturo Rosales, *Chicano!: The History of the Mexican American Civil Rights Movement*, Arte Público Press, 1996, p. 250.
10 *Phoenix Gazette*, January 9, 1975.
11 Ibid., May 26, 1975.
12 Ibid., June 12, 1975.
13 Ibid., September 16, 1975.
14 Ibid., April 24, 1975.
15 Ibid., March 5, 1976.
16 Ibid., March 18, 1976.
17 Ibid., March 1, 1976.
18 Ibid.
19 Ibid.
20 Ibid., June 19, 1975, and March 23, 1974.
21 Ibid., June 19, 1975.
22 Ibid., June 20, 1975.
23 Ibid.
24 Ely v. Klahr, 403 US 108, 1971.
25 "'Welfare Queen' Becomes Issue in Reagan Campaign," *Washington Star*, February 14, 1976.
26 Ibid.
27 *Phoenix Gazette*, September 5, 1975.

28 *Washington Post*, May 28, 1997.
29 "Battling obscurity, Babbitt leads with chin," *New York Times*, January 28, 1988.
30 *Arizona Republic*, July 28, 1983.
31 Jonathan Rosenblum, *Copper Crucible: How the Arizona Miners' Strike of 1983 Recast Labor-Management Relations in America*, Cornell University Press, 1998, p. 52.
32 Ibid., p. 53.
33 Ibid., p. 59.
34 Ibid., p. 92.
35 *Arizona Daily Star*, August 6, 1983.
36 Barbara Kingsolver, *Holding the Line: Women in the Great Arizona Mine Strike of 1983*, ILR Press, 1989, pp. 42–3.
37 Rosenblum, *Copper Crucible*, p. 102.
38 Ibid., p. 113.
39 *Phoenix New Times*, February 6, 1991.

Chapter 6: Torture at the Border
1 US Department of Justice, Annual Reports of the Immigration and Naturalization Service.
2 Joseph Nevins, *Operation Gatekeeper: The Rise of the "Illegal Alien" and the Making of the US–Mexico Boundary*, Routledge, 2002, p. 63.
3 Ibid., p. 64.
4 Ibid., p. 63.
5 Vernon M. Briggs, Jr., "Methods of Analysis of Illegal Immigration into the United States" (1984), Articles & Chapters, Paper 6, digitalcommons.ilr.cornell.edu/articles/6.
6 Nevins, *Operation Gatekeeper*, p. 64.
7 Rodolfo Acuña, *Occupied America*, 4th ed., Pearson Publishers, 1999, p. 405.
8 Armando Navarro, *The Immigration Crisis*, Altamira Press, 2009, p. 101.

9 Acuña, *Occupied America*, p. 404.

10 This discussion draws on an interview with Jose de Jesus Rivera conducted by the author.

11 Bill Ong Hing, *Defining America Through Immigration Policy*, Temple University Press, 2004, pp. 156–8.

12 Gutiérrez, *Walls and Mirrors*, p. 201.

13 Hing, *Defining America*, p. 159.

14 *Phoenix Gazette*, January 23, 1981.

15 Hayes-Bautista, *La Nueva California*, p. 34.

16 Rodriguez, *Mongrels*, p. 226.

17 Kenneth Prewitt, "Public Statistics and Democratic Politics," in William Alonso and Paul Starr (eds), *The Politics of Numbers*, Russell Sage, 1987, p. 271.

18 Raul Yzaguirre and Charles Kamasaki, "Comment on the Latino Civil Rights Crisis: A Research Conference," Civil Rights Project/Proyecto Derechos Civiles, University of California, Los Angeles.

19 Rodriguez, *Mongrels*, p. 226.

20 Ibid.

21 Thomas Sowell, *Ethnic America: A History*, Basic Books, 1981, p. 261.

22 Ibid.

23 Christine Marie Sierra, "In Search of National Power," in David Montejano (ed.), *Chicano Politics and Society in the Late Twentieth Century*, University of Texas Press, 1999, p. 145.

24 Ibid., p. 146.

Chapter 7: Proposition 187

1 http://www.reagan.utexas.edu/archives/speeches/1986/110686b.htm.

2 Hing, *Defining America*, p. 160.

3 Ibid., p. 166.

4 United States Border Patrol Statistics, Fiscal Year 1925–2011, *Apprehensions*.

5 Jorge Durand, Douglas S. Massey, and Emilio A. Parrado, "The New Era of Mexican Migration to the United States," *Journal of American History*, September 1999.

6 Ibid.

7 IRCA 1986, HR Rep no 99-6821(I), 99th Congress.

8 Hoffman Plastic Compounds, Inc. v. NLRB, 535 US 137 (2002).

9 Kathleen Stanton, "The Price of Power," *Phoenix New Times*, February 6, 1991.

10 Kathleen Stanton, "Checkmate: Pacificorp's Bold Ad Campaign Has Left Pinwest Looking Like a Dork," *Phoenix New Times*, July 4, 1990.

11 Andrew Wroe, *The Republican Party and Immigration Politics: From Proposition 187 to George W. Bush*, Palgrave Macmillan, 2008, p. 47.

12 *Los Angeles Times*, June 28, 1992.

13 "The L.A. Riots: 15 years after Rodney King," *Time Magazine-CNN Specials*, April 27, 2007.

14 *Los Angeles Times*, "Six Months After the Unrest," October 9–14, 1992.

15 Wroe, *The Republican Party*, p. 43.

16 Ibid.

17 Hayes-Bautista, *La Nueva California*, p. 126.

18 Wroe, *The Republican Party*, p. 44.

19 Ibid., pp. 43–5.

20 Ibid, pp. 44–7.

21 Wroe, *The Republican Party*, p. 223.

22 Rodriguez, *Mongrels*, p. 240.

23 "Prop 187 Turns Up Heat in U.S. Immigration Debate," *Los Angeles Times*, August 10, 1994, A1.

24 Hayes-Bautista, *La Nueva California*, pp. 126–7.

25 Ibid., p. 128.

26 Nevins, *Operation Gatekeeper*, p. 61.

27 Hayes-Bautista, *La Nueva California*, p. 128.

28 Wroe, *The Republican Party*, p. 42.

29 Hayes-Bautista, *La Nueva California*, p. 127.

30 *Los Angeles Times*, November 15, 1997.

31 Ken Ellingwood, *Hard Line: Life and Death on the US-Mexico Border*, Pantheon Books, 2004, pp. 39–40.

32 Hing, *Defining America*, p. 189.

33 *Arizona Daily Star*, July 16, 2010.

34 Hing, *Defining America*, p. 189.

35 Ibid., p. 194.

Chapter 8: An Immigration Policy without Moral Consideration

1 *Los Angeles Times*, October 26, 1994.

2 Certificate of Incorporation, The Pioneer Fund, Filed Pursuant to the Membership Corporations Law, The State of New York, February 27, 1937.

3 The Pioneer Fund, Inc., "About Us," pioneerfund.org, July 2012.

4 Francis Galton, "Hereditary Character and Talent," originally published in *Macmillan's Magazine*, vol. 12, 1865, available at galton.org.

5 *Arizona Republic*, August 7, 2004.

6 Special Report, Center for New Community, August 2004.

7 Transcript, *Rachel Maddow Show*, April 20, 2010.

8 *Washington Times*, September 30, 2004.

9 *In These Times*, April 24, 2006.

10 *New York Times*, April 17, 2011.

11 Ibid.

12 Paul Lombardo, Eugenics Laws Restricting Immigration, Image Archive on the American Eugenics Movement, University of Virginia, Dolan DNA Learning Center, Cold Spring Harbor Laboratory, February 2000.

13 John Heilemann, "Do You Know the Way to Ban José?" *Wired*, August 1996.

14 *Time,* July 30, 2001.

15 Susan Carroll "Mexico's Top Envoy Lobbies For Migrants," *Tuscon Citizen,* June 22, 2001.

16 Chris Hadal, "Border Security: The Role of the Border Patrol," Congressional Research Service, 2010.

17 ICE Reports: 1: ICE Budget 2010, from ICE Fact Sheet 2010, Estimated Budget, November 5, 2009; 2: Testimony of Michael Doughtery, ICE Director of Operations, House Judiciary Committee, February 25, 2004.

18 Hadal, "Border Security"

19 "Winning the Immigration Issue: Requiring Legal Status for Illegal Immigrants," Lake Research Partners, Hart Research, and Greenberg Quinlan Rosner, July 24, 2008.

20 Tom Barry, "Immigration Reform: Democratic Accomplishments, July 2008," Center for American Progress, available at alainet.org.

21 Eugene Scott, "Group of Hispanic leaders announce support of Obama," *Arizona Republic,* January 22, 2008.

22 Transcript "Obama Addresses the National Council of La Raza," *Washington Post,* July 15, 2008.

23 Elizabeth Alexander, *Praise Song for the Day,* Graywolf Press, 2009.

24 David Goldman, *CNN Money,* January 9, 2009.

25 *New York Times,* April 8, 2009.

26 *Arizona Republic,* February 2, 2008.

27 Testimony of Janet Napolitano, Senate Judiciary Committee, May 6, 2009.

28 Ajmel Quereshi, "The Family Values of Local Enforcement of Federal Immigration Law," *Wisconsin Journal of Law, Gender and Society,* December 28, 2010, pp. 264–5.

29 Quereshi, "Family Values," p. 268.

30 Ibid., p. 274.

31 Press release, NIF, June 3, 2009.

32 Ibid.

33 Roberto Lovato, "Of América," blog post, August 10, 2009, ofamerica.wordpress.com.

34 ICE Fiscal Year 2008 Annual Report.

35 "Issue Briefing Series, Issue #3: 287(g) and Secure Communities: The Facts about Local Immigration Law Enforcement," Migration and Refugee Services/Office of Migration Policy and Public Affairs, United States Conference of Catholic Bishops, May 2011.

36 This discussion is based on interviews with Carlos Roa and Gaby Pacheco conducted by the author.

37 Hans Nichols, "White House Resists Push to Stop Deportations"," *Bloomberg News*, April 4, 2011.

38 Julia Preston, "Obama to Permit Young Migrants to Remain in U.S., *New York Times*, June 15, 2011."

39 *Arizona Republic*, June 13, 2005.

40 Ruben Navarrete, *Tribune Media News*, August 8, 2010.

41 Melissa del Bosque, "Children of the Exodus," *Texas Observer*, November 4, 2010.

42 Ibid.

Acknowledgements

This work came about because of the extraordinary support of three persons, Douglas Patiño, Bette DeGraw and most of all because of the relentless encouragement of Sharon Zapata. My sincere gratitude to each of them.

I am also deeply grateful to Herman Gallegos for his guidance and clear recollection of a bygone era and finally I would be remiss to not acknowledge the always cheerful assistance of the librarians at Burton Barr Library.

Index

Index

Box, John, 4
Boxer, Barbara, 172
Bracero Program
  cancellation of, 68
  description of, 23–25
  extension of, 25–26, 31–33
  labor organization opposition to, 22–23
  Latino organization opposition to, 21
  proposal reestablishing, 108
Bracho, America, 221
Brotherhood of Railroad Trainmen, 5
Brotherhood of Railway and Airline Clerks, 148
Brown, Don, 109
Brown, Jerry, 120
Brown, Kathleen, 172
Brown, Pat, 68
Brown, Willie, 172
Brown v. Board of Education, 47
Brownell, Herbert, 28
Bush, George W., 198, 200, 211
Business Week, 126
Bustamante, Antonio, 140–1, 144

C
Caldes, Ted, 73
California Civil Rights Commission, 68
California Coalition for Immigration Reform, 176
California Department of Labor, 146
California Highway Patrol, 170
Calles Administration (Mexico), 11, 19
Camp of the Saints, 195
Campaign Against Illegal Aliens, 102
Campbell, Cloves, 93
Campesino, Teatro, 70
"capacity building" for barrio organizations, 77
Carbajal, José, 11
Cardozo Immigrant Justice Clinic, 216
CARECEN, 214
Carillo, Yahaira, 223
Carnegie, Andrew, 3
Carpenter, Carol, 168
Carter, Jimmy
  Alfredo Gutierrez in campaign of, 115
  Alien Adjustment and Employment Act, 145
  immigration reform efforts of, 164, 196
  Leonel Castillo as INS commissioner, 137
  Raul Castro ambassadorship, 109, 115
  Stansfield Turner as CIA director, 138
CASA (Center for Autonomous Social Action-General Brotherhood of Workers), 147
Castañeda, Jorge, 199
Castillo, Leonel, 137
Castro, Fidel, 58
Castro, Raul, 105–11, 115
casualty rates of Mexican-Americans in military, 45–47
Catholic Social Services, 164
Catholicism, Mexican policies against, 11, 19
CBS News, 32

Celler, Emanuel, 67
Center for American Progress, 201–3, 213, 221
Center for Autonomous Social Action-General Brotherhood of Workers (CASA), 147
Center for Community Change, 201–2, 213
Center for Constitutional Rights, 216
Center for Immigration Studies, 194–5
Central Intelligence Agency (CIA), 136, 138
Chapman, Leonard, 136–7
Chavez, Cesar
  Campaign Against Illegal Aliens of, 102
  Chicano Movement and, 70–73, 101–4
  as Chicanos organizer, 63–65
  Community Services Organization and, 62–63, 76
  employer sanctions opposed by, 146
  farm worker focus of, 84
  fasting of, 93
  Kennedy campaign of 1968 and, 74
Chicano Moratorium, 46, 100
Chicano Movement, 66–96
  Cesar Chavez and, 70–73
  demographics and, 69–70
  development of, 66–68
  Interagency Committee on Mexican-American Affairs, 85–87
  Mexican American Students Organization, 73–76, 87–90
  Mexican-American sociological status and, 83–85
  National Council of La Raza, 91–95
  Southwest Council of La Raza, 77–80, 90–91
  War on Poverty, 80–83
Chicano Movement, ending of, 96–133
  Arizona state legislature and, 111–6
  Bruce Babbitt as Arizona governor and, 116–9
  Cesar Chavez and, 101–4
  Chicano Moratorium, 100
  La Raza Unida Party, 98–100
  Medicaid and, 119–21
  National Chicano Youth Liberation Conference, 97–98
  Phelps Dodge Mining Corporation strike and, 125–34
  Raul Castro as Arizona Governor and, 105–11
  War on Poverty and, 104–5
  Welfare-to-Work programs and, 121–5
Chicanos, wars as theme of, 44–65
  American GI Forum, 50–52
  anti-immigrant hysteria, 52–54
  Asociación Nacional Mexico-Americana as Mexican community voice, 55–60
  Cesar Chavez as organizer of, 63–65
  Community Services Organization, 61–62
  International Union of Mine, Mill and Smelter Workers as Mexican community voice, 54–55
  Latino presence in U.S. wars, 44–45
  League of United Latin American Citizens and, 47–49

INDEX

Mexican-American disproportionate casualty rate, 45–47
Mexican-American Political Association, 62–63
U.S. Census "Mexican" classification, 49–50
Chicanos Por La Causa (CPLC), 75–76, 78, 109, 221
Children of Sanchez (Lewis), 70
Chinese Exclusion Act of 1882, 4
CIA (Central Intelligence Agency), 136, 138
CIO (Congress of industrial Organizations), 29, 54
Citizens Informer, 193
Civiletti, Benjamin, 141
Clean Elections, 186
Clifton-Morenci mining district, strikes in, 14–15
Clinton, Bill, 124, 131, 171, 181, 205
Clinton, Hilary, 205
Cloward, Richard, 80
CNN, 208
coercive sterilization laws, 3
COFEM (Consejo de Federaciones Mexicanas en Norteamérica), 222
COLA (Cost of Living Adjustment), 128
Colby, William, 136
Cold War atmosphere, unionization in, 60
Columbia University, 76, 80, 152
Committee on Immigration and Naturalization, U.S. House of Representatives, 196
Community Services Organization (CSO), 61–62, 76
Compean, Mario, 98
Comprehensive Immigration Reform Act of 2007, 200–1
Congress of Industrial Organizations (CIO), 29, 54
Congressional Budget Office, 160
Congressional Record, 45
Consejo de Federaciones Mexicanas en Norteamérica (COFEM), 222
Constitution of Republic of Texas (1836), 49
consumer rights bill, 114
conversos (Jews forced to convert), 11
Copper Crucible (Rosenblum), 126
Cornyn, John, 200
Corona, Bert
  Asociación Nacional Mexico-Americana and, 57–58, 60
  on California Civil Rights Commission, 68–69
  Center for Autonomous Social Action-General Brotherhood of Workers (CASA) and, 147
  Interagency Committee on Mexican-American Affairs (ICMAA) and, 85
  Kennedy campaign of 1968 and, 74
  Mexican American Political Association and, 55, 57, 62
  Southwest Council of La Raza and, 77
  Special Agricultural Workers legalization program and, 157

Corrections Corporation of America, 161
Corwin, Arthur E., 137–8
Council of Conservative Citizens, 193
CPLC (Chicanos Por La Causa), 75–76, 78, 109, 221
Cristero War (Mexico, 1926-1929), 11, 19
CSO (Community Services Organization), 61–62, 76
Cuban Liberation movement, 58
culture
  isolation of, 19
  mining, 63–64
  of poverty, 150
  traditional folk, 83–84

D
Darwinian-Galtonian perspective, Pioneer Fund and, 192
Daub, Hal, 160
Davis, Gray, 178
de Bright, Josefina Fierro, 40
de Dawson, Aurora Santana, 58
de la Guerra, Pablo, 48
de la Guerra, Pablo case (CA, 1870s), 190–1
de Uriarte, Richard, 223
DeCanas v. Bica (1972), 146
DeConcini, Dennis, 131, 148
deferments from military service, 46
Defining America Through Immigration (Hing), 187
DeGraw, Bette, 123
del Bosque, Melissa, 224–5
Delinquency and Opportunity (Ohlin and Cloward), 80
Delinquency Commission, 80
DelRio Independent School District, Salvatierra v. (1931), 47
Demography, 163
Denali National Park, 3
denaturalization of immigrants (McCarran-Walter Act of 1952), 26
deportations
  Cesar Chavez support of, 103
  Clifton-Morenci mining district strikes and, 14–15
  in Ford administration, 136–7
  Gila County Welfare Association coordination of, 8
  in Great Depression, 6
  of Gutierrez's father, 1–2
  in Obama's first term, 5
Derechos Humanos desert rescue group, 188
Desarrollo Integral de la Familia (DIF, Mexican government agency), 225
deterrence, immigration prevention by, 179–80, 187, 211
DHS (U.S. Department of Homeland Security), 5, 203, 207, 215
Dies, Martin, 6
DiGiorgio Corporation, 33
discrimination, 14, 54–55
Doak, William, 5–6
Doe, Plyer v. (1982), 175
Domínguez, Cesario, 188
Dream Act, 200, 209, 217–20, 223

243

Index

Index

Index

Index

287(g) section of Immigration Act of 1990, 210–12, 215

U
UAW (United Auto Workers), 78, 86–87
underclass, permanent, 156
undocumented persons. *See* deportations; illegal immigration
union busting. *See* Phelps Dodge Mining Corporation strike
United Auto Workers (UAW), 78, 86–87
United Farm Workers
   AgJob compromise and, 200
   DeCanas v. Bica case and, 146
   illegal alien deportation supported by, 102, 136
   Obama and, 205
   Special Agricultural Workers compromise and, 157
United States Employment Service, 24
United Steelworkers Union, 53, 126
University of California, Berkeley, 76
University of Guadalajara (Mexico), 162
University of Maine, 94
University of Michigan, 194
University of Notre Dame, 68, 116, 148
Univision television network, 219
Unzueta, Tania, 223
urban renewal as racial cleansing, 15
U.S. Census
   1930, 7
   1940, 18
   1960, 45
   1970, 67
   Laughlin use of (1924), 196
   Mexican-American classification in, 38, 49–50
   Mexican-American underutilization of programs from, 153–4
   Prewitt as director of, 152
U.S. Constitution, fourteenth amendment to, 38, 172
U.S. Department of Health and Human Services, 160
U.S. Department of Health and Welfare, 120
U.S. Department of Homeland Security (DHS), 5, 203, 207, 215
U.S. Department of Justice, 141
U.S. Department of Labor, 5–6, 82, 123
U.S. House of Representatives, 196
U.S. Justice Department, 102
U.S. Supreme Court, 116, 146, 164, 175, 178
USA Today, 172
US-VISIT screening program, 204

V
Valdez, Luis, 70
Van Dyke, Cleve, 7, 15

Vanderbilt University, 3
Vasconcelos, José, 70
VCT (Voices of Citizens Together), 176–7
Vega, Fortunato, 9–10
Velázquez, Braulia, 57
veterans organizations, segregation in, 44–45
Vietnam, Chicano veterans of, 45, 100
Villa, Pancho, 27
violence, controlling, 81
visas, 135, 197
Visel, Charles, 6
VISTA anti-poverty program, 116
Voices of Citizens Together (VCT), 176–7
"voluntary departures" (deportations), 8–9
voter registration initiatives, 79, 88

W
War on Poverty, 79–84, 104–5
Washington Post, 172
Washington Times, 193
water code, rewriting, 118
Weber, Max, 83
Wechsler, Burt, 141
"welfare reservation," U.S. as (Corwin), 138
Welfare-to-Work programs, 121–5
Western Growers Association, 157
Western Mining Federation, 14
Westminster, Mendez v., 47
Weyher, Harry, 195
White, Jim, 108
White House Conference on Civil Rights, 85
Williams, Jack, 93
Williams, Russ, 106
Wilson, Pete
   ethical crossroads of, 169–170
   on fourteenth amendment to U.S. Constitution, 171–2
   Mexican border visit of (1994), 173
   National Guard deployed by, 171
   pre-natal care for undocumented women opposition of, 173–4
   Proposition 187 and, 157, 174, 177–8, 191
   re-election of, 177
Wilson, Woodrow, 14
Winning the Immigration Issue: Requiring Legal Status for Illegal Immigrants report (2008), 202–3
women's role, *Salt of the Earth* (film) on, 56

X
Ximenes, Vicente T., 85

Y
Yoldi, Frank, 93
Yzaguirre, Raul, 152–4